Robert Peel Ritchie

The Early Days of the Royall Colledge of Phisitians, Edinburgh

Robert Peel Ritchie

The Early Days of the Royall Colledge of Phisitians, Edinburgh

ISBN/EAN: 9783337161408

Printed in Europe, USA, Canada, Australia, Japan

Cover: Foto ©ninafisch / pixelio.de

More available books at **www.hansebooks.com**

SIR ROBERT SIBBALD OF KIPPS, M.D.

THE EARLY DAYS OF
THE ROYALL COLLEDGE OF PHISITIANS, EDINBURGH

THE EXTENDED ORATION OF THE HARVEIAN SOCIETY, EDINBURGH DELIVERED AT THE 114TH FESTIVAL

BY THE PRESIDENT

ROBERT PEEL RITCHIE

M.D.EDIN., F.R.C.P.E., F.R.S.E., ETC.

EDINBURGH

GEORGE P. JOHNSTON

1899

Edinburgh: T. and A. CONSTABLE, Printers to Her Majesty

TO THE

FELLOWS OF THE HARVEIAN SOCIETY OF EDINBURGH

AND TO THE

PRESIDENT, FELLOWS, MEMBERS, AND LICENTIATES OF THE

ROYAL COLLEGE OF PHYSICIANS OF EDINBURGH

THIS EXTENDED ORATION, THE 114TH

IS WITH ALL RESPECT

DEDICATED

BY THEIR PAST-PRESIDENT

THE AUTHOR

PREFACE

In submitting the following pages to the reader, a word in explanation of the numerous Extracts from Authorities is necessary. In my Oration, as delivered, the Statements were given as facts and without the proofs which substantiated them. This was objected to by some; and the necessity, therefore, to back up my views, where they differ from those generally accepted, became urgent. After consideration, the only course left me, in order to make the history complete, was, not to give a reference merely, but the quotations themselves from the old Minute Books of the Royal College of Physicians. For permission to make use of them and also of several of the Portraits, my very hearty thanks are due to the President, Sir John Batty Tuke, and to the Council of the Royal College. Having given these extracts from its private Records, I found it also advisable, to make my narrative complete and distinct, to follow the same method with the other Authorities referred to, so that any dubiety or misunderstanding might be obviated.

My desire to be strictly accurate as to the dates upon which much of my argument depends, to prevent misstatement of the views of other writers, and to sufficiently substantiate my reasons for differing from the opinions of those Authorities I may be at variance with, will, I trust, be held as ample excuse for any inelegance which the quotations, and in some instances their repetition, occasion.

I have also to express my regret that circumstances have prevented me from sooner preparing this extended Oration for publication, and from gratifying the wishes of interested inquirers.

When the printing of the extended Oration was well advanced, my attention was directed by Mr. J. M. Shaw, M.A., the Superintendent, to a volume relating to the Minutes of the Royal College of Physicians, which he had found in an unused room in the College Hall, and which did not appear to have been at any time one of the catalogued books belonging to the Library. On examination I found it to be a copy of the Minutes of the College from the Early Minute Books, made under direction of Alexander Boswell, W.S., Clerk to the Royal College, and to whom reference is made in the Oration. But in addition to the Minute Books which were submitted to me by Mr. Christopher Douglas, W.S., the late Clerk, as containing all the existing old Records of the College, I found this copy also contained a portion of vol. iii., recording the Minutes from 21st March 1693 to 6th December 1694. As this additional record of one year and nine months throws further light on some of the questions touched on in my story, I have thought it right to give an abstract of these Minutes, so that all that can be learned of the proceedings of the years succeeding The Early Days may be deduced. During these twenty-one months, twenty-nine Sederunts of the Royal College were minuted, and of the Original Fellows, the names of eleven only were entered as having been present. Of these the President, Sir Archibald Stevensone, was present at twenty-eight Meetings, Dr. Cranstoune was also at twenty-eight, Drs. Trotter and Pitcairn at twenty-four each, Dr. Halkett at fifteen, Dr. Learmont at five, and Drs. St. Clare and Halyburton were each present at one.

Sir Andrew Balfour attended the first nine; but then his health appeared to have given way, and after 21st December 1693 he was not again present. Sir Robert Sibbald attended regularly sixteen consecutive Meetings till 5th July 1694, but then ceased his attendance, apparently because though one of the five yearly Examinators, he did not approve of the new form of Examination.

Dr. Brisbane was present on three occasions, but ceased attending after he was declared by vote to be only an Honorary Member. Attendance at the Dispensary on the sick poor was given by Drs. Robertson and Smelholme, who had been appointed for that duty.

The Pharmacopœia, too, received some attention; for on 23rd October 1694 it was remitted to the President (Stevensone) that there should be a Pharmacopœia, and that it would be fit to commit it to one person to make a Scheme of it, and thereafter that he should communicate it to two or more of the College, to be at a later stage referred to a Committee for revision, but there is no after Report by the President regarding it.

The Discourses continued to be given before the College, and I have to modify the opinion expressed in the Oration as regards two of the Fellows. Sir Archibald Stevensone gave one, divided into two parts, upon Diabetes, but the second part does not appear to have ever been delivered before the College.

The other reference is to Dr. Pitcairn, for I find on 1st November 1694, that 'Dr. Pittcairne had (at Dr. Halyburton's desyre) a Discourse, *De febribus*, and that the Colledge were very well satisfied yr with and returned him the thanks of the Board.' It still remains, however, that when at a later period he was desired to give a Discourse on his own account he persistently omitted to do so, and was regularly fined for his neglect to be present.

The remaining matters of interest in these Minutes are the Intrants' Examinations, and they appear to me to substantiate the view expressed regarding them in the Oration. The difficulty experienced when I wrote it was to determine when the change in the appointment of Examinators took place. I concluded it was at an earlier period than I now find it was, for these Minutes fix the date to have been on 14th December 1693. At that Meeting Stevensone, Balfour, Sibbald, Cranstoune, and Pitcairne, of the original Fellows, were present, as also was Dr. Eccles, a recently admitted Socius. The Minute states: 'Qlk day the Colledge having taken into consideratione the regulatione of Examinationes, Doe think fitt that there be fyve Examinators appoynted, to continue till the next Election of the President, and that they be nominated by the President and Colledge from year to year, But prejudice to the Colledge to continue all or any one or more of the said Examinators as they shall think fitt and there shall be no Examinatione unless thrie of these Examinators be present and the President or propreses, and as many of the Colledge as with the Examinators present shall make up a full quorum. And it is ordered that for the greater Solemnity the whole Members be warned to be present at the Examination of Intrants.'

At the next meeting, 21st December, Drs. Learmont, Trotter, Halkett, and Olyphant, were present, as well as those at the preceding meeting, when the College ratified what was done at the last meeting anent Examinations. And 'the Colledge appoynts, Doctors Sibbald, Trotter, Pittcairn, Eccles, and Olyphant, to be Examinators.'

The effect of this was to make a great change in the character of the Examinations, and I cannot but regard that change as a retrograde movement, by whomsoever it was suggested. It was also recommended, to the several Members of the Colledge, to consider and give their opinion, what further tryall shall be imposed upon Intrants after the said Examinatione; and on 4th January 1694 six of the above-named Fellows being present, Balfour, Trotter, Learmont, and Pitcairn being absent, the College resolved, that after 'his Examinatione, they have thought fitt, that the Intrant should have a subject of a Discourse prescribed him, by the Colledge upon which he is to treat when appoynted, either to be delivered *vivâ voce* or by Paper.'

When these lately found Minutes begin, on 21st March 1693, they open with the words, 'The q[lk] day, Doctor Olyphant, having undergone his first tryall, according to the last sederunt, the Colledge unanimously approves of his ans[rs], and finds him sufficiently qualified upon that subject, and admitts him to his second tryall, which is to be upon Tuesday the 4th Apryll; and

Sir Robert Sibbald and Doctor Eccles to be his Examinators—each of them to Examine him upon a separat Apphorisme of Hippocrates.' On that day he is approved of by the College, 'And appoynts his third and last tryall to be upon Monday the 17th inst., upon two practicable (practicall) cases—one by Dr. Trotter and the other by Dr. Learmont. And the Colledge having heard Dr. Olyphant upon his third and last tryall, Doe find him sufficiently qualified and therefore licenses him to practise.' This is the original form, and is a much more thorough Examination than the new form to which Dr. Andrew Melvill was subjected on 24th June 1694. 'The 9th day the Colledge having mett, according to ye order of ye last dyet, proceeded to ye tryall of Dr. Melvill, and he being examined by the whole fyve Examinators was unanimously approven by the Colledge, and he haveing payed into Dr. Olyphant, Treasurer, ane hundreth Merks Scots, the Colledge appoynts Thursday the fyft of July for him to discourse upon ye *Vertigo*—and adjourn to that day.' The next Minute records, 'that the Colledge having heard the Discourse *De Vertigine*, according to the order of the last dyet, Doe unanimously approve of the Discourse and Licentiat him to practise.'

Sir Robert Sibbald was present on that occasion, but did not again attend until the 14th September 1695, the day upon which Sir Archibald Stevensone locked the door of the College, and refused to give up the keys. And yet, he had previously been most regular in his attendance. . . . On 17th January 1695, for the second time, five Examinators were elected, but Sibbald was not one of them. Sir Archibald Stevensone takes his place, and

Dr. Trotter being now President, is succeeded by Dr. Halkett. Sibbald's disapproval of the change of form is marked, and at the meeting of 14th September it is put to the vote, whether the old or new rule for Examinations is to be followed? It is carried by a plurality of votes that the old law should be observed, and the new one abrogated. This, after the necessary voting upon the question, became the law, and the Examination of Dr. Gilbert Rule, delayed till the form was settled, was then carried out in the original three 'tryall' form, with this alteration, without remark, that on 25th September Dr. Gilbert Rule 'was examined by Sir Thomas Burnet and Dr. Eizat upon ye *Institutions of Medicine*, for his first tryall.'

Two things are noticeable here: the one, that upon the return to the original form, Stevensone and Pitcairn were not present; and the other is the use of the title 'Institutions of Medicine,' which is minuted as if it were the customary subject of the 'tryall' previous to the change.

For his third trial, on October 2nd, Dr. Rule is examined 'on a particular case, "Apoplexy,"' by Dr. St. Clare, and it is not till the next candidate, Dr. Freer, is examined, five days later, on 7th October, that the return to a 'Practical Case' is made. All this, it seems to me, supports my contention in the Oration, that from the first the Practical Cases as the subject of the third 'tryall' were a distinctive feature of the Royal College Examination, and may be associated with Sibbald, Balfour, Burnet, and their supporters, but it may be questioned whether I am correct in assigning the introduction of the title 'Institutions' to Dr. Archibald Pitcairn.

During this period of twenty-one months, the following nine Physicians were admitted Socii—Drs. Charles Olyphant, Andrew Melvill, Thomas Dalrymple, James Robertson, David Dicksone, George Stirling, John Smelholme, George Hepburn, and Robert Carmichael. With the exception of Dr. Dalrymple, they were all examined.

It is necessary to make these preliminary explanations for accuracy and in support of the views I have expressed in the course of the extended Oration.

It may be added that at the suggestion of some of the Council of the College, the title of the Oration has been modified as being more suited for a book, and at the same time sufficiently comprehensive.

My thanks are due to the President and Council of the Royal College of Surgeons for their courteous permission to reproduce the Portrait of Dr. Archibald Pitcairn in their possession.

EDINBURGH, *October* 1899.

CONTENTS

PART I

THE EPOCH OF WILLIAM HARVEY

PART II

A COLLEDGE OF PHISITIANS IN SCOTLAND

PART III

THE EARLY DAYS OF THE ROYALL COLLEDGE

PART IV

THE FIRST KNIGHTS

PART V

AFTERWARDS

ILLUSTRATIONS

PART I

WILLIAM HARVEY

THE MEDICAL INSTITUTIONS OF HIS TIME IN ENGLAND, IRELAND, AND SCOTLAND

PART I

WILLIAM HARVEY

GENTLEMEN,—In the preface of Dr. R. Willis to his work on Harvey and his Life (*William Harvey, a History of the Discovery of the Circulation of the Blood*: London, 1878) are the words, 'I always hoped . . . I might one day be enabled to accomplish my purpose of writing a Life of Harvey . . . and by reference to the writings of the great anatomists of the period of the Renaissance especially, to trace the gradual approximation to truer interpretations of function, through better apprehension of structure, until Physiology for the first time, and in the highest sense of the word, received its birth from the genius of Harvey, and the foundations of rational Medicine were laid.' **Introduction.**

Accepting this expression of opinion as correct, and now universally admitted to be true, I desire at this time, the 114th celebration of the Festival of our Harveian Society, to carry our thoughts forward, and to consider the effect of Harvey's work, his discovery, his writings, and his teaching upon the progress of Medicine in Great Britain. **William Harvey and the effect of his work.**

I put aside the question—for in my opinion it has been fully considered in the past, and may be held to be proved to the satisfaction of all disinterested inquirers—Who was the discoverer of the circulation of the blood? for only one answer can be given to this question, and it is that which Professor, now Sir John, Struthers, a recent holder of the position I by your favour occupy, gave us in his interesting address at the 1894 Festival—'William Harvey.'

Harvey, the discoverer of the circulation of the blood.

My course is therefore cleared. To Harvey must be assigned the honour of being the discoverer of the circulation of the blood, as we now understand what these words imply; and when his observations and investigations are considered, we cannot but agree with Willis, that to him also must be given the high distinction of promulgating the early stage of a true Physiology, upon which the rational practice of the Medical Art could be placed on a scientific basis. And it has occurred to me that it would be interesting were we to consider at this time the result, in this country, which followed Harvey's teaching, upon the advancement of Medicine—as shown by the institution of Medical Schools, Colleges, or Lectureships for the instruction of those entering the profession, societies for the consideration of Medical and Surgical or cognate scientific questions, or the foundation of establishments for the treatment and relief of the sick poor and the instruction of pupils.

Proposed subject of the Oration.

To do this effectively, it will be necessary to consider what sources of instruction in Medicine were at Harvey's age in existence in England, Scotland, and Ireland. The subject is large, and at this time must necessarily be very much condensed; otherwise the trespass on your patience would be greater than you would be inclined to permit.

Harvey, born 1578, died 1657, in 80th year.

William Harvey was born at Folkestone on 1st April 1578. He died 3rd June 1657, in his eightieth year—239 years ago—and was buried at Hampstead in Essex. At the age of sixteen he entered Caius College, Cambridge, and at the age of nineteen obtained his B.A. degree.

He then proceeded to Padua to study Medicine, and in his twenty-fourth year, in 1602, obtained the degree of Doctor of

Medicine. Returning to England, he had the degree of Doctor of Medicine conferred upon him by his *Alma Mater* without examination. At this time there was a Professor of Physic at Cambridge, the Chair having been founded in 1540, while at Oxford there had been a Professor of Medicine since 1535.

Medical Professors at Cambridge and Oxford.

In 1615 Harvey first lectured at the College of Physicians in London, and published in 1628 his *Exercitatio Anatomica de Motu Cordis et Sanguinis*: 'An Anatomical Disquisition on the Motion of the Heart and Blood in Animals.'

Harvey first lectured at Physicians' Hall in 1615. *Exercitatio* published in 1628.

It will be observed that Harvey obtained his doctorate after seven years' University training, and yet we find Dr. Ralph Winterton, Professor of Physic at Cambridge, in a letter to the President of the College of Physicians of London, August 25, 1635, excusing himself for not licensing some of the Continental doctors on account of the shortness of their University study, which he considers should be 'twelve years' study in the University,' and requesting the College to solicit Dr. Clayton, his Majesty's Professor of Oxford, and my Lord Grace of Canterbury 'to doe the like'; although there was only one Professor at each University to teach such students as were resident, no opportunity for practical instruction, and no Hospital!

Professor Winterton on length of study required for a licence.

Harvey lectured at the College of Physicians for forty years as Lumleian Lecturer. He resigned that position in 1656 owing to failing health. Sir Dyce Duckworth in his recent Lumleian Lectures (*The Lancet*, 28th March 1896) tells us it was the intention of the founders that in these lectures some surgical question should be discussed, but the attendance at the chirurgical lectures was scant, whilst Harvey's discourses, mainly Anatomical and Physiological, were more attractive. Harvey was appointed to this position soon after his return to England, and settling in London. It gave him the opportunity to elucidate and annunciate his views upon these subjects.

Lumleian Lecturer for forty years, and resigned in 1656.

Summary.

At the time, therefore, of Harvey's birth, and at the time of his entering on his studies as a student of Medicine, in 1598, the opportunity to study and be instructed in its science and art in England consisted in there being a Professor of Medicine at Oxford and one of Physic at Cambridge Universities, and two Hospitals in London, St. Bartholomew's and St. Thomas's, which even at that period seem to have partaken more of the priestly than of the medical spirit of charity. And even at the time of his death in 1657, although he had been Physician to St. Bartholomew's, with the exception of the appointment of the Tomlins Prælector of Anatomy at Oxford in 1623, and the foundation of a Reader in Anatomy at Barber Surgeons' Hall in 1645, little or no advance had been made in the public teaching of Medicine in the Metropolis and the two University centres. I should however mention that, according to John Aubrey, *Lives of Eminent Men*, pp. 482, 483, Dr., afterwards Sir, William Petty was resident at Oxford from 1648 to 1652, having entered himself of Brasenose College. 'Here he taught Anatomie to the Young Scholars,' and he adds, 'Anatomy was then but little understood by the University.' He was a private teacher, and this was subsequent to Harvey leaving Oxford and returning to London.

Tomlins Prælector at Oxford, and Reader at Barber Surgeons' Hall in the Metropolis.

Bartholomew's and St. Thomas's Hospitals.

Bartholomew's Hospital does not appear to have been used for the instruction of students till a much later period; and in 1609, when Harvey was appointed Physician, it was under the foundation given it in Henry the Eighth's time (Royal Charters of 1544 and 1547), after the separation from the Church, and seems to have contained upwards of 100 beds devoted to the treatment of sick persons. According to Mr. D'Arcy Power, from the first, the Hospital 'had an independent constitution and a separate estate, though it was for some purposes under the control of the Priory' (*Brit. Med. Journ.*, July 20, 1895).

At St. Thomas's Hospital, subsequently to 1571, attention was paid to the Medical and Surgical treatment of the inmates; and Mr. D'Arcy Power in his recent papers, just referred to, states that after 1694, when the Hospital was rebuilt, 'the first mention of a Medical School occurs'; and in later years it entered into alliance with Guy's in the eighteenth century. There was evidently no teaching given in it in Harvey's time, nor for long afterwards.

First mention of Medical Schools, 1694.

The other Medical Hospitals in London originated in and subsequently to the eighteenth century. The London Hospital started in 1740. Mr. Harrison delivered a course of lectures in the Hospital on Surgery in 1749, and Mr. Power observes, 'This School was therefore one of the earliest in England.'

and London Hospital, 1749.

Of the Provincial general Institutions, the earliest was that at Bristol in 1735; and it is noteworthy that it is styled an *Infirmary*. It occurs to me that this is indicative of its having arisen from a charitable public, rather than of its being part of the priestly organisation of a previous age, when such places are mentioned as Hospitals. Thus 'Hospital' is described by Baily in his Dictionary as derived from the Latin *hospitalium,* through the French *hôpital,* and defined as 'a house erected out of charity for the entertainment and relief of the poor, sick, impotent, or aged people.' Such a place was not likely before Harvey's time to be made use of for the instruction of students of Medicine in the diseases of the sick inmates. Addenbrook Hospital at Cambridge (and in relation to Dr. Winterton's high-sounding declaration, it seems, to say the least, remarkable, when it appears it was made 100 years before the means of Hospital instruction was obtainable at Cambridge) was not founded till 1740; and with the exception of the Bellott's Mineral Water Hospital at Bath in 1610, the Royal Hants Hospital at Winchester (1736), and the Bethel Hospital at Norwich, all the other general

Provincial Institutions. Bristol the first Infirmary or Hospital.

Addenbrook Hospital founded 1740.

Bellott's Hospital at Bath and Royal Hants, 1736. Bethel Hospital, Norwich.

Infirmaries or Medical or Surgical Hospitals in England are subsequent to that date.

Universities and College of Physicians and Incorporation of Surgeons.

But to return to the Universities and College of Physicians and Incorporation of Surgeons.

Evidently the rousing of the Medical teaching spirit had not commenced in England before the time of Harvey. It was stimulated by his lectures at the College of Physicians during his lifetime, but was not developed till long after his death. The aspirants to Medical instruction and titles had therefore to visit the Continental Universities and Schools to be indoctrinated in the healing art, unless they were content with such information and instruction as could be obtained from the Surgeon or Apothecary each was apprenticed to, or as the servant or pupil of a Physician.

London qualification for practice.

To practise as Physician or Surgeon in London, it was necessary to have the licence of the Bishop of London or the Dean of St. Paul's granted after examination, under guidance of four Physicians of the College, or of four Surgeons, but of what nature or scope these examinations were I can find no distinct evidence. They do not seem to have been of a practical character.

Scope of examination not known.

Licence of College of Physicians.

For the Physician the licence of the College was also necessary, but again the nature of the examination does not appear, further than that it was to be conducted by the President and Elects.

Apothecaries' examinations.

That of the Apothecaries is better defined; and although a Physician supervised, it was distinctly upon drugs. These examinations, as well as those of the College of Physicians, appear to have been conducted in private. It may be suggested that there were the Anatomical demonstrations by the Physicians and Surgeons on the 'Anatomies'—six by the Physicians and four by the Surgeons yearly—and it is possible that the apprentices, pupils, or students may have been admitted to these; but I take it the demonstrations were intended for the benefit of the Fellows

The Anatomies.

or Freemen of the Incorporation, and not for students in their apprentice stage unless as a favour. Judging from the pictures extant of such scenes, the spectators seem to have been of the grave and reverend seignior stamp, rather than of the gay ingenuous youth type, and afford a demonstration of the adage that it is never too late to learn.

London College of Physicians and teaching.

It is noteworthy, in connection with the constitution of the College of Physicians at this period, that there is no clause regarding 'teaching.' It had certainly the privilege of teaching, and the power to do so, as the permission to obtain four bodies granted by Queen Elizabeth; and afterwards increased by King James the First to six bodies yearly for *Anatomics* shows; but the Lumleian Lectures in Harvey's time would seem to have been the only means of teaching made use of.

London Barber Surgeons made use of the *Anatomics*.

It occurs to me that, seeing they originally partook of a surgical nature, and in Harvey's time were anatomical, they were intended to make a practical use of the 'Anatomics.' From the elegant volume published in 1890, *The Annals of the Barber Surgeons of London, Compiled from their Records and other Sources*, by Mr. Sidney Young, it is seen that the Surgeons not only made use of their privilege of claiming the four bodies yearly by their officers, who frequently had a hard fight to obtain possession of them, but that fines were exacted from those members who did not attend the dissections, and if the Surgeons did not appear in the prescribed dress, there was a fine of three shillings and fourpence. The dissector was also paid forty shillings. The dissections could not have been very minute, as the bodies were buried the next day or soon after.

Fines for non-attendance, etc.

Lectures read in 1566 by Dr. Wm. Cunningham.

Caldwal and Arris Reader founded in 1645.

Mr. Young states that Lectures were read at the Hall as early as 1566, or even before that date, when Dr. William Cunningham was Reader. But before Harvey's death there was some evidence of progress in the Company. In 1645 Alderman Edward Arris, one of their number, an enlightened and liberal-hearted man, acquainted their Court that a friend of his did by him freely offer to give the sum of £250 to the end and on the condition 'that a human body be once in every year hereafter publicly dissected, and six lectures thereupon be read in the Hall.' This was to furnish a stipend for the Reader. At the separation of the Barbers and Surgeons in George the Second's time, the amount of Arris benefaction, then £510, was transferred by the Barbers to the Surgeons.

From the *Description of the Pictures, etc., in the Hall and Court Room of the Worshipful Company of Barbers*, by Mr. Charles John Shoppee, 1883, it would appear, there was also a Lecture about this time (1645) founded at the Barber Surgeons' Hall by Dr. Richard Caldwal. It is not quite clear to me whether these benefactions were not related to each other, that Caldwal was the friend mentioned by Arris, and that the latter afterwards continued and extended the yearly amount of the benefaction to £30. According to Mr. Young, Dr. Scarborough was elected Anatomical Reader on the 12th October 1649; and according to Mr. Shoppee he read the Caldwal Lecture in the Hall 'for sixteen or seventeen years with great applause.' In his remarks on the portrait of Sir Charles Scarborough, it is observed: 'This picture represents this eminent physician when thirty-six years of age, delivering a lecture on anatomy, with Alderman Edward Arris as his demonstrating surgeon.' Beneath is an inscription in Latin, the first two lines of which are thus translated by Mr. Shoppee: 'This to thee, Scarborough, Arris dedicates, whose spirit and thine inwardly studies the noble framework of the human body.' Arris, manifestly having dedicated the portrait, economically makes use of it to immortalise and perpetuate his interest in the lecture which is being delivered by Scarborough with his assistance.

Dr. Charles Scarborough Reader in 1649.

Shoppee's Statement.

Sir Charles Scarborough Lumleian and Caldwal Lecturer.

Sir Charles Scarborough had therefore held the two positions, and was at the same time Lumleian Lecturer at the Royal College

SIR CHARLES SCARBOROUGH AT AGE OF 30.

of Physicians, and Caldwal and Arris Anatomical Reader to the Company of Barber Surgeons.

London private teaching begun by Cheselden.

As to private teaching in London, that may be said to have begun with Cheselden, Surgeon of St. Thomas's Hospital, in 1711; who thereby incurred the displeasure of the Barber Surgeons Company shortly afterwards, when he interfered with their prerogatives conferred by Henry the Eighth, by obtaining the dead bodies of persons executed and dissecting them, not for his own instruction but for that of his pupils.

Provincial Practice.

Rules for practice throughout the country were in force and were similar in nature to those in the Metropolis, but of course the means of instruction were no better. I should add, however, as regards the teaching at Oxford, that Broderick (the Hon. G. C. Brodrick, D.C.L.), in his *History of the University of Oxford*, London, 1891, at p. 72, in his remarks on Lynacre (who was elected Fellow of All Souls' in 1484, after being Professor of Medicine at Padua, and the first President of the College of Physicians), states that 'his principal claim to gratitude at Oxford consists in his posthumous foundation of two Readerships in Physiology at Merton College, which have since been consolidated into a Professorship of Anatomy. The new studies, however, met with violent opposition.'

Oxford.

Lynacre's Readerships in Physiology at Merton College.

Tomlins Prælectorship in Anatomy, 1623.

In Harvey's time the Tomlins Prælectorship in Anatomy was founded in 1623. This is the only new Medical University Foundation in England during the seventeenth century; but, after earnest inquiry at Oxford, I have failed to find its connection with the great Harvey or his teaching; nor have the Oxford authorities been able to favour me with any information regarding its originator. Like Linacre's Readerships, it was founded in connection with Merton College, of which Harvey was afterwards involuntarily Warden for the year 1645, and where he was for the first time associated with Charles Scarborough, who worked with him on his inquiry regarding generation. So far as I can determine, the Prælectorship is a coincidence, and not a consequence of Harvey's teaching. Dr. Caldwal's Readership at Barber Surgeons' Hall I incline to think resulted from Harvey's teaching and its effect upon at least one or two enlightened men.

As bearing on the College, and the Incorporation, and Society of London, I may state that Messrs. Jacob Bell and Theophilus Redwood in their *Historical Sketch of the Progress of Pharmacy in Great Britain*: London, Pharmaceutical Society, 1880, quote from Dr. Goodall's *History of the College of Physicians* as follows: The first Act of Parliament relating to the Medical Profession was passed in the year 1511, and is entitled, 'An Act for the Appointing of Physicians and Surgeons,' 3 Henry VIII. c. 9, and is thus worded: 'Be it therefore (to the surety and comfort of all manner of people) by the authority of this present Parliament enacted: That no person within the City London, nor within seven miles of the same, take upon him to exercise and occupy as a Physician or Surgeon, except he be first examined, approved, and admitted, by the Bishop of London, or by the Dean of St. Paul's, for the time being, calling to him or them, four Doctors of Physic, and for Surgery, other expert persons of that Faculty: and for the first examination such as they shall think convenient, and afterwards four of them that have been so approved,' etc. And further, 'that no person out of the said city and precinct of seven miles of the same, except he have been (as is aforesaid) approved in the same, take upon him to exercise and occupy as a Physician or Surgeon in any diocese within this realm, but if he be first examined and approved by the Bishop of the same diocese, or, he being out of the diocese, by his Vicar-General: either of them calling to them such expert persons in the said Faculties as their discretion shall think convenient.'

Dr. Goodall's *History of the College of Physicians.*

Qualifications for Practice in London and country.

Bell also states: 'The Physicians' assistants or dispensars were styled Apothecaries; and they, gradually acquiring information respecting the properties of drugs, began to transact business on

Apothecaries, origin of.

their own account.' From this it appears that the Apothecaries owed their existence to the Physicians. In 1518, Dr. Thomas Linacre, Physician of Henry the Eighth, proposed the establishment of a College of Physicians, which was accomplished on 23rd September 1518. Its powers were extended in 1540, and it was empowered to supervise the body it had caused to arise, by visiting the Apothecaries' shops, and inspecting their drugs. In 1723 the College of Physicians was again empowered by Act of Parliament, 10 Geo. I. c. 22, accompanied by the Master or Wardens of the Grocers' Company to visit and examine the Apothecaries' shops.

Supervision of, and of their shops.

The same authority informs us that the Barbers and Surgeons were also in 1540 erected into a Company; 'but the Surgeons were prohibited from shaving, and the Barbers were restricted from performing any surgical operations, except tooth-drawing. The Physicians were allowed to practise Surgery.'

Barber Surgeons erected into a Company in 1552.

Dr. Goodall in 1684 published a History of the Proceedings against Empirics, from which we learn that in 1552 the Lord Mayor decided it was illegal for Surgeons to practise Medicine, and in 1595 the College of Physicians issued a letter prohibiting their interference with Medical Practice.

Lord Mayor on Surgical and Medical Practice in 1552.

Goodall further states that in 1595, in the case of Read *v.* Jenkins, the Chief Justice decided 'that no Surgeon, as a Surgeon, might practise Physic for any disease'; and that 'no man, though never so learned a Physician or Doctour, might practise in London, or within seven miles, without the College Licence.'

Chief Justice's decision as to necessity for College of Physic Licence in 1595.

It is on record that the College interdicted in 1627 'Dr. Alexander Leighton . . . from Practice, being found unqualified on examination by the President and Censors'; but the nature of the examination does not appear.

From Bell and Redwood we also learn that in 1617 the Apothecaries formed a 'Dispensary,' 'for the purpose of making some of the most important preparations for the use of their own

Apothecaries' Dispensary of 1617.

Members.' This was at the time when the Apothecaries separated from the Grocers. The word 'Dispensary' is here used in its Pharmaceutical, not in its Medical signification. The education of the Apothecary was strictly insisted on. His apprenticeship extended to eight years, so that by his own observation he might acquaint himself with drugs and plants by the frequent use of them. He had also to visit the Physic Garden, and on several set days in the summer 'the Company have to go into the country on purpose to make acquaintance with all the vegetable tribes, the senior and more experienced instructing the juniors' (Bell and Redwood). There was also an 'Elaboratory' at their Hall. The same authorities state that 'the plan for preventing the further increase of Apothecaries consisted in the institution of a strict *examination for apprentices in Latin and Greek*, public lectures at the Hall, instruction in practical Pharmacy, and *an examination at the close of apprenticeship*, prior to the granting of a Licence to practise as an Apothecary.' This was in 1704.

Education of Apothecaries chiefly practical.

Reason for strict preliminary in 1704.

Ireland.

In Ireland Medical matters do not seem to have been more advanced, although the oldest of its Educational Institutions, the University of Dublin, Trinity College, dates from 1591. The first Medical Chair was founded in 1637, about a century later than those at the English Universities. It was the Regius Chair of 'Physic.'

Dublin University first Medical Chair 1637.

An Anatomic Chair was founded in 1716, whilst Chairs of Anatomy and Surgery, Chemistry and Botany, were founded in 1785.

Royal College of Physicians, 1660,

of Surgeons, 1784.

Apothecaries' Hall, 1791.

Medical Schools.

The Royal College of Physicians of Ireland dates from 1660. It was and is a Licensing Corporation, and does not teach. The Royal College of Surgeons only dates from 1784. It too is a Licensing Corporation, whilst the Apothecaries' Hall, also Licensing, was established in 1791. The Medical Schools and Hospitals in Ireland in the present day number seventeen. Mercer's Hospital, one of the oldest in the kingdom, dates from 1707. Jervis Street Hospital was founded in 1718, and Dr. Steeven's Hospital was established in 1720; but these are only used for Clinical tuition, and I have failed to find when they were first so used.

The Rotunda seems to have been used from an early period of its existence, which began in 1745, for giving Clinical instruction in Midwifery and diseases of women.

Let us next consider the position of Scotland previous to 1578, and also during the time of Harvey. Before he was born three Universities had already been established; but, like those in England, they were devoted to Classics and Philosophy rather than to Science and the Medical Art. The oldest of these Institutions was the University of St. Andrews.

Scotland.

Three Universities before Harvey.

It had been already in existence 167 years, having been founded in the year 1411 by Wardlaw, Bishop of St. Andrews, and two years later was sanctioned by Papal Bull of Benedict the Thirteenth.

University of St. Andrews founded 1411.

The Faculties of Arts, Theology, and Common Law existed from its beginning; and in the sixteenth century it comprised three distinct Corporate Colleges—St. Salvator's founded in 1455, St. Leonard's in 1512, and St. Mary's in 1537. Now, however, according to the Calendar of 1895, after undergoing various changes, it 'consists of three distinct corporations, viz.—the United College of St. Salvator and St. Leonard, with its Principal and nine Professors; St. Mary's College, with its Principal, who is also Primarius Professor, and three Professors; and the University, comprising the Members of both Colleges, and of which the Senior Principal (senior according to priority of office) is also President.'

Faculties of Arts, Theology, and Common Law from the beginning.

In sixteenth century three distinct Corporate Colleges.

This University even now, according to the Calendar of 1897-98, has only a Professor of Medicine, one of Natural History, and one of Chemistry; whilst Lecturers have recently been appointed in Botany, Anatomy, Materia Medica, and Physiology.

From Calendar of 1897-98.

By the new ordinances, women may now become matriculated students, and enter upon the various curricula with a view to graduation in Arts, Science, or Medicine—*Calendar*, p. iv.

In Harvey's time there existed only the Professorship of Chemistry.

I am indebted for the following information to Mr. J. Maitland Anderson, Secretary and Librarian to the University. Regarding the Medical Graduation System at the close of the seventeenth and beginning of the eighteenth centuries, under date 7th March 1896, he writes, 'Unfortunately it appears to be impossible to learn anything about that period. Before 1696 there are no records of Senatus at all, and between that date and 1711 I cannot find any trace of Medical degrees having been conferred. From 1711 onwards they have been granted continuously. From 1711 to 1826 they were conferred in two ways, *in presentiâ* and *in absentiâ*. In the former case there was an examination, in the latter there was none—the degree being granted on the basis of testimonials from three or more Medical men. Since 1826 the two methods have been combined, all candidates having to produce testimonials as well as to undergo an examination.'

Medical Graduation System in seventeenth and eighteenth centuries.

No record of Medical degrees between 1696 and 1711.

From 1711 to 1826 conferred in two ways.

Since 1826 two methods combined.

As indicating the method of procedure at St. Andrews, I may state that, in reply to a further inquiry as to the conferring the degree of Doctor of Medicine upon John Clerk, afterwards admitted Socius of the Royal College of Physicians of Edinburgh, Mr. Maitland Anderson has favoured me with the following: 'St. Andrews, 25th June 1711, the said the University being met, there was produced by the Rector a letter from Dr. Pitcairn in favour of one, Mr. Clerk, desiring a diploma to him, whereby he is to be graduat Dr. of Medicine, which the University, taking to their consideration, desired the Rector to write to Dr. Pitcairn that the University is willing to grant a diploma upon the attestation of three known Physicians, and this diploma is to be free of all charges, except the Beddals dues.' 'There is

St. Andrews University, 1711.

John Clerk, how degree conferred.

nothing more about Clerk in the Minutes, so I presume, from what you say, that he had produced the certificates, and got the diploma.' He did so without examination.

Dr. John Clerk was afterwards a distinguished Physician of his day, but the College of Physicians of Edinburgh, being obliged to receive all Candidates holding Scottish University degrees, without being subjected to its examination, naturally resented this obligation, and viewed such graduates with scant satisfaction, more especially when foreign graduates, whose qualifications had been already tested by a Continental University, could not be received as Socii until they had been subjected to examination by Fellows of the College.

Dr. John Gairdner's views.

According to Dr. J. Gairdner, in his *Sketch of the Early History of the Medical Profession in Edinburgh*, delivered at the College of Surgeons in January 1864: 'In St. Andrews, the celebrated Dr. John Arbuthnott appears to be the first Doctor in Physic created (September 11, 1696). He was subjected to a trial before a board of Physicians. From the tenour of the Minute, it appears that the conferring of Medical degrees was then a new thing, and no more were conferred for six years after.' Dr. Gairdner obtained this information from the late Dr. Oswald H. Bell, Professor of Medicine at St. Andrews University.

The University of Glasgow founded 1450.

The University of Glasgow dates from 1450. King James the Second, at the instigation of Bishop Turnbull, obtained a Bull of Pope Nicholas the Fifth for its foundation. It taught from its foundation Canon and Civil Law, Theology, and the Arts; and had power to grant degrees in all the Faculties.

Before Harvey a Principal and three Professors.

The year before Harvey's birth, in 1577, King James the Sixth granted a Charter known as the *Nova Erectio*, by which provision was made for the support of a Principal, who also taught Theology, and of three Regents in Philosophy.

First Medical Chair, 1713.

It was not, however, until 1713 that the first acting Medical Chair was founded, that of Practice of Medicine, whilst that of

Anatomy was not established till 1718, 103 years after Harvey first lectured at the College of Physicians in London on the circulation of the blood.

The Chair of Chemistry at this University was not founded till 1817. It was preceded by those of Natural History in 1807, and Surgery and Midwifery in 1815; and was succeeded by those of Materia Medica in 1831, and Forensic Medicine and Physiology in 1839. Clearly, therefore, Harvey could have received no instruction here. The spirit of his teaching was long in reaching this University, and it is evident it owed nothing directly to his influence.

Dr. John Gairdner's observations.

Minute of 1712.

Dr. John Gairdner considers that the graduates in Medicine were inconsiderable in number in the sixteenth and seventeenth centuries. He further observes, 'On 6th November 1712 there is a Minute to the effect that "the Faculty, considering that the professions of Law and Medicine have of a long time been neglected, and that the Royal visitation in the year 1664 did find that the said professions ought to be revived," agreed that they should be revived. Accordingly, Dr. John Johnstoun was made Professor of Medicine, 1st June 1714; and some years after, 29th September 1720, a Mr. Andrew Grahame was made Doctor in absence.' He refers to the *Institutes* of the University of Glasgow printed by the Maitland Club.

First Medical Graduate, 1720.

University of Aberdeen, founded 1494, consisted of King's College, 1494, and Marischal College, 1593.

The third Scottish University was that of Aberdeen. But originally, and until 1860, it consisted of the University and King's College of Aberdeen, founded in 1494 by Bishop William Elphinstone of Aberdeen, and was also sanctioned by Papal Bull obtained by James the Fourth; whilst Marischal College and University of Aberdeen was founded in 1593.

When Harvey, therefore, was fifteen years old, and just thinking about going to Caius College, Cambridge, Marischal College was founded, under a Charter ratified by Parliament, by George Keith, Earl Marischal; and from this it has its title.

Aberdeen University takes rank, however, in virtue of the foundation of King's College being in 1494.

In the Faculty of Medicine the oldest Chairs were in connection with the original College. The Chair of Chemistry was founded in 1505; and, after an interval of eighty-eight years, it was followed by that of Natural History in 1593.

Chemistry founded in 1505.

Practice of Medicine was not founded till 1700, forty-three years after Harvey's death, and next came Anatomy in 1839! And yet Aberdeen was a recognised source of Medical degrees before 1700, and its officials objected, for that reason, to the Edinburgh College of Physicians being formed.

Whilst the dates of the foundation of the Chairs which I have given are those now entered in recent official returns, it must be borne in mind that the Chair at present designated as 'Chemistry,' and founded in 1505, was originally also one of Medicine, and the holder of it was known as the 'Mediciner.'

The Chair of 1505 was held by the Mediciner.

Chambers, in the second volume of *Domestic Annals of Scotland*, quotes from the *Spalding Club Miscellany*, vol. ii. p. 73, the following interesting paragraph, under date April 1st, 1636: 'On the application of Mr. William Gordon, Professor of Medicine and Anatomy in the University of Aberdeen, who had hitherto been obliged to illustrate his lessons by dissecting beasts, the Privy Council gave consent to the Sheriffs and Magistrates of Aberdeen to allow him the bodies of a couple of malefactors for the service of his class, if such could be had; but, failing these, the bodies of any poor people who might die in Hospitals or otherwise, and have no friends to take exception; this being with the approbation of the Bishop of Aberdeen, Chancellor of the University.' But so late as 1788 or 1790, Mrs. Rodgers, in her book of *Aberdeen Doctors*, tells the origin of the Medical Students' Society about this time; and at page 56 observes, 'Once a week a dog was dissected, and the parts divided, each man demonstrating on his own portion. This was all the Anatomical instruction the

Application for bodies for dissection by the Mediciner of 1636.

Medical Students' Society of 1790.

Medical Students of Aberdeen received'; and at another place she remarks, 'The want of proper Medical instruction was greatly felt in the North of Scotland, despite the two Colleges in Aberdeen.'

Since writing the preceding page, I have seen the Aberdeen University Calendar for 1895-96, and at page 13, under the head of 'University and King's College,' I find the following statement regarding the Professor of Medicine in that University: 'The duties of the Doctor or Professor of Medicine (Mediciner), originally intended to embrace instruction in all the branches of Medical education, were in 1839 restricted to the teaching of Chemistry. In its original form, this Chair constitutes the most ancient foundation for instruction in Medicine in Great Britain.' You may remember the Oxford Chair of Medicine was established in 1535.

Duties of the Mediciner or Professor of Medicine.

The list of 'Mediciners,' as given in the Calendar, commences with the name of 'James Cumyne,' who was Mediciner before 1522. The Chair in the seventeenth century was held in 1619 by Patrick Dun, afterwards Principal of Marischal. In 1632 William Gordon, mentioned as desiring to improve the teaching of Anatomy, was appointed. He held the Chair for eight years. After being vacant for some years, Andrew Moore was elected in 1649, and seems to have been in possession for twenty-three years. Patrick Urquhart was appointed his successor in 1672. He must have been the holder of the Chair when the Royal College of Physicians of Edinburgh was founded, and the opposer of its erection, for the next recorded appointment to the Chair was fifty-three years after, when James Gregory the elder was elected in 1725.

Professor Sir John Struthers, in his notes on the progress of Aberdeen University, gives interesting particulars as to the examinations and their development at this University, and remarks: 'There was, of course, the old-fashioned and still existing

Examinations at University.

"paper," and there was the "oral" examination, a conversation across a table-cover, but no dissections or laboratory work or clinical testing.' Professor Struthers in his remarks seems to ignore the progressive improvement in teaching, and the appliances for and the means of teaching; and the 'conversation across a table-cover' was undoubtedly an improvement on the time when there was no examination whatever, and this again on the degree being given without the candidate appearing at all, but merely sending testimonials. Mr. Robert Sangster Rait tells us in *The Universities of Aberdeen, a History* (1895) that up to 1817 degrees in Medicine were given on the recommendation of some Physicians of eminence, but, after this date, an account of the candidate's education was required, of the lectures he had attended, and of any public examination he may have undergone, as well as certificates from two Physicians. This was the system followed at King's College till the union in 1860, whilst at Marischal College up to 1825 the honorary degree of M.D. was conferred upon the recommendation of known Doctors; but in April of that year regulations were made that personal examination would henceforth be essential. It seems rather late in the ages of the University to come to such a resolution, and there can be no wonder that, when the Edinburgh College of Physicians began its work in 1681, the Fellows seem to have regarded with distaste the obligatory admission of such University Graduates to its Society, without any examination or trial by the Fellows of the Royal College.

Mr. Rait's Accounts of Medical degrees given up to 1817 and to 1860.

Marischal College after 1825 requires personal examination.

One word more before leaving Mr. Rait's *History* and the University of Aberdeen. At page 360 he remarks, 'The greatest expansion, however, has been in the Faculty of Medicine. The reputation of the Aberdeen Medical School has been made since 1860, and its success has been in large measure due to the exertions of Professor Struthers, who occupied the Chair of Anatomy from 1863 to 1889.' This is a note of well deserved praise to one whom

Medical School expands under Professor Struthers after 1860.

his sovereign has recently honoured, and to a former holder of the Harveian Society Presidentship.

Bower's error as to early Medical Professors in Scotland.

According to Bower (*The History of the University of Edinburgh, etc.*, by Alexander Bower: Edinburgh, 1817, vol. i. p. 41), 'The earliest notice which I have been able to discover of any Professor of Medicine in Scotland, is in Glasgow in 1637.' A statement for which he refers to the *Statistical Account*, vol. xxi. p. 25. 'It seems, however, to have been merely a nominal office, and that no regular course of Lectures was delivered upon that science for a very long time after.'

Bower is, as I have shown, in error in this statement, for the erection of the Medical Chair at Aberdeen, now designated 'Chemistry,' was in 1505; and I have mentioned that Professor William Gordon in April 1636 obtained 'Anatomies' from which to teach, and had then held the Chair of Medicine in Aberdeen for four years.

Graduates as early as 1556.

Dr. John Gairdner in his *Sketch*, p. 16, considers that Gilbert Skene, Professor of Medicine at Aberdeen in 1556, was probably a graduate of the University. He further observes: 'It does not appear to me that there was any considerable number of Aberdeen graduates in the sixteenth century or even in the seventeenth.' Towards the close of the seventeenth the Medical degree would seem to have been very easily obtained.

THE UNIVERSITY OF EDINBURGH

Edinburgh University.

The fourth of the Scottish Universities, but now second to none in all its Faculties, but especially so in the Medical, is that of Edinburgh. It was established nearly 100 years after that of Aberdeen. In 1582, when Harvey was four years old, James the Sixth founded it. At first it was designated 'Academia Jacobi Sexti,' or 'King James's College.'

Originated in 1558.

Its origination was really twenty-four years before that date,

KING JAMES VI.

QUEEN ANNE OF DENMARK.

for in 1558 Bishop Reid of Orkney made a bequest to the Town Council of Edinburgh for the erection of a College. The money did not immediately pass into their hands, for it was retained by the Abbot of Kinloss. On the faith that ultimately it would be received, the Town Council purchased land, Queen Mary granted a Charter of Presentation to some confiscated Church property, and a building was commenced in 1581. The University was incorporated in the year following, 1582, by Royal Charter by King James the Sixth, and the original grants of Queen Mary were increased.

Incorporated by James Sixth in 1582.

Teaching in this University does not appear to have commenced until 1583, and at first the Professors or Regents were only in Humanity and Greek, Mathematics and Natural Philosophy, Logic, Metaphysics, Moral Philosophy, and Divinity.

Teaching begun in 1583.

It was not until about 100 years later that a Medical Faculty was thought of. The Chair of Anatomy is claimed to have been founded in 1705, but whether quite accurately or not we shall presently see. Assuming for the present that period to be correct, it was not until ninety years after the first lecture was delivered by Harvey in London, and seventy-seven years after the publication of his *Disquisition*, that the governing patrons of the 'Academia Jacobi Sexti' woke up to the importance of adding a degree in Medicine to their University curriculum. But this was not the first Chair, neither was it the name of Harvey, nor the importance of his discovery which directly led to its being created. It was due to local influences and Medical aspirations arising around the University, afterwards stimulated by the Royal College of Physicians; and, as I hope to show you, it was through it indirectly connected with Harvey and some of his pupils and followers.

Medical Faculty thought of, 1685. Anatomy in 1705.

Its association with the Royal College of Physicians, and indirectly with Harvey and his followers.

One authority (*Oliver and Boyd's Almanac*, 1889) remarks regarding this University: 'Its medical fame, which arose under Dr. Alexander Monro after 1720, is second to that of no

Professor Alex. Monro, 1720.

University in Europe'; but that was not until fifteen years after the foundation of the Chair of Anatomy, which by the same authority is stated to have been founded in 1705. As I shall later show, there was a gradual development, and in that development the Royal College of Physicians through one of its original Fellows played the initial part.

Botany claimed to be founded in 1676.

The University seems to claim the origination of its Chair of Botany in 1676, but at that time the University had no good reason to regard the institution of the Botanic Garden by Sibbald and Balfour as connected with it. The idea was quite distinct from University influence, nor does it appear from Sibbald's account that the University contributed at first in any way towards the intendant's expenses. There can be little or no doubt that the institution of the Botanic Garden by Sibbald was for the instruction of students in Botany, next for the enlightenment of Apothecaries in the vegetable Materia Medica, and that it was associated in Sibbald's mind with the issuing of a Pharmacopœia, which he strove hard to produce as one of the first efforts of the College of Physicians. At first, too, the garden was not associated with the Town Council, the patrons of the University. Their relation to it was secondary, and began when its promoters obtained from them a lease of the Trinity College garden ground, subsequently termed, from the use it was put to, the Physic Garden. The Town Council allowed Mr. Sutherland the intendant, at a later period, £20 a year, but it would seem rather as keeper or intendant of the Garden than as a University Professor.

The Physic Garden in Trinity College grounds.

Arrangement with Surgeon Apothecaries for pupils.

Mr. Sutherland also had relations subsequently with the Corporation of Surgeons and Apothecaries; for in 1695 they made an arrangement for their apprentices and pupils to receive instruction at the Physic Garden at a fee of one guinea each. The Garden was also benefited by the patronage and subscriptions of members of the College of Justice. I delay the further consideration of this matter, as it will again be referred to in the concluding part of this Oration.

It was not till after the erection of the College of Physicians that a Medical Professor was elected, and the first Medical Professor was Sir Robert Sibbald. The wording of the Minute of 25th March 1685 of the meeting of Town Council held on that day indicates that the University was 'indowed with the previleges of erecting professions of all sorts, particularly of Mediceen,' and that there is 'a necessity ther be ane professour of Physick in the said Colledge, therefor as Patrons of the said Colledge and University unanimously elect, nominate, and choyse the sd Sir Robert Sibbald to be Professor of Physick in ye sd University.' Here the appointment in 1685 is distinctly to the University. Preston, the botanist, in 1712 was elected Professor of Botany of 'this City.' He was the *Town's* botanist rather than the *University* Professor, though allied to it. Further on, on 4th September 1685, the Council Minute of that day intimates 'that the Counsell appoynts two Professors of Mediceen to be joyned with Sir Robert Sibbald in the University.' On the 9th September the Minute records: 'Considering that ther is ane necessity ther be more Professors of Mediceen in the said University, and understanding the abilityes and great qualifications of Doctor James Halkit and Doctor Archibald Pitcairne, Doctors of Mediceen, and ther fitness to teatch the airt of Mediceen in the said University, Doe therfore elect, nominate, and choyse ye sds two Doctors to be joyned with the said Sir Robert Sibbald, his Majestie's Phisitian in ordinary, to be Professors of Mediceen in the sd University,' etc. etc. I have afterwards to refer to these appointments, and meantime point out that they were the first, and were evidently intended to form a Medical Faculty in the University.

First Medical Professor of Physic, 1685.

Two more Professors of Medicine.

Dr. James Halkit. Dr. Arch. Pitcairne.

Intended to form a Medical Faculty.

In December 1713 a further addition was made to the Medical Staff of the University by the appointment of Dr. James Crawfurd

1713. Professor of Medicine and Chemistry succeeds.

as Professor of Physic and Chemistry. He, like the three Medical Professors just alluded to, was a Fellow of the College of Physicians, and had studied at Leyden under Boerhaave. According to Bower (*op. cit.*) he only lectured at times, so that the encouragement he received did not induce him to deliver an annual course. At first he had no salary, but afterwards was allowed seven hundred merks, and in 1719 this sum was increased to nine hundred.

Professor A. Pitcairn a supporter of Harvey.

Dr. Archibald Pitcairn, who does not appear to have lectured as Professor of Medicine in the University, died in 1713. He supported the views of Harvey and Bellini, and in connection with the rise of the Anatomical Department of the Medical School of Edinburgh, at first outside the University, he performed an important part as suggestor and instigator; for by him efforts were made so early as 1694 to obtain more opportunity for human dissection. In this he was associated with his friend Alexander Monteath, a member of the Corporation of Surgeons, who was regarded by Pitcairn as an excellent man, an eminent Surgeon, and well acquainted with Chemistry. With the sanction of the Corporation he had already delivered lectures on Chemistry and Materia Medica.

Suggestor of improved Anatomical teaching along with Alexander Monteath.

Chambers's account of rise of Edinburgh Medical School.

Chambers, in his *Domestic Annals of Scotland*, in the third volume, makes the following statement: 'Previous to 1705, when the first Professor of Anatomy was appointed in the University of Edinburgh, there were only a few irregular attempts in the Scottish capital to give instruction in that department of Medical education. We first hear of dissection of the dead body in our city in the latter part of the year 1694, a little before which time the celebrated Dr. Archibald Pitcairn had left a distinguished position as Professor of Medicine in the University of Leyden, and marrying an Edinburgh lady, had been induced finally to settle there in practice. On the 14th October Pitcairn wrote to his friend, Dr. Robert Gray of London' (he was afterwards elected an

Honorary Fellow of the Edinburgh Royal College of Physicians), 'that he was taking part in an effort to obtain subjects for dissection from the Town Council, requesting from them the bodies of those who die in the Correction House called Paul's Work, and have none to bury them. "We offer," he says, "to wait on these poor for nothing, and bury them after dissection at our own charges, which now the town does; yet there is great opposition by the chief Surgeons, who neither eat hay nor suffer the oxen to eat it. I do propose, if this be granted, to make better improvements in Anatomy than have been made at Leyden these thirty years; for I think most or all Anatomists have neglected or not known what is most useful for a Physician."' Dr. Chambers continues: 'The person ostensibly moving in the matter was Mr. Alexander Monteath, an eminent Surgeon, and a friend of Pitcairn. In compliance with this request the Town Council (October 24) gave him a grant of the dead bodies of those dying in the Correction House, and of foundlings who die on the breast, allowing at the same time a room for dissection, and freedom to inter the remains in the College Kirk Cemetery, but stipulating that they bury the intestines within forty-eight hours, and the remainder of the body within ten days, and that his prelections should only be during the winter half of the year.' Having quoted so much from Chambers, it is only fair I should quote the conclusion. He further observes: 'Monteath's brethren did not present any opposition to his movement generally. They only disrelished his getting the Council's gift exclusively to himself. Professing to give demonstrations in Anatomy also, they preferred a petition to the Town Council, asking the unclaimed bodies of persons dying in the streets; and foundlings who died off the breast; and the request was complied with on condition of their undertaking to have a regular Anatomical Theatre ready before the term of Michaelmas 1697. Such were the beginnings of the Medical School of Edinburgh.'

Dr. Archibald Pitcairn's action along with Dr. Monteath stimulated the action of Incorporation of Chirurgeons.

First Anatomical Theatre.

The Surgeons were also to have a public Anatomical dissection in their theatre once a year.

Robert Elliot, the Public Dissector of Incorporation of Chirurgeons.

In 1705, Robert Elliot, Chirurgeon Apothecary and Burgess of the city, was by an Act of the Incorporation of the Chirurgeon Apothecaries unanimously elected their Public Dissector of Anatomy. He applied to the Town Council for encouragement in his 'intention to make a public profession and teaching thereof for the instruction of youth.' The Town Council signified its approval. 'And, for the petitioner's encouragement to go on in the said profession, they allow the petitioner £15 sterling of yearly salary during the Council's pleasure.' This was on the 29th August 1705 (Bower, vol. ii. p. 161, from Council Regist., vol. xxxviii. p. 352). 'Mr. Elliot was accordingly regularly inducted, and was the first Professor of Anatomy in the University of Edinburgh.' It will be noted he was the nominee of the Chirurgeons, and adopted by the Town Council (*op. cit.*). He died early in 1714, and on 24th October following the Patrons nominated Dr. Adam Drummond his successor. As he was engaged in extensive practice, Mr. John Macgill, 'a young man of an enterprising temper,' was united with him, and received half the emoluments.

Inducted first Professor of Anatomy in University.

His successors, Drummond and Macgill.

1720, Alexander Monro appointed.

In January 1720 they both demitted their position as Professors in favour of Dr. Alexander Monro, who, having been specially trained for the office of Professor or Teacher of Anatomy, became their distinguished successor, and the establisher of the Anatomical fame of the Edinburgh University and Medical School, with the magnificent allowance of £15 sterling of yearly stipend.

1705, first degree in Medicine conferred.

The Medical Faculty of the University of Edinburgh arose therefore long after the day of Harvey, and it was not till 1705 that the first degree in Medicine was conferred by this University, in the manner I shall afterwards narrate. *From the first its Medical degree was conferred after examination*, and the Professor of Anatomy did not take part in the examination.

SCOTTISH MEDICAL CORPORATIONS

At the time of Harvey's birth in 1578, one only of the Scottish Corporations had existence, and was originally incorporated, in association with the Barbers, on 1st July 1505, and also subsequently with the Apothecaries. The association of the Barbers and Chirurgeons was traceable in its origin to monkish times, when shaving was done as a mystic ecclesiastical right by the one, whilst the enjoined periodical bleeding was performed by the other. On 1st July the Surgeons and Barbers presented a petition to the Magistrates and Town Council of Edinburgh that their society might be recognised as one of the Guilds of Craftsmen of Edinburgh, with the exclusive privilege of exercising their craft, which was granted and ratified. This was also ratified by King James the Fourth on 13th October 1506. In 1613 King James the Sixth confirmed the original seal of cause. In 1657 the association of the Surgeons and Apothecaries appears, for on 25th February 1657 the Town Council, on the petition of the Apothecaries and Surgeon Apothecaries in the burgh, enact that no person shall be admitted to practise the art in the burgh unless under certain restrictions, and that from time to time the bailies and two or more Apothecaries shall inspect the drugs that are for sale in the burgh, but this act was not to be held as erecting them into a Corporation. On 23rd August 1670 Parliament again confirmed all previously confirmed Acts, and confirmed the Acts of the Town Council in favour of both the Incorporation of the Surgeons and Barbers, and the brotherhood of Apothecaries and Surgeon Apothecaries, and anew ordained the Magistrates to maintain the privileges of the two bodies. In 1694 the Surgeons received a gift and patent from the Crown which was ratified by Parliament, and in 1778 they received a Royal Charter (see *A Collection of Royal Grants in relation to the Royal College of Surgeons in Edinburgh*, 1505-1817: Edinburgh, 1818).

Scottish Medical Corporations.

Barber Surgeons incorporated in 1505 as one of the Guilds of the City, and later associated with the Apothecaries.

Enactment of 1657.

In 1778 received a Royal Charter.

Incorporations of Barbers and Surgeons dissolved.

As in London, so in Edinburgh, in the course of time the Incorporation of Barbers and Surgeons was dissolved.

Physicians and Apothecaries in London.

The Physicians of London having first instituted and encouraged the Apothecaries there, after a time finding that they were becoming too powerful, then entered into controversy with them and endeavoured to depress them. The effect of this was to have a stimulating influence upon the Apothecaries, who had originated with the Grocers, and this ultimately ended in the development of a new order of Medical Practitioners in London. In Edinburgh, on the other hand, the question of the association between Apothecaries and Surgeons introduced that Corporation to the Court of Session, and this indirectly led to the formation of a College of Physicians.

Effects of association of Apothecaries and Surgeons in Edinburgh.

The separation of the Surgeons from the Barbers and Apothecaries was undoubtedly very favourable for the Surgeons. As one of the trade corporations of the city, the Surgeons had a right to send their elected head, their so-called 'Deacon,' to represent their interests, as one of the members of the Town Council of the city; and as such, in the past generations the Surgeons were the professional guardians of the health of the town and its burgesses, and the guiders of the sanitation of the municipality. They also claimed the right to supervise the shops of the Apothecaries, and to inspect the quality of their drugs. This was one of the points on which they objected to the establishment of the College of Physicians, and for many years was the cause of great dissatisfaction between the two Colleges, for the newly erected body of the Physicians had obtained this privilege in their Charter.

Deacons of the Surgeons.

With the passing of the Burgh Reform Act of 1833, the Surgeons with the other Guilds and Corporations lost the right to send their Deacon to the Council Board of the town; but at the times when the Physicians of the city were endeavouring to obtain a position and a Charter of Incorporation, the intimate relations which existed between the Surgeons and the Town

Effect of Burgh Reform on Deacon's position.

Council on the one hand, and the Town Council and Edinburgh University on the other, of which they were the Patrons or Governors, along with the Church dignitaries, who occupied such positions as Chancellors of the Universities, rendered the opposition of the Surgeons a very formidable matter.

Incorporation of Surgeons, their opposition to formation of a College of Physicians.

In their early Association or Corporation, dating from 1st July 1505, the Chirurgeons do not appear to have done much as a teaching body; although they had the privilege to teach—and not only so, but had a certain right, though more limited than that of the London Barber Surgeons—as regards the study of Anatomy, for they could obtain the body of one executed criminal each year for this use; but so far as I have been able to determine, it does not appear that, previous to the incorporation of the College of Physicians of Edinburgh (which had tried, but ineffectually, to have a like privilege conferred upon it) in 1681, this right had been of much benefit to any one. Yet from the earliest period candidates for admission to the Corporation had to pass an examination of a certain kind in Anatomy.

Chirurgeons' Incorporation dates from 1505 as a teaching body.

Entrance examination.

It does not seem to have occurred to any one to suggest an increase in the number of subjects to be dissected, until Dr. Archibald Pitcairn, one of the original Fellows of the College of Physicians, at this time still in association with it, and not connected with the Surgeons' Incorporation, who had recently returned from being a Professor of Medicine at the University of Leyden, agitated in this matter. He obtained, in conjunction with Mr. Alexander Monteath, as already narrated, an important concession as regards bodies for Anatomical purposes from the Town Council which were to be used for private teaching. His venture does not appear to have been so successful as the sanguine Pitcairn expected, and after giving it a trial, Monteath relinquished it, and returned to teach Chemistry at the Hall of the Chirurgeons.

Effects of Pitcairn's suggestion.

Monteath's venture fails, but has a stimulating effect on Incorporation of Chirurgeons.

This episode would seem to be confirmatory of the surmise

that he, like the previous University Professors of 1685, was before the time, and that there was not a sufficient number of pupils. In other words, that there was as yet no attraction of students from a distance. But this display of energy had a good effect. The Corporation of Chirurgeons was thereby stimulated to act in protection of their interests and privileges, and in its corporate capacity applied to the Town Council to be allowed more subjects. The Council were astute men and meant business, but not at the Town's expense. To give this second application due importance, they granted it on condition that what was wanting in the city should be supplied at the cost of the Incorporation, viz., a suitable Anatomical Theatre, within a fixed time, and in which a public demonstration might be given once a year.

Intra and extra Academical Medical School assured.

Thereafter the success of the movement was assured, and it ultimately led to the establishment of the intra and extra Academical Medical School. But it was long after Harvey's death, and the first stimulus was given, as I have shown, by Dr. Archibald Pitcairn, a recognised supporter of his views and defender of his discovery, a Professor of Medicine in the University, and one of the founders of the Royal College of Physicians.

First stimulated by Dr. Pitcairn, a Physician.

Pitcairn's action at this time intensifies one's desire to know the real reason for his not discharging the duties of a Professor in the University, seeing he was appointed by the Town Council one of the three to form a Medical Faculty nine years before. The reputation associated with his short career at Leyden eminently bears testimony to his capability at this period of his life for the brilliant performance of a prælector's function.

1595, Chirurgeons protect themselves against outsiders.

So early as 1595 the Corporation of Chirurgeons was earnest in protecting its rights, for, according to Chambers (*op. cit.*), in that year 'complaint made to Town Council, against a French Surgeon M. Arvin practising his art within the liberties of the city, by the Corporation of Surgeons'; and in consequence he was restricted to cutting for stone, ruptures, and cataracts, curing the pestilence, and diseases of women consequent on childbirth.

From the *Traditions of Edinburgh, Chronologically Arranged*: Edinburgh, W. Rutherford, 1848, and also from Dr. John Gairdner's *Historical Sketch of the Royal College of Surgeons*, an address delivered at the College 19th January 1860, the nature of the intrants' examination in 1505 is learned. Previous to the admission of a member, he required to be a freeman and burgess of the city and 'that he be worthy and expert in all the poyntis belangand the saidis Craftis deligentlie and avysitlie examinit and admittit be the maisteris of the said craft. . . . And als that everie man that is to be maid frieman and maister amangis be examinit and previt in thir poyntis following:—That is to say that he knaw anatomei nature and complexioun of everie member of humanis bodie: And in lykewayes he knaw all the vaynis of the samyn thatt he may mak flewbothomea in dew tyme. And alsua that he knaw in quhilk member the signe hes domination for the tyme; for everie man aucht to knaw the nature and substance of everie thing he wirkis or ellis he is negligent, and thatt we may have ains in the Zeir ane condampnit man efter he be deid to mak anatomea of, quhair throw we may haif experience. Ilk ane to instruct utheris and we sall do sufferage for the soule.' The amount of preliminary instruction was also specified. 'Item that na maisteris of the said craft sall tak ane prenteis or feit man in tyme cuming to use the surregeane craft without he can baith wryte and reid.'

Chirurgeons' original intrants' examination, 1505.

THE FACULTY OF PHYSICIANS AND SURGEONS OF GLASGOW

Faculty of Physicians and Surgeons, Glasgow.

When Harvey began his Medical studies at Padua in 1598, the Faculty of Physicians and Surgeons of Glasgow was merely in its inceptive stage, and it was not constituted until the dawn of the seventeenth century. It was instituted by Royal Charter in 1599, nearly a hundred years after the Edinburgh College of Surgeons took its rise, and was like it in association with the Barbers.

Founded by Dr. Peter Lowe, 1599.

It was founded by Dr. Peter Lowe, an account of whose works and life has within recent years been written by Dr. James Finlayson, a Fellow of the Faculty. Mr. Alexander Duncan, B.A. Lond., the Librarian and Secretary of the Faculty, has also this year (1896) published the interesting *Memorials of the Faculty of Physicians and Surgeons of Glasgow*, 1599-1850, etc.: Glasgow, 1896.

Duties, fiscal and examining, not teaching.

It does not appear that the 'Faculty' ever was a teaching body, but only privileged to exercise Medical and Fiscal supervision over the Baronie of Glasgow, and the neighbouring counties, Renfrew, Dumbarton, Lanark, and Ayr, and to examine candidates for admission to practise therein, as Licentiates and Fellows of the Incorporation.

It was founded when Harvey was twenty-one years old, the year after he went to study at Padua, and sixteen years before his first lecture at the College of Physicians in London. His influence, therefore, had nothing to do with its conception or origin.

System of examination.

The system of examination, even from an early period, seems to have been for the age very good and thorough. The system of apprenticeship was at first in full force, but gradually gave way before the extension of Medical School teaching, and at last ceased to be necessary. Most of the Glasgow Surgeons of the early days were trained solely by apprenticeship, at first extending over seven years. If seeking to be admitted to the Faculty, the candidate was examined three times—first at the end of three years, then at five, and lastly at seven, when 'he examinat upon the holl particulars of his airt, of the definitions, causes, signs, accidents, and cures of all diseases pertaining to his airt, w[t] the composition of, nature, and fit medicaments,' etc. etc. In 1602 part of the examination was to be in writing, and 'many circumstances tend to prove that the examinations were to a considerable extent practical,' and 'even the Clinical was not always awanting in the examinations of these early days.' In the eighteenth century Surgeons were admitted only after examination, and the test was divided into two parts,—the first the 'private,' the last the 'public,' trial. The first was the more important. The candidate was tested in both the theory and practice of his profession. At the public examination he had to dissect a prescribed part, to discourse on a set Surgical or Medical theme, and to make up a Pharmaceutical preparation. About 1740 the Faculty gave up the examinations being conducted in its presence, and the first examination was conducted by a committee selected on each occasion, but ultimately a yearly standing committee of examiners was appointed.

Eighteenth century private and public trials.

Had Harvey, when starting in life, turned his face to Scotland, it is evident he could have received no Medical training there, either at University or Corporation, nor would he have met with any encouragement in the prosecution of his Anatomical studies, for it is not until 1636 that we find the Professor of Medicine at Aberdeen preferring his request to the Town Council there, that he may have human subjects given him, on which to illustrate his lessons, instead of having to do so from dead beasts. The year is significant,—could Professor William Gordon of Aberdeen have been a pupil or been influenced by Harvey's teaching? There is no record. With the exception of this

No training for Harvey in Scotland.

Was Prof. Gordon of Aberdeen a pupil of Harvey's?

indication of progress at Aberdeen, twenty-one years after Harvey first lectured at the College of Physicians in London and eight years after the publication of his *Exercitatio Anatomica* there is no evidence of any Medical School in Scotland previously. It may be said there were no organised Scottish Medical Schools until subsequent to Drs. Pitcairn's and Monteath's movement in 1694. Before then there may have been individual teaching but there was no public organisation.

No organised Scottish School till after 1694.

Anderson College in Glasgow only assumed its form as an educational establishment in 1796. Whilst the Edinburgh School, although attempted previously, cannot be said to have become established till the close of the seventeenth and beginning of the eighteenth centuries.

No Medical Hospital.

No Medical Hospital was in existence in Scotland in the days of Harvey. The first to arise was the Royal Infirmary of Edinburgh. The Hospitals, with perhaps an exception in favour of special places of *detention* but I cannot say for *treatment* of cases of Leprosy, Grandgore or Syphilis, and the Pest or Plague, bore the impress of the Church, and were rather places of entertainment or support for the aged, or correctional, such as Paul's Work, or residential places for education of the young. The special places were intended for the protection of the healthy by the isolation of the diseased therein, as is shown by the Grandgore cases being sent from Edinburgh to Inchkeith.

Scottish Special Hospitals.

Royal Infirmary of Edinburgh, 1736.

The Royal Infirmary of Edinburgh was incorporated in 1736, but its origin was of earlier date. Although the name of Lord Provost Drummond is generally associated with the institution of the Royal Infirmary, I cannot but regard the originators of it to have been the Royal College of Physicians of Edinburgh, and I shall fully enter into this subject when your attention is directed to the Early Days of the Royal College. As the Dispensary system had been carried on by the Fellows of the College for fifty-four years, the difficulty in getting the

Infirmary established would have been, and must have been, very great, but for the assistance and active endeavours of the resolute, energetic, intelligent, and benevolent Provost Drummond. Its legend is significant of the actions and wants of the Fellows. 'I was sick and ye visited me' was what they had done; 'I was a stranger and ye took me in' was the difficulty they had to encounter, when they had no place to treat necessitous and serious cases except in the wretched and insanitary abodes of the poor of this city. Hence arose first a Sick-house, and upon this foundation was raised the greater institution, 'patet omnibus.'

It was a Medical charity.

I cannot but again direct attention to the title, as showing that it was to be eminently a *Medical* charity and not a Church one. It was not to be a Hospital, but from the first an Infirmary, and its boast still is, that it is a place for the sick and hurt, not a place for malingerers nor for the old and imbecile, but for the poor, suffering from disease from which there is a reasonable prospect of relief being obtained by treatment. The Surgeons do not appear at first to have supported a joint movement, but established a Surgical Hospital for themselves in 1738. They gave individual support only to the Infirmary. The scheme did not receive at first the united approval of the College.

Not supported at first by the College of Surgeons.

Aberdeen Royal Infirmary dates next in 1739.

The Aberdeen Royal Infirmary was established in 1739, and, following the lead of that of Edinburgh, has developed into another important teaching and educational centre for Medical men and nurses.

Scottish Dispensaries—Royal established in 1776.

Of the Dispensaries in Scotland the earliest was that of the College of Physicians, which developed into the Royal Infirmary. The next in Scotland was also connected with the Physicians. It was founded in 1776 by Dr. Andrew Duncan senior, Professor of the Institutes of Medicine, Fellow and President of the College of Physicians. He originated it as a Dispensary for the sick poor on similar lines to those of the first, the College Dispensary. It was officered originally by the Fellows of the

Its connection with College of Physicians.

College of Physicians, and at one time had a branch in the New Town, for which the College provided suitable rooms at its expense in its Hall in George Street. It was originally intended as an adjunct to the Royal Infirmary for the treatment of cases not suitable for, nor requiring residential, Infirmary treatment, and, whilst it was a charitable institution, it was also from its commencement an educational one; and the charity, as now, was supported largely by the fees of the students attending it. When the Infirmary was opened, the College Dispensary continued for some time thereafter. The Dumfries and Galloway Infirmary also dates from 1776, and the Kelso Dispensary from 1777. The other Infirmaries, Hospitals, and Dispensaries are subsequent to that date. Although the Glasgow Faculty dates from 1599, the Royal Infirmary of that city was not established till 1791.

Infirmary of Dumfries and Galloway and Kelso Dispensary.

Glasgow Infirmary, 1791.

Scottish Medical Societies.

Royal Medical, 1737.

Of the Medical Societies in Scotland I shall show that their basis was in the College of Physicians; but undoubtedly the oldest existing society is the deservedly honoured Royal Medical, and it is interesting to note how soon it originated (in 1737) after the establishment of the Royal Infirmary. It bears evidence of the vitality and energy which characterised the Medical School then centred in the University; and, although now in the mature age of 159 years, its vitality is undiminished, its vigour unabated, and its usefulness in developing talent and preparing our future teachers, lecturers, and orators, unimpaired.

Harveian.

Aberdeen Medico-Chirurgical.

Our own Harveian, also an Edinburgh Society, now in its 114th year, ranks next, whilst the Medico-Chirurgical of Aberdeen takes third place with a venerable age of 107 years.

This concludes the Retrospect of the English, Irish, and Scottish Medical Institutions before, during, and subsequent to Harvey's time; and, so far as I have gone, after careful search, I have failed to discover the influence of that great man or his teaching directly affecting more than one of them.

One Scottish Medical Institution yet remains to be particularised —the Royal College of Physicians of Edinburgh, and it is my pleasing duty to show you the difficulties it had to contend with before it obtained an existence, and how these difficulties were overcome; and although, as Harvey was dead, I am unable to say that he personally was related to it, I expect you will agree with me, before this address is concluded, that indirectly he assisted at its inception, and that his spirit influenced its Early Days and First Knights—and that the original College was in touch with the great master.

One Scottish Institution yet to be described —the Royal College of Physicians.

PART II

A COLLEDGE OF PHISITIANS IN SCOTLAND

THE FOUR ATTEMPTS TO FOUND IT

JAMES, THE FOURTH EARL OF PERTH, AFTERWARDS THE FIRST DUKE OF PERTH; SIR CHARLES SCARBOROUGH; AND JAMES, DUKE OF YORK, AFTERWARDS JAMES THE SEVENTH

PART II

ERECTION OF A ROYAL COLLEDGE OF PHISITIANS IN EDINBURGH

ROM the consideration of the foregoing introductory statement regarding the Medical Institutions and the dates of their origin in England, Scotland, and Ireland, it is evident that there was no University nor Medical School sufficiently equipped in the time of Harvey to offer the capability of a Medical education. Educational instruction was obtained from their masters by the apprentices of individual Practitioners, or from what the students themselves were able to pick up or observe at their practical attendance upon patients at their own homes, in the surgery, or in the shops of their employers. Human Anatomy could only occasionally be learned in the course of the year from the inspection of a malefactor's body; and that only in some favoured places, whilst general Anatomy was learned by the dissection of the lower animals.

Erection of a Royal College of Physicians in Edinburgh.

No equipped School in Harvey's day.

In 1615, at the age of thirty-seven, Harvey first lectured at the Royal College of Physicians in London; and in 1628 his *Anatomical Disquisition on the Motion of the Heart and Blood in Animals* was published.

Harvey first lectured in 1615.

Disquisition published in 1628.

Unless, as I have mentioned, the endowment of the Tomlins Prælectorship of Anatomy at the University of Oxford in 1623 and of the Caldwal Reader at the Barber Surgeons' Hall in 1645

Tomlins Prælectorship and Caldwal Reader

only evidence of Medical progress in England.

were the result of his teaching and stimulation of scientific inquiry, there are no other evidences in England, during the seventeenth century, of progress in Anatomy or Physiology, as shown by the creation of Professorships, Lectureships or Medical Schools: nor in Scotland before the establishment of the College of Physicians, except the application of Professor William Gordon, Mediciner at the University of Aberdeen, for human subjects for dissection by himself, not by his pupils apparently, in 1636.

In Scotland Gordon's application. Till erection of Royal College of Physicians of Edinburgh.

Anatomy first taught at Cambridge in 1707. In Edinburgh before 1694 once a year.

It was not until the year 1707 that Anatomy was taught in Cambridge. Previous to 1694 it had been taught once a year in Edinburgh from the malefactor's body, but seemingly in a very imperfect manner.

The great indication of progress was manifested in Scotland, in the early efforts for a College of Physicians in Edinburgh, and ultimately by its erection in 1681.

Royal College of Physicians of Edinburgh in 1681 the great indication of progress. Its association with Harvey.

As it seems to me, that there is a connection between it and Harvey, I shall shortly endeavour to submit my views; and I expect that you will, if not altogether convinced, at least allow that I have made out this, that the spirit of Harvey's teaching had a good deal to do with the early inception of the College, and certainly with the ultimate success of the efforts of the earnest and enlightened men who were its first Fellows. I dare say that to some of you the facts may seem stale. I cannot but think, however, that you will consider my handling of them in many respects new.

Four attempts—three defeated.

Four attempts were made to establish a College of Physicians in Edinburgh, and three times these attempts were opposed and defeated. The forces arrayed against the movement had intimate relations, the one with the other. They were the Town Council of Edinburgh, the Universities, the two Medical and Surgical Incorporations, and the Clergy. The Town Council were the Patrons of the University of Edinburgh, the Clergy, especially the Episcopal, were intimately associated with the Universities,

The opposing forces.

whilst the Surgeons were closely related to the Town Council through their 'Deacon' representing the Incorporation, as one of the civic rulers.

On each of the occasions the Town Council of Edinburgh and the Clergy as represented by the Archbishops and Bishops were vigorous in their opposition. **The Town Council.**

As regards the Clergy, Dr. Beilby, the President, in his Oration delivered in 1847 at the opening of the present College Hall in Queen Street, observes, that the first attempt was frustrated 'chiefly through the influence of the Bishops, whose prescriptive privileges were thereby affected; and who suspected, whether justly or not, that the Physicians, as to their religious or rather ecclesiastical opinions, had too much sympathy with the popular party, which was not very favourable to Episcopal rule.' **The clergy.** **Dr. Beilby's views.**

Upon this point I would remark that, whilst in England the Bishops had an interest in regulating Medical and even Surgical practice, and the title of Doctor of Medicine was conferred by certain dignitaries of the Church, probably from their being officially connected with the Universities, I have been unable to find that in Scotland the reformed clergymen ever claimed the right to confer degrees in Medicine. **Position of Episcopal dignities in England and Scotland.**

The present Professor of Church History, the Rev. Malcolm C. Taylor, D.D., has favoured me with his opinion of the reason for the opposition of the Clergy and writes me: 'The opposition . . . must, I imagine, be traced to the relation of the Clergy to the *Universities*, and be explained as an opposition in the interests, real or supposed, of the Universities, and of their exclusive rights to confer the degree. In Episcopal times the Archbishops and Bishops were the Chancellors of the three older Universities. Hence the identity of interests between the Bishops and Universities. During the Presbyterian period to which you refer, the General Assembly claimed the right of exercising a considerable amount of supervision over the Universities, although **Professor of Church History's view.**

the relation between the General Assembly and them was not so definite. The result, however, was the same in respect of an identity of interest.'

The Chirurgeons' opposition.

The opposition of the Surgeons seems to have been only natural. Dr. John Gairdner, in his *Sketch of the Early History of the Medical Profession in Edinburgh*, remarks: 'The self-conceit of the Physicians of those days took a dangerous direction, for they thought themselves the proper persons to govern the untitled members of the profession.' He also characterises their early efforts as 'degrading conspiracies.'

Scope of proposed Charters of College of Physicians.

The Physicians were by the first proposed Charters to have the right to practise Surgery, whilst the Surgeons were to be debarred from practising Medicine. The practice of the Surgeons was to be curtailed, and in certain cases it was required to have the consent of a Physician in consultation. In one of the proposed Charters the desire of the Physicians was to have subjects for Anatomy allotted to them. This gave rise to opposition; whilst the Faculty of Glasgow objected to powers being granted, by which their privileges over the district assigned by their constitution might be interfered with, for the Physicians, in one at least of their attempts, proposed that their right to practise or to supervise it should extend all over Scotland, and not be limited merely to Edinburgh and its neighbourhood.

The Faculty of Glasgow's objection.

College relation to Harvey.

The first attempt 1617.

I desire to direct your attention to the following facts as bearing on the relation of the College of Physicians to Harvey, and its association with him. The *First* attempt to found a College of Physicians was made in 1617, when James the First revisited Scotland. *Harvey two years previously had been chosen to teach and lecture* in London.

The second attempt 1630.

The *Second* attempt was made in 1630, and *again, two years previously, his great work, 'Exercitatio anatomica de Motu Cordis et Sanguinis, in animalibus,' had been published.*

The third attempt 1657.

The *Third* attempt was made in 1657, in Cromwell's time,

whose approval it received. Shortly before this, Harvey's teaching had drawn to a close, and he had handed over the Lumleian Lectureship to his dear friend and successor, Sir Charles Scarborough.

Increased desire for Anatomy subjects.

The death of the Protector stopped further proceedings. It is in this attempt that, *for the first time, direct evidence of the stimulus of Harvey's teaching is shown as regards Anatomy*; for evidently the necessity for more instruction in it and attention to it than it was then receiving in Scotland is indicated by the desire to obtain bodies for dissection. Scientific Medicine in Edinburgh was undergoing development, and the necessity for more light was being felt. You will, however, recollect that the Surgeons had the privilege of obtaining one body at this period. The Physicians did not on this occasion limit the number they wanted. I may here remark parenthetically that it is difficult to understand how, with the privilege of obtaining only one body a year for Anatomy, the candidates for admission to the Incorporation of Barbers and Surgeons of 1505, in addition to being freemen and burgesses of the city, were to obtain the information, as already mentioned, required for the examination 'that he knaws anatomie, nature and complexioun of everie member of humanis bodie; and in lykewayes, he knaws all the vaynis of the samyn, that he may mak flewbothomea in dew tyme' (Rutherford's *Traditions of Edinburgh*, 1848, p. 67). It seems as if the students' Anatomy, as in Aberdeen before, and even after 1636, had been learned from beasts!

Not mere coincidences but results of Harvey's teaching.

I cannot but regard these associations with Harvey's times and teaching, as more than mere coincidences. They rather appear to me to result from them.

Effects of the third attempt on Incorporation of Surgeons—'the plot of 1657.'

It is of interest, in connection with this third attempt of 1657, to note some of the effects upon the Incorporation of Surgeons, of what Gairdner in his ***Historical Sketch*** terms 'the plot of 1657.' Referring to the minute of meeting of the Surgeons held 22nd August 1672, in a footnote he observes, page 9: 'The chairman produced to the meeting a proposed Act of Parliament "for erecting the Colledge of Edinburgh into ane Universitie." He stated that this Act had been "given to him by ane confident person, to consider if the calling might be concerned yrin or not."' There was a division of opinion—but a report framed by James Borthwick was adopted—'supporting the Act, under certain conditions, as one calculated to be useful,' and to be a 'caveat against all hazards by a Colledge of Physitians!"' We shall see before I conclude this Oration the relations which ultimately existed between the 'Universitie' and the 'Colledge of Physitians,' and how largely instrumental the latter has been in aiding the development of the Medical Faculty in the former—and assuring the high standard *from the first* of its degree in Medicine.

Fourth attempt 1681.

I now come to the fourth and successful attempt to erect a College of Physicians in Edinburgh.

With this the names of the Duke of York, the Earl of Perth and Dr. Robert Sibbald have hitherto been usually associated. I shall not trouble you with the repetition of Dr. Beilby's statement and the accounts given in the Library Catalogue Prefaces, or the *Historical Sketch*, published in 1891; but I propound the question—How was it that, in spite of 'the most strenuous opposition' of the same four opponents, whose combined efforts had always hitherto been successfully exerted, and were united in common interest still, the fourth attempt to establish the College succeeded? To arrive at a clear understanding we must look to Sibbald's autobiography for the explanation. If we accept his views and accounts of the three previous attempts, we are bound to accept his statements as to the fourth.

How was it that the fourth attempt succeeded?

The law cases which led to the combination of the Physicians.

I must first direct your attention to the law cases which led to the combined action of the Physicians of Edinburgh. From the supplement to the *Dictionary of Decisions* by M. P. Browne, Esq., advocate, vol. iii., containing decisions reported by Sir John Lauder of Fountainhall, I find that Dr. Beilby refers to the wrong year, 1680, when he refers to the disputed case before the Court of Session. The case is dated according to the *Dictionary* July 7th, 1681, and is entered as '*The Chirurgeons of Edinburgh* against *The Apothecaries*' in these words: 'In the mutual declarations between the *Chirurgeons* and *Apothecaries* in Edinburgh, the Lords before advising, named of their number to call for three Physicians, Hay, Stevenson, and Balfour, and thereafter added Burnet, to take their advice and opinion anent the true limits and distinctions of Chirurgery and Pharmacy. And they having made a Report to the prejudice of the privileges of the Chirurgeons, and the Lords having advised the controverted points betwixt them, on the 19th July they found Phlebotomy, or blood-letting, only belonged to the Incorporation of the Chirurgeons of Edinburgh, within the town, upon citizens and burgesses. But if extended *ad pomaria urbis*, to the suburbs and liberties of it; and if they should have the sole right and power to exercise it upon strangers within the town, they desire to hear that further debated and cleared; and found others than Chirurgeons might breathe a vein, and let blood, even upon burgesses within the town in the cases either of imminent necessity (where a Chirurgeon is not so near as another, who may be, chances to be present) or charity to the poor.'

Chirurgeons against the Apothecaries.

Four Physicians called to advise.

Deliverance of the Court.

'As for sear clothes, found the sole application of them belonged to Chirurgeons, where there was any named operation by evisceration, incision, and extenteration: and in other cases, that the Apothecaries might apply them as well as they. And *quoad* the summary way of Chirurgeons arresting unfreemen and offering to prove the contrasertions by their oath; the Lords discharge the further using of that, (even though they gave in a special condescendence of time, place, and persons,) till they heard that point further reasoned in their own presence.'

I may say in passing that this case in various phases was carried on till 1687, but it is of interest to note that, on January

24th, 1682, 'His Royal Highness the Duke of Albany and York came to the session and was present at the debate between the Chirurgeons and Apothecaries.'

After the opportunity was given to the Physicians by their joint meeting regarding the union of Surgery and Pharmacy in July 1681, they had lost no time in advancing their application to the King's Commissioner, the Duke of York, for in spite of the combined opposition, within five months they obtained the Charter or Patent.

The leaders in the matter must have been earnest, determined, and resolute men. They must also have been backed by powerful influence with the Duke.

The Duke of York. The Commissioner's general policy.

The Duke of York's policy, whilst he was at Holyrood at this time, was one of conciliation, in which he was well aided by the Duchess and his daughter by his first marriage, the Lady Anne, afterwards Queen Anne. Now, to place himself in direct opposition to the Clergy, the Universities, the Town Council, from whom he had received so much honour and respect, not to mention pecuniary gifts, and the Chirurgeons, was acting quite contrary to his policy.—On the one hand were four powerful organisations of old, indeed it might be said of ancient, standing, and his policy of conciliation,—and on the other, twenty-one men without Incorporation, but actuated, their leaders at least, by high professional motives, and the strong desire to benefit their fellow-citizens and countrymen by an improved Medical service. Surely the policy of conciliation was not to be advanced by resisting the prayer of four institutions, including so many learned and influential men, appealing also to the noblemen to help their cause! And yet the Duke threw them over, and granted the request of the twenty-one earnest Medical reformers. For the explanation of this strange thing we must look to Sibbald for enlightenment. It is fortunate for his own justification by posterity that Sir Robert Sibbald left a fragmentary manuscript bearing the title 'Life of Sir Robert Sibbald, Knight, written by

He acts contrary to it in supporting a College.

Sibbald's Autobiography.

himself.' This is the manuscript in the possession of the Boswells, referred to in the *Life of Samuel Johnson*, and it probably got into the possession of that family by the hands of, or through their interest in, Sibbald, one of the early Clerks to the College having been A. Boswell, Writer to the Signet. The minute of the College of 11th December 1684 bears that Hugh Stevensone was continued clerk. Then comes a hiatus, and on the board of vol. ii. of the minutes is written, 'Minute-Book No. I. contains merely minutes from 18th January 1682 to 22nd December 1684 engrossed in this book' (initialed A. B.); and below, 'Minutes from 22nd December 1684 to 21st March 1693 not in Mr. Boswell's possession,' and then follows another note, 'Vide Minutes, 12th and 19th January 1704 for the reason of sundry minutes being deleted (initialed A. B.).'

A. Boswell, W.S., Clerk to College of Physicians.

It is from Sibbald's Autobiography that the origin of the College of Physicians of Edinburgh can be learned.

Preliminary to the agitation for the establishment of the College, it is recorded by Sibbald, page 28, that, in the year 1680, he induced some of the Physicians in town, especially Dr. Burnet, Dr. Stevenson, Dr. Balfour, and Dr. Pitcairn, to meet at his lodging, *i.e.* his house, once a fourth night or so 'when we had conferences.' The matters discoursed upon varied, the meetings seem to have been continued till the College was erected, and one of the early arrangements of the College, was a continuance of these Medical and Scientific conferences monthly, by each of the Fellows in rotation. So much importance did Sibbald assign to these meetings that, in his Summary of his Life (p. 43), he says, 'The Conferences were kept up likewise during my tyme and the discourses were made.' These meetings in 1680 seem to be the earliest instances of a Medical and Scientific Society in Edinburgh.

Origin of College as given by Dr. Robert Sibbald.

Conferences commenced in 1680 by Sibbald.

The first Medical and Scientific Society in Edinburgh.

Sir Robert then proceeds to tell the precursory stages of the formation of the College. It is from him, I suspect, rather than from the Law Records of Fountainhall that Dr. Beilby had taken

Precursory stages of the formation of College of Physicians.

his account. There is a little variance between Sibbald's account and that of Fountainhall, for, whilst the former says that 'Mr. Cunninghame, a chirurgeon, had been refused his admission amongst the Chirurgeon Apothecaries, and ill-used by them, he had engaged the Apothecaries in town upon his syde, and had raised ane action before the Lords of Session anent the rights of these employments,' the latter in his Reports of the Decisions already mentioned, states the action as being raised by 'the Chirurgeons of Edinburgh against the Apothecaries.' Probably who raised the action is of little importance; but, as Cunninghame's action was in 1680 and the Surgeons' action in 1681, it antedates the meeting of the Physicians. Fountainhall's *Decisions* fixed it in July 1681.

Sibbald puts the question at issue clearly enough, but when he states, 'The Lords had required the opinion of Dr. Hay, Dr. Burnet, Dr. Steenson, and Dr. Balfour,' he had evidently been writing some years after the event and his memory made a slip, for according to Fountainhall, Hay, Stevenson, and Balfour were appointed first 'and thereafter added Burnet, to take their advice and opinion anent the true limits and distinctions of Chirurgery and Pharmacy.'

Sibbald continues, The opinion of these Physicians was required 'about the Chirurgion Apothecaries, whither ther were any such conjunction of these employments in other countryes, and whither or not it was expedient for the Leidges, they should be joined in one persone here. They were pleased to take the opinion of the rest of the Physitians in Town anent these matters, and accordingly they mett all togither at Dr. Hay his lodging. After . . . they had agreed to the report that ther was no such conjunction of these arts elsewhere, and that it was very prejudicial both to the Leidges and to the Physitians,'—true to the great object he had at heart and to the trust confided to him by his uncle, Dr. George Sibbald,—Sir Robert adds, 'I took occasion to represent to them, that this being the first tyme we had all mett, I thought it was our interest to improve the meeting to some furder use, and I down right proposed we might take into consideration the establishment of a Colledge, to secure our priviledges belonged to us as Doctors, and defend us against the incroachments of the Chirurgion Apothecaries which were insupportable.' And so, for the fourth time, the idea of originating a College of Physicians was propounded. The Physicians present appear to have readily assented. They only wanted a leader, the leader was ready, imbued with the responsibility transmitted and transferred to him from his uncle, Dr. George Sibbald, who had been chiefly responsible for one of the previous efforts. Can we doubt that, fired with the desire to succeed where his uncle and others had failed, the zeal, enthusiasm, and determination of Dr. Robert were aroused, stimulated, and carried to a successful termination? 'This gave the first ryse to our meetings thereabout,' and at these meetings we can imagine the earnestness with which he enunciated his scheme.

Proposed scheme.

Profiting by the miscarriages of the past attempts, he and those associated with him avoided with politic care,—in which I fancy can be traced the counsel of the judicious Balfour,—the rocks upon which the former ventures were wrecked, and one can imagine him declaring, The College must be Metropolitan not National. 'The Chirurgeons,—divided amongst themselves upon the point, as to who was to supervise the drug shops?—the Chirurgeons, the Apothecaries, or the Municipality? We the College shall do that, for the quality of the drugs sold is one of the strong points upon which the agitation for the establishment of a College of Physicians is based, and as the Physicians order the drugs, it should, therefore, be their place to supervise them, and to see that the public get the right thing. The Surgeons also it will be our endeavour to satisfy. We shall not go in for teaching, nor rival them in trying to obtain the body of one malefactor a year for dissection,—and the Universities, and through them the Clergy, will be conciliated by our relinquishing the idea of giving degrees, whilst their opposition will still further be disarmed by our agreeing to admit Scotch University Graduates in Medicine to the College licence to practise, and ultimately to the Fellowship or Socius of our proposed Society without examination; but we will adhere to our claim to have authority to supervise Medical Practice in the City, Suburbs, and Liberties thereof, and to practise Medicine therein shall only be permitted to those Physicians licensed by the Fellows of the College after trial and examination, and no one shall be admitted Socius until he has first obtained the licence to practise from the College. Better have the College established, though more restricted than we desire, than to have no College at all!'

Question of how to obtain the Charter.

The preliminaries having been agreed on, the important question came to be, how to obtain the Charter or Patent of Constitution; for the four opponents were still vigorous, and strong in their opposition to any College. Sibbald's explanation divides itself into four heads; and, after careful consideration, I incline to regard the influence of the Earl of Perth, who usually, next to Sibbald, gets the chief share of praise, as only secondary to Sir Charles Scarborough, on whom the mantle of the great William Harvey descended and through whom I claim for the College of Physicians of Edinburgh an interest in the immortal Harvey. Although as I have said Harvey cannot be considered to have had a direct connection with the creation of the College, still, when it is recalled that Andrew Balfour was his pupil, and Archibald Pitcairn the avowed teacher of his anatomical and circulatory views, and the defender of his discovery, that Sibbald had been trained at Leyden, from whence, a few years before he went there, Wallaeus's letters and Drake's theses had issued—we can imagine, though dead, that he had an influence over these earnest and intelligent men in favouring the conception of the scheme

Earl of Perth's action secondary to that of Sir Charles Scarborough.

Influence of Harvey.

SIR CHARLES SCARBOROUGH

and the preparation of its design, and also picture their vexation because teaching and the means of extending a knowledge of Anatomy were for politic reasons excluded. Further, when it appears that Sir Charles Scarborough—the favourer and fosterer of the scheme, its advocate and adviser,—had been so intimately associated with Harvey, and was the personal friend of some of those I have named, I come to regard the College as related to the great Harvey, and as a worthy tribute to his genius. For as I have endeavoured to show it was the only Medical Institution reared, at the time of its erection, as bearing testimony to the enlarging influence of his Anatomical and Physiological teaching, the extension of more correct Medical ideas, and the higher aspiration for Medical dignity, purity, and self-respect, by the Physicians of Scotland; and their desire to be freed from the trammels of wretched and limited speculations in Science, and to be separated from an ignoble trafficking in bad drugs and deception.

The College related to Harvey and a worthy tribute to his genius.

The time was propitious for the movement being made. The Chirurgeons themselves the followers of Surgery as an art and science desired to be separated from those who compounded and sold drugs. Their opposition was therefore likely to be less powerful when divided, than when it was that of a united association, or corporation, and the Universities, and therefore the Clergy not being so inimical, the Municipality was likely to be less determined in its opposition, seeing the divided position of the Chirurgeons and Apothecaries, and the opinion which the Court of Session had expressed tended to the same result.

The time was propitious.

Division amongst Chirurgeons and Apothecaries.

In 1679, James, the Duke of Albany and York, came to Edinburgh, in the autumn of the year, as the Commissioner of his brother King Charles, and he was shortly after followed by his physician, Sir Charles Scarborough, and to Sir Charles the schemers determined to go. He was also the King's medical adviser, in which position he had succeeded Harvey. So as Sibbald has it, 'And Sir Charles Scarborough, his Majesty's first

The Duke of York.

Sir Charles Scarborough, his position at Court.

Physician, followed him soon after that, wee consulted with Sir Charles, and found him our great friend, and very ready to give us his best assistance, with the King and the Duke who was by this tyme High Commissioner.'

Earl of Perth.

The Earl of Perth, to whom it seems to me we have in the past attributed too great influence, was also made use of by the chief schemer, Sibbald, who took advantage of the close intimacy between them. He observes, 'I got the Earl of Perth and his brother Melfort, to be our great friends, and they brought over many of the Nobility to favour the design,' so that he and his brother had their duty assigned them. The error associated with Perth, it seems to me, is in supposing him to have been Chancellor at this time. Sibbald as his friend had done his best to dissuade Perth from engaging in a political career, but he determined, for his own ambitious nature and reduced financial condition, to embark in it; though at this time his foot was just on the first rung of the ladder. He was a member of the Privy Council but not yet nominated an Extraordinary Lord of Session, which he became in 1682. Next he was promoted to be the Lord President or Justice-General, and it was only in 1684, three years after the Royal College was established, that he schemed with Queensberry to get Aberdeen turned out of the position of Chancellor, on the plea that his wife went to conventicles, and to have himself appointed to that high position; and to finish his career, so far as it influenced the College, it was to secure his maintenance of that high honour against the charges of Queensberry that in 1685 he seceded to the Church of Rome. No doubt in 1681 his influence was becoming great, but it does not seem to have been so with the King; and the greater influence would, without doubt, be in the hands of the trusted Scarborough, 'the first Physitian' to King Charles, and now in attendance upon the Duke of York and his family.

Dr. Andrew Balfour, when in London, had known Scar-

JAMES DRUMMOND, FOURTH EARL AND FIRST DUKE OF PERTH.

borough; and, when the Earl of Rochester was confided to his care, would probably again meet him, especially when he was introduced to King Charles. Another bond of interest would doubtless be that before Balfour went abroad to complete his Medical studies he had been the pupil and follower of the great master, William Harvey.

His former acquaintance with Dr. A. Balfour.

In Pitcairn, too, at this period, Scarborough would find a sympathy in congenial tastes, for he was in his intellectual prime, and free from those lower habits which seem to have conduced to his premature decease. Both were earnest students of Mathematics, and herein had further mutual interest, and above all he would be attracted to the genial, social, and witty Pitcairn, as recognising in him one of the most talented and outspoken supporters of the revered master's views upon the circulation of the blood. Whilst in Burnet, he would also be interested as being the distinguished author of the *Thesaurus Medicinæ Practicæ*, etc., which had been first published in London in 1673, and who at this date was also a Royal Physician. For Sibbald he must have had a sincere regard. The intimacy seems to have commenced at an earlier period, most likely in the end of 1662, when Sibbald stayed in London on his return from studying at Leyden and graduating at Angers.

Interest in Dr. A. Pitcairn

and in Dr. Thomas Burnet the author.

His regard for Sibbald.

It may interest you that I should recall some of the records of Sir Charles's life, and for which, for the most part, I am indebted to Dr. Munk's *Roll of the Royal College of Physicians*. His name is therein spelled 'Scarburgh,' although in most Scottish references to it, it is 'Scarborough.' He was a native of London. He received his early education at St. Paul's School, and thereafter proceeded to Caius College, Cambridge, where he graduated Bachelor in 1636, was Master of Arts in 1639, and was chosen a Fellow. He then engaged in teaching, his spare time being devoted to the study of Mathematics, which he regarded as the best preparation to the practice of Medicine,

Records of Sir Charles Scarborough's life.

which was to be the business of his life. Scarborough being a Royalist lost his Fellowship at Cambridge, and proceeded to Oxford, then favourable to Charles's cause. He enrolled himself at Merton College, of which Harvey was then Master for the year 1645, the year subsequent to the defeat of the Royalists by Cromwell at Marston Moor. Scarborough was thus brought into relation with Harvey, obtained his friendship, and assisted him in the preparation of his work, *De generatione Animalium.*

Ten years after graduating B.A., and seven after obtaining the Master's degree at Cambridge, he was created Doctor of Medicine at Oxford in 1646, in his thirty-second year, 'by virtue of letters from the Chancellor of the University,' and his 'letters testimonial from Harvey stated that he was well learned in Physic, Philosophy, and Mathematics.' This appears to have been (apart from his private study and the information obtained from his master), all the examination required by the University of Oxford at this time. One cannot, therefore, be surprised that Universities possessing less of a national reputation on this side of the Tweed should have adopted a similar mode of 'creating' their Medical graduates. He was incorporated subsequently, in 1660, at his own University of Cambridge, monarchy having been restored in May of that year.

He removed to London for practice in 1647, and, the same year, was admitted 'candidate' at the College of Physicians, and elected Fellow in 1650. Subsequently he held various offices. Was Censor in 1655, and Elect, in place of Dr. Glisson, from 1677 to 1691, when he resigned. Whilst in Edinburgh, therefore, he was one of the Council of the London College. In 1656, nine years after settling in London, when Harvey resigned the Lumleian Lectureship, he transferred it to Scarborough. In 1658 his reputation, it is said, was now established, and for many years (since 1649) he had read anatomical lectures in London at Barber Surgeons' Hall.

About this time he was appointed Physician to Charles II., then in exile. He was knighted in 1669, and in 1685 he attended Charles in his last illness, and has left an account of it. But what more especially concerns our present inquiry is that he was, in 1681, Physician in attendance upon the Duke of York at Holyrood, whose regard for him must have been great; for, when he ascended the throne, as James the Second, Scarborough was still in attendance upon him.

We have seen that he followed the Duke to Edinburgh, and, as showing that his reputation was quite independent of his Church or political views—purely professional—he was appointed after this Physician to the Tower and to King William the Third.

He must have been a man of cultured mind, of philosophic thought, a clear and eloquent lecturer, of polished manners, and of amiable disposition; for Harvey in his will bequeathed his 'velvet gowne to my lovinge friend, Mr. Doctor Scarburgh,' and 'all my little silver instruments of Surgerie' (Munk, p. 254). Oughtred in his preface to the *Clavis Mathematica* mentions him in high terms. His library is also stated to have been 'incomparable.'

A man of such a genial, intelligent, and intellectual nature was just the one likely to aid the ardent organisers of the Edinburgh College, and to help their cause with the Duke and King. It was to Sir Charles that Sibbald and his fellow-workers, therefore, first went to secure the help and good offices of him to whom the 'velvet gowne' of the immortal Harvey had been specially bequeathed as the man best qualified to succeed him, and maintain his Anatomical and Physiological views and discoveries. Sibbald next tells us of great opposition now aroused by the Town of Edinburgh, the Chirurgeon Apothecaries, the Universities, the Clergy, and the Nobles. The Earl of Perth appears to have been useful in bringing over the nobility to favour the design, but he is never mentioned as being otherwise of use. This, no doubt, was an important part, but it was evidently quite a secondary one to that of Scarborough.

That Sibbald had made a most favourable impression upon Scarborough is still further borne out by the two facts, that, it was through him, concerted along with the Earl of Perth, that in the beginning of 1682 Sibbald was one Saturday night advertised to bring with him, next day, Dr. Steinson and Dr. Balfour, 'to waitt upon his Royall Highness the Duke of York, after the forenoon Sermon.' 'Wee indeed knew nothing of the design, but thought we had been sent for to receive his Royal Highnesses Commands anent the Colledge, for he was to goe away shortly.' (He left on 6th March.) 'But to our surprisall, there was ane carpet layed, and we were ordered to kneel, and were each of us knighted by his Royal Highnesse, then Commissioner.'

Sir Charles thus again figures as the active agent in the honour conferred upon the College of Physicians of Edinburgh, and Sir Robert Sibbald, when he was introduced by Scarborough, and admitted an Honorary Fellow of the London College of Physicians. I believe he is the only Fellow of his College upon whom a like honour has ever been conferred.

Dr. George Rolleston, Fellow of Merton College (of which Harvey was warden), in his Harveian oration at the Royal College of Physicians in London in 1873, observes that in the Register of Merton, the name of Charles Scarborough, the *protégé* of Harvey, appears, and at page 71 of his published address remarks, 'Whatever else of Aubrey's tales of Harvey I may disbelieve, I can believe that the words addressed to Charles Scarborough, "Prithee, leave off thy gunning and stay here," are his,'—and it was fortunate for the cause of Medicine and Scotland that he did.

This, then, was the man whose help and counsel Sibbald and his *confrères* sought to aid them in obtaining a Charter for a

KING CHARLES II.

College of Physicians, and through whom—the *protégé*, the pupil, the friend, and the successor of Harvey—I claim for the College an interest in and connection with that great man.

After long discussion before the Privie Council, by the insertion of some conditions in their favour, the Universities became favourable to, and even solicitous for the College, 'so that, after long debates, the matter was concerted.'

Sibbald, however, was not yet at the end of his resources; he had one in reserve, and cautious, energetic enthusiast that he was, he bided his time to bring it forward, and to make thoroughly secure the goodwill and concurrence of the Duke. He states, 'And I having recovered ane warrand of King James the Sixt of happie memorie (that obtained by his uncle Dr. George Sibbald and left in his care), directed to the Commissioner and Estaits of Parliament then sitting in Scotland, dated the 3rd July 1621, with ane reference by the Parliament thereanent, to the Lords of Secret Counsell with power to doe therein what they thought fitt and that their determination therein sould have the form of ane Act of Parliament, dated the Second of August 1621, . . . produced this to his Royall Highness, who, as soon as he saw it superscribed by King James, said with much satisfaction "he knew his grandfather's hand and he would see our bussiness done," and from that moment acted vigorously for us.'

Sibbald's reserved resource.

King James the Sixth's warrand—obtained from his uncle, Dr. George Sibbald.

That he carried out his intention in spite of the disputings in the Privie Council, in due course had its effect, and the draft of the Patent agreed to by the Council was sent to, and very soon returned, signed by King Charles the Second.

Patent soon returned signed by King Charles,

Sibbald states that the next day he gave the Charter its classic form, and translated it into Latin, and winds up his account by stating that the day after he 'gave it to the Chancery Chamber, and waited upon it till it was written in Parchment, and ready for the great seall, which was appended to it upon the 29th of November 1681, being St. Andrew's Day.' Success had, after long

and translated next day by Sibbald into Latin.

The great seall appended 29th Nov. 1681.

years, at last attended the determined efforts of the Physicians of Edinburgh to obtain recognition and organisation as a body of United Medical Practitioners, and we who now enjoy the benefits of our ancestors' persistent labours, can quite agree,—although they did not succeed in gaining all they wanted and especially the authority to teach,—with the verdict of the originator and earnest advocate of the fourth attempt that 'the Patent is very honourable for our Society and contains a jurisdiction within ourselves, which the Publick judicatures are obliged to see executed.'

Sibbald's opinion of the Patent.

The most emphatic testimony as to the part Sibbald took in the whole matter and of the esteem with which at least the majority of the Fellows, his coadjutors, regarded him, is well vouched for by the following: 'Upon the Patents passing the seal, I was ordererd by the Colledge to have a discourse of thanks to his Royall Highness in the Colledge name, which I delivered in the Chamber of Presence.' But even in these early days the spirit of jealousy existed; and although he had proved himself the most capable business man amongst the original lot, and had been by them appointed to be the first Secretary, even this little honour was grudged him, for he adds, 'this occasioned much envy to me, that I was taken notice of at the Court.' Alas, how unlike the spirit of professional large-heartedness of the great Harvey! It was but the precursor of the opposition his efforts met with in The Early Days, when envy gave place to malice.

PART III

THE EARLY DAYS OF THE ROYALL COLLEDGE

THE ATTENDANCE OF THE FELLOWS

THE FOUR EFFORTS FOR PROFESSIONAL ADVANCEMENT

FIRST .	THE PHARMACOPŒIA
SECOND .	THE DISPENSARY
THIRD .	THE EXAMINATION FOR LICENCE
FOURTH .	THE MEDICAL CONFERENCES

PART III

THE EARLY DAYS OF THE ROYALL COLLEDGE

AT last, after many years of struggle and disappointment, the Physicians of Edinburgh as the reward of their fourth attempt had succeeded. They had obtained organisation in the form of a Patent from Charles the Second for the erection of a Royal College of Physicians in Edinburgh. I have just shown how the tact of Dr. Robert Sibbald and his associates had overcome all the difficulties. They had got the Charter after honourable contest and the question might have been asked, What will they do with it? As was feared by some of those opposed to them, might not they use it merely to advance their own personal interests? The Physicians, on the contrary, were influenced by high and patriotic impulses in all the attempts they had made. It was not merely for their own protection and advantage that they had fought the good fight and won. It was for the advancement of Medical Science and its interests, and for the benefit of their fellow-countrymen, as well as for the general professional gain that attends upon strength-giving union and organisation, and which is secured thereby when these are disinterestedly exercised. As a result of the disunion and dissension in the stronghold of their opponents, the opportunity without being sought for by them presented itself. The astute and quick perception of Sibbald suggested and led to united action, and his earnest determination along with the discreet activity of his

The Early Days. After years of struggle the fourth attempt succeeded.

The Charter obtained. What will he done with it?

The Physicians' high impulses were not selfish, but for the advancement of Medical Science.

Obtained after sixty-four years of waiting.

associates were crowned with success, and a College of Physicians was at last, after sixty-four years of waiting, an accomplished fact.

Original Fellows number twenty-one.

The number of its original Fellows was twenty-one. Some of them were well advanced in years, some of them were ailing and weakly, but the majority were men in the prime of life, in the flower of their age, and in the possession of matured judgment and formed resolves.

Preliminary meeting at which the course was arranged.

Four Efforts ready to be submitted to College.

Before any record of the College meetings was preserved the active minds had been at work in advance; and, almost as soon as the College had its form, four great Efforts were ready to be submitted for its approval and adoption, and the first steps towards their being carried out were taken. They were all characterised by the intention to advance Medical Science, to benefit the people of Scotland and of Edinburgh, to promote the mutual improvement of the Fellows by interchange of thought on professional knowledge, the improvement of professional education, and the maintenance of professional respectability. Had the College been granted the power to teach as well as to examine, it is probable the Medical School of Edinburgh would have been started some years sooner than it was.

Date of Incorporation, 29th November 1681.

The twenty-one original Fellows.

Incorporated by Royal Charter of date 29th November 1681, the original College consisted of the following twenty-one Fellows; the names, for the most part, are subscribed according to seniority, and each was the possessor of a University Degree of Doctor of Medicine obtained at a foreign University—1. David Hay; 2. Thomas Burnet; 3. Mathew Brisbane; 4. Archibald Stevensone, Steinson, or Steenson; 5. Robert Sibbald; 6. James Livingstone or Livingstoun; 7. Andrew Balfour; 8. Robert Craufurd; 9. Robert Trotter; 10. Matthew St. Clare, or Sinclare, or Sinclair; 11. James Stewart; 12. Alexander Cranstone or Cranstoune; 13. John Hutton or Huttoune; 14. John M'Gill; 15. John Learmonth; 16. William Stevensone, termed in the Minutes 'Younger,' to distinguish him from Archibald the 'Elder'; 17. James Halkett or Halkit; 18. William Wright; 19. Patrick Halyburton; 20. William Lauder; 21. Archibald Pitcairn or Pittcairne.

For my information regarding 'The Early Days' of the 'College of Phisitians,' I am chiefly indebted to the recorded Minutes, for reference to which, and for permission to make extracts from them, I have to render my thanks to the President and the Council, the Representatives of the College. Thanks to representatives of the College for permission to use old Minutes.

There must have been preliminary meetings of those Physicians of Edinburgh I have named, before the College was constituted, and after the Patent was received, previously to the Minutes being kept. It must be believed that the Fellows at the commencement would pay every possible attention to the conditions of the Patent or Charter. An election meeting would therefore be held early in December, for that of 1682 was held on St. Andrew's Day of that year. The first election could not have been held on St. Andrew's Day of 1681, for it was on that day that Sibbald had the Patent, immediately on receiving it, turned into Latin—pronounced by a competent authority to be very good Latin—had registered, and had had the Great Seal appended to it. First meetings before those recorded.

The Minutes have not been regularly nor continuously engrossed, and in The Early Days, and even subsequently, have been kept in as few words as possible, and indicate that the first Clerks of the College were by no means the most enlightened or intelligent of writers.

The Minute of the first recorded sederunt of the Royal College is dated 18th January 1682. First Sederunt recorded, 18th January 1682.

Of the twenty-one Fellows, twelve were present. They were the President, Dr. Archibald Stevensone, and Drs. Balfour, Burnet, Sibbald, W. Stevensone, Cranstoune, R. Craufurd, Huttoune, Pitcairne, J. Learmont, M'Gill, and Halyburtoune. By comparing subsequent Minutes it is made out that the following were the first office-bearers of the College, and being Twelve present.

The first Office-bearers.

all University Doctors of Medicine, they were necessarily previously 'Laureated' Masters of Arts—

President, .	Dr. Archibald Stevensone.
Censors,	,, Andrew Balfour. ,, James Livingstoun.
Secretary, . .	,, Robert Sibbald.
Treasurers, .	,, John Huttoune, until 1st May. ,, William Stevensone, from 1st May.
Council, .	,, Thomas Burnet. ,, Andrew Balfour. ,, Robert Sibbald. ,, James Livingstoun. ,, James Stewart. ,, Alexander Cranstoun.
Procurator Fiscall,	,, Archibald Pitcairne.
Clerk, . . .	Mr. Hugh Stevensone, W.S.

The first death, Dr. James Livingstoun, May 1682.

Drs. Craufurd, Trotter, St. Clare, M'Gill, Learmont, Halkitt, Wright, Halyburton, and Lauder, did not hold office; nor did Dr. William Stevensone till Huttoune retired on 1st May. The first death vacancy occurred in May. Dr. James Livingstoun had probably been in bad health before the College was erected, for his name is only once entered as present, at the second meeting. He died in this month. Dr. Robert Trotter, the ninth name on the Roll of Fellows, was elected to succeed him as a Member of Council, and Sibbald was appointed a Censor in his place.

Drs. Hay and Brisbane were Honorary Fellows.

As some indication of the feeling existing amongst the twenty-one original Fellows, it may be noted that during the first year Drs. Hay and Brisbane, as they did not pay their share of the preliminary expenses, were made 'Honorarie Fellows,' and did not attend any meeting. They were Numbers 1 and 3 on the Roll.

Dr. Matthew St. Clare.

Dr. Matthew St. Clare was not present till first election day, 30th November 1682. He was Number 10 on the Roll.

Dr. John Huttoune was a regular attender for six months, and then resigned on going 'furth the kingdome.' He was No. 13 on the Roll, and Dr. William Stevensone succeeded him as Treasurer. Dr. John Hutton.

Dr. James Halkitt, No. 17, was present at no meeting till 6th December 1683—the election meeting. Dr. James Halkitt.

Dr. William Wright, No. 18, was present at only three out of twelve meetings. Dr. William Wright.

Some changes are observed in the regularity of attendance on taking a retrospect of the whole of The Early Days, when forty-one recorded meetings of the College, and three of the Council are minuted. It is found that at these forty-four meetings, Dr. Archibald Stevensone and Dr. Robert Sibbald, the President and Secretary, were each present at forty-one meetings.

Dr.	Andrew Balfour,	at 39	meetings.
,,	Alex. Cranstoune,	,, 37	,,
,,	Archibald Pitcairne,	,, 36	,,
,,	Robert Trotter,	,, 28	,,
,,	John Learmont,	,, 27	,,
,,	John M'Gill,	,, 26	,,
,,	Thomas Burnet,	,, 24	,,
,,	Robert Craufurd,	,, 22	,,
,,	William Stevensone,	,, 21	,,

Dr. Robert Trotter, although present at twenty-eight meetings, and Dr. John Learmont, at twenty-seven, do not seem to have taken a very active share in the work of Medical Reform, nor did Dr. Stewart continue so regular after the first year. His health gave way, and he died in January 1684, before the Early Days were ended; whilst Dr. Huttoune left Edinburgh in the course of the first year.

The praise due for the early successes of the College must be assigned to these thirteen earnest and intelligent men.

Dr. Patrick Halyburton, No. 19, only attended three meetings in 1682; and the election meeting, 30th November 1684. Dr. Patrick Halyburton.

Dr. William Lauder.

Dr. William Lauder, No. 20, to end of 1684 was present only once on 28th April 1682; so that practically the work of the College during its Early Days, from 18th January 1682 to 22nd December 1684, when the Minutes cease (and are not resumed till 21st March 1693, nor preserved in book till 6th December 1694), was done by twelve or thirteen Fellows. Some of these were most regular in their attendance: thus, during the first year, Burnet was absent from only two out of fifteen meetings; President Stevensone was equally attentive; Sibbald was absent on only one occasion; Balfour was absent twice.

Craufurd	was present	6	times out of	13	meetings.	
Trotter	,,	6	,,	14	,,	
Stewart	,,	10	,,	15	,,	
Cranstoun	,,	12	,,	15	,,	
Huttoune	,,	9	,,	10	,,	before he left.
M'Gill	,,	8	,,	13	,,	
Learmonth	,,	10	,,	13	,,	
Wm. Stevensone	,,	11	,,	13	,,	
Pitcairne	,,	13	,,	13	,,	

There is nothing stated in the Minutes to account for the absence of St. Clare, Halkitt, Wright, Halyburton, and Lauder.

The Early Days.

As I have stated, the Minute of the first Sederunt of the Royal College of Physicians in Edinburgh indicates it to have been held on 18th January 1682; and the Minutes of the Sederunts are continued regularly until 22nd December 1684—a period of two years and eleven months. A break then occurs without any explanation. I understand in other institutions in this city (such as the early Stent Books, wanting from 1682 to 1693) irregularity in the record of their proceedings also occurs—evidence of the unsettled state of the country before, and at the Revolution period. In a note reference is made to the Minutes, from December 1684 to 21st March 1693, not being in

Reason for so naming them.

the possession of the Clerk of the College, but from 6th December 1694 the Minutes are again preserved continuously.

It is the first period of two years and eleven months that I have designated 'The Early Days' of the Royal College of Physicians of Edinburgh. The Early Days.

THE PHARMACOPŒIA

In my introductory remarks I desired to show you the professional wants and shortcomings in England, Ireland, and Scotland. The desire of the College was, so far as Scotland was concerned, to rectify these; and as far as possible to supply them. It first addressed itself to the relations between Physicians and their patients as regarded drugs. They were unsatisfactory, not only as to their supply and the accuracy of dispensing them, but also as to their quality and cost. The first Effort. The Pharmacopœia.

The College in the Patent had obtained power to visit the Apothecaries' shops, to inspect their drugs, and, if necessary, to condemn them. But that was not all that was wanted. They required to have the control of the prescribing, as well as the dispensing of pure and reliable drugs, in their own hands. The Pharmacopœia of the College of Physicians of London was not binding on the Scottish Apothecary. Its jurisdiction extended only as far north as Berwick. Nor were the Scottish Physicians restricted to the use of it. Consequently there was room and opportunity for evasion in supplying the drug ordered, and one preparation might be substituted for another. Sibbald and Balfour had established the Physic Garden, with Mr. James Sutherland as the Intendant, not merely with the intention of non-professionals learning the rudiments of Botany, but also in order that students or pupils of Practitioners of Medicine and Surgery and the Apothecaries might study the vegetable Materia Medica, and the latter also obtain supplies of the fresh plants to be used

Sphere of London Pharmacopœia.

The Physic Garden.

in the preparation of the galenicals. So far as I have made out, these gardens, in their first days, were unconnected with the University, but by the Minute of Town Council of 8th September 1676, Mr. Sutherland the present Botanist who professes the said art was appointed a yearly salary of £20, and for the better flourishing of the University College that the said profession be joined to the rest of the liberal sciences taught therein. As the garden was established before the Royal College, its only connection with it was when its patronage was solicited. Nor did the Municipality at first aid it; but it was helped by individual Physicians and others. Indeed it would appear that the Law Faculty, next to Murray of Livingstone, Balfour and Sibbald, had been its early and chief benefactors.

As might have been expected, therefore, the first effort the Royal College made was to place the Materia Medica in an organised and authorised position by the preparation of a 'Pharmacopœia,' so that Physicians might understand what to put in their 'bills,' and Apothecaries how to prepare the materials so prescribed.

Pharmacopœia Committee was named in the preliminary meetings.

It appears by the first reported Minute of Sederunt that, at a previous meeting, a committee had been named; for on 18th January 1682, it was remitted to the former committee named for forming a Pharmacopœia, 'to meet and prepare the samen as appoynted.' Who were the members of the first committee are not mentioned; but, at the fourth sederunt, on 8th March 1682, it is minuted that Drs. R. Craufurd, Trotter, M'Gill, Learmont, and Halyburton, were appointed a Pharmacopœia committee. Of these I have shown that Craufurd and Trotter were not very constant in their attendance during the first year, and Halyburton was noted for having been present at only four meetings in three years—that is in all 'The Early Days.' It is not surprising, therefore, to find at the fifth sederunt of the College, that only two members of this first and very important committee

Members of new Pharmacopœia Committee.

were present, and that the President Stevensone, Drs. Burnet, Balfour, Sibbald, and Stewart were 'appointed an additional Pharmacopœia committee to revise the severall parts.' Additional Pharmacopœia Committee.

In the course of the meetings of the College, at the seventh sederunt, a remit to the College from the Privie Council concerning the case of James Aikenhead, Apothecary, and his servant, for selling poisons, came up for consideration. As the witnesses were not present, it was remitted to Drs. Sibbald and Trotter to examine them and report. This they did, and at the ninth sederunt their Report was approved, and ordered to be given to the King's Council. Remit from Privie Council as to sale of poisons. Drs. Sibbald and Trotter's Report.

There is no fresh notice of the Pharmacopœia till the twentieth sederunt, held on 13th August 1683. Dr. Balfour is then recommended 'to bring in his part of the Pharmacopœia, the next meeting, being this day seventh night,' and so far advanced was it, that, at the twenty-first sederunt, held on 20th August 1683, 'Doctor Sibbald gave account that he had agried with David Lindsay for printing the Pharmacopœia, who had undertaken to give the Colledge copies of each of the Impressions for the use of the Colledge, where to the Colledge agries, and appoynts each member to revise their own part, and the Præses, Doctors Balfour, Sibbald, and Pitcairne to be revisers of the haill, and that the Præses, Doctors Balfour and Sibbald, or any two of them enter into a contract with the printer.' 13th August 1683, Dr. Balfour to bring in his part of the Pharmacopœia. 20th August 1683, Sibbald reports agreement for publishing it. The haill to be revised and printed.

The spirit of opposition was now shown, by whom the Minutes do not indicate; but, for more than a year, no mention is made of the Pharmacopœia till Sibbald was elected President on 2nd December 1684. Opposition is shown. Set aside till Sibbald President.

He tried to overcome the opposition when he was in that position; and it is minuted, 'the President, Doctors Trotter, St. Clair, Stevenson younger, M'Gill, Cranstoune, Learmonth, and Halkitt appoynted to be a quorum for considering the Pharmacopœia and the improvement of Medicine.' The absence of Burnet's name from this committee is noteworthy. Renewed Effort by Sibbald.

The blank in the Minute Book.

Then comes the blank in the Minutes, and when the College is again recorded as meeting, Sir Archibald Stevensone is once more President, and the only original Fellows present are Drs. Trotter, Cranstoun, and Pitcairne; the latter returned from his Leyden Professorship, and now the son-in-law of Stevensone. The next Minute, under date 6th February 1696, referring to the Pharmacopœia, shows where the cause in the delay of its publication arose: 'The same day ye College appoynted Dr. St. Claire and Dr. Dundas to goe to Dr. Stevensone and ye late clerk Mr. Alexander Hume, and require from him ye copie of ye Pharmacopœia compiled by ye Colledge qt other papers belong to ye Colledge in yr hands.' Then follows this Minute, 'the same day ye colledge name Sir Thomas Burnet, Sir Robert Sibbald, Doctors Eizat, Mitchel, Blackader, Dundas, and Dicksone to revise ye Pharmacopœia and make yr report to ye Colledge.'

Copy of Pharmacopœia to be required from Dr. Stevensone.

Pharmacopœia to be again revised, 9th March 1697,

On March 9th, 1697, the subject is once more taken up, 'the qlk day the Colledge, taking into consideration the several papers relating to the Dispensatory now given in by the severall comittee with their remarks upon them, they appoynt Sir Robert Sibbald, Drs. Cranstoune, St. Clair, Eizat, and Mitchel to revise the whole, and make yr report of the same to ye Colledge.' Sibbald, disgusted apparently by the continued delays to this early Effort of the College, which he regarded as of first importance, having retired from the Committee, Dr. Trotter on 30th August 1697 took his place. At last, on 24th March 1699, 'The College being so satisfied with the draught yrof (the Dispensatory) ordains the same to be printed and appoynts the President, Doctor Eizat, or in any of their absence, Doctor Mitchel, to agrie with the printer, revise the sheets, and correct the proof. (Signed) MATTHEW ST. CLAIR, President.'

and Committee named.

Dr. Sibbald retires from the Committee.

24th March 1699, ordered to be printed.

Sir Robert Sibbald had been present as well as Burnet at the meeting on 1st February 1699, but neither of them was at that of 24th March. One can imagine the mingled feelings of regret and satisfaction which would fill the generous breast of Sibbald, when he heard that at last, after eighteen weary years, the Pharmacopœia of the Edinburgh College of Physicians was now to be brought forth. His feeling, too, must have been one of intense disappointment that so many precious years had been wasted, and that hindrances had been obtruded of a most serious nature from one especially, from whom the College and the Profession of the day might have expected a more enlightened and generous line of action, when he recalled that, sixteen years before, he and David Lindsay had agreed upon the terms, upon which the latter would print and publish the Pharmacopœia, and that Dr. Stevensone, Dr. Balfour, Dr. Pitcairne, and himself were to be 'the revisers of the haill,' and that he, the Præses, and Dr. Balfour were to 'enter into a contract with the Printer.'

Pharmacopœia to be issued after sixteen years' delay.

Sir Robert, in his Autobiography, at page 42, gives the following account of the matter, and I have shown from the Minutes, with whom originally the obstruction arose: 'When I was President, the Dispensatorie or Pharmacopœa for this place was compleated. I caused transcribe two copies of it, one for the Colledge in folio, which was delivered by me to Dr. Balfour, at his election to be Præses, and another in quarto for myself, which I payed for out of my own money. I got the Chancellor's Licence for it, and did agrie with David Lindsay for printing it upon the saide David his charge, and he obliged himself to deliver copies of each of the impressions both in folio and 12mo for the use of the Colledge, whereto the Colledge did agrie, as appears by their Minute Booke, and yett a faction obstructed them,' just as I have shown you by the quotations I have made. Again Sibbald, at page 35 of his Autobiography, observes, 'In the tyme I was President, our Patent was ratified in Parliament, The Pharmacopœa Edinburgensis was composed and licensed to be printed by the Chancellor, and the printer agreed to print it gratis, and give the College a competent number of copies, and take his hazard of vending the

Sir Robert Sibbald's account in Autobiography.

rest'; and he concludes with those significant words, 'but by the malice of some it was laid aside for ten years thereafter.'

Necessity for a Scottish Pharmacopœia.

It was necessary that a Pharmacopœia for Scotland should be prepared, for whilst the Royal Proclamation prefixed to the London Pharmacopœia made it binding for the Apothecaries of England, Scotland was not mentioned. The druggists of Scotland, as has been said, were not bound to recognise the London Pharmacopœia, and could make such variations in their preparations as they pleased; but when the College of Edinburgh issued their volume, tardily though it was, the Scottish Apothecaries became under control as to what they dispensed, and were ruled by the Edinburgh Pharmacopœia, until the issue of the British Pharmacopœia of the General Medical Council in 1864.

Possible opposition of the Apothecaries influenced Sir Archibald Stevensone.

It is possible that opposition by the Apothecaries to the introduction of a Pharmacopœia may have influenced Stevensone in the course he followed, for at first he seemed favourable to it. Although the publication of this first useful Effort of the Royal College was so long delayed, it was ready for issue before the expiry of The Early Days; and the merit is not lessened of the good intentions of Balfour, Burnet, and Sibbald and those supporting them for trying to carry out one of the great reasons for which the establishment of the College of Physicians was considered necessary. But, though thwarted, it at last prevailed, and was not unworthy of the age in which it was produced.

Pharmacopœa Collegii Regii Medicorum Edimburgensium.

As some of you may be interested in the 'Pharmacopœa Collegii Regii Medicorum Edimburgensium—Edimburgi—*Apud Hæredes* Andreæ Anderson, Anno Domi: MDCXCIX,' I show you the original copy from the Library which bears on the title-page the arms of the city, and the legends of the city and of Scotland, the latter surrounding a serpent coiled round a rugged staff. It is in size duodecimo; and, including the Index, numbers 236 pages. It is dedicated to 'Serenissimo Gulielmo II. D. G., Scotiae, Angliae, Franciae, et Hiberniae Regi, Fidei

Defensori, Collegium Medicorum Edimburgensium, Pharmacopœam hanc, Tanquam observantiae Tesseram Humillime offert consecrat que.' Then follows a preface in Latin, but it contains no observation explaining the delay in the publication of the volume.

The recognition of the system of Galen is testified to at pages 156 and 157, where four greater warm seeds and four lesser—four greater cold seeds and four lesser, are given, with cordial flowers and fragments of precious stones.

The following extracts from the Minutes may be of interest to some of you, although not regarded as necessary to be mentioned in my story :—

Subsequent Minutes bearing on the Pharmacopœia.

'Decr. 25, 1696.—The Colledge appoynts Dr. Eizat and Dr. Mitchell to revise ye Materia Medica, and to give yrs thoughts of it; and from the Aquae Stillatitiæ, to yt part of ye Pharmacopœia, ye Pilulae, to Dr. Rule and Dr. Frier; and from Pilula to the end, to Drs. Dicksone, Dundas, and Forrest; and yt they be sedulous in revising ye sd Pharmacopœia, and to make report of yr diligence as soon as possible.'

'June 7, 1697.—The Colledge unanimously agried upon the simple waters to be inserted in the Pharmacopœia.'

'June 29, 1697.—The Præses represented to the Colledge that the African Company desyred two or more of the Members of the Colledge wold visit the drogs that are come home for their use, which desyre the Colledge thought fitt to comply with,' etc.

'5th July 1697.—Dr. Dicksone brought in a receipt of Epileptic water, which the Colledge heard read, and considered; and appoynted every Member to take a copy of it, and consider against next meeting.'

'Doctor St. Clair gave in a receipt of ane anti-Scorbutic water, which being read, they ordered to be considered against next meeting.'

'Doctor Mitchell reported that he thought the Aq. Theriacalis should be kept in, as in the London Dispensatorie, which the Colledge agried to.'

'Appoynt Doctors Mitchell and Dicksone to bring in a receipt of Tincture of Opium, and Drs. Eizat and Forrest to bring a receipt of the Tincture of Castor.'

'Sept. 12, 1698.—The qlk day, the Colledge heard all ye objections made against the Pharmacopœia and the oyles, and have approven so far.'

Animal substances in the first Pharmacopœia.

The following are some of the animal simples and preparations named in the Pharmacopœia.

Urina juvenis sani impuberis—in Aqua stiptica.

Spiritus, Sal Volatile, et Oleum, Cranii Hominis violentâ morte extincti.

Spiritus, Sal Volatile, et Oleum, Lumbricorum, ex Lumbricis terrestribus Aqua ablutis et modice exiccatis.

Spiritus, Sal Volatile, et Oleum, millepedum.

Spiritus, Sal Volatile, et Oleum, Viperarum ex Viperis exiccatis.

The Emplastrum de Ranis cum Mercurio, contains,
Ranas vivas numero duodecim,
Lumbricorum terrestrium purgatorum uncias quotuor.

Oleum Vulpinum, from the boiled down adult fox.

Oleum Scorpionum, forms part of Oleum Masticхinum.

Carnis Viperarum exsiccatae, uncias tres in Theriaca Adromachi.

Ventris Scinci ʒ ii ss, are in Mithridatium Damocratis.

{ Jecorum cum felle anguillarum exiccatorum, ʒ ii,
{ Testiculorum Caballinorum in Clibano siccatorum, ℥ i,
form part of Pulvis ad Partum.

The Pulvis de Gutteta contains Ungulae Alcis, et Cranii Hominis violenta morte extincti ʒ iij.

The Edinburgh College Pharmacopœia soon asserted its position. It occurs to me as possible that, whilst it served to maintain the importance of the Edinburgh College, it was also intended to prevent the encroachment of that of London ; and for these reasons Sibbald was anxious to have the New College in Edinburgh issue its distinctive Pharmacopœia. The College must have been quite aware of the importance of its Pharmacopœia being brought up to date. Accordingly under 25th May 1721, there is the following Minute :—'The which day the Colledge appoynt the President (Dr. Forrest), Dr. Robert Trotter, Sir Edward Eizatt, Dr. William Eccles, Dr. David Dicksone, Dr. John Drummond, Dr. James Craufurd, Dr. John Clerk, and Dr. John Learmont, as a Committee to revise their former Dispensatory, and to take cair that a New Edition be made thereof, after it shall be revised, compared, and remended, and their first meeting to be Colledge Hall upon —— there after to adjorne from tyme to tyme as they shall think convenient.' Also before it was sent to press, a Committee of the Chirurgeons was requested to meet with Dr. John Clerk and Dr. John Learmonth to revise the Dispensatory or the Methodus Componendi. This was on 5th September, and on 7th November 1721 it is reported that 'the Chirurgeons were satisfied with the Dispensatory as it then stood.' The committee were so diligent that the New Pharmacopœia was published towards the end of 1721.

Intentions of publishing the Pharmacopœia.

Edition of 1721.

The London College, whose first Pharmacopœia was published in 1618, issued a new edition in 1724, dedicated to King George, by the Grace of God King of Great Britain, France, and Ireland. It also contains a proclamation by the king, commanding Apothecaries to follow the Dispensatory compiled by the College of Physicians of London, after narrating the advantages of it, and that it be compiled in the Latin tongue. It continues : 'Being persuaded the establishing the general use of the said book may tend to the prevention of such deceits in the making and com-

London Pharmacopœia first published in 1618.

Edition of 1724 contains Proclamation by the King.

pounding medicines, wherein the lives and health of our subjects are so highly concerned . . . we therefore strictly require, charge, and command all and singular Apothecaries and others whose business it is to compound medicines or distilled oyles or waters, or such other extracts within any part of our Kingdom of *Great Britain* called *England*, dominion of *Wales*, or Town of *Berwick* upon *Tweed*, that they and every of them immediately after the said Pharmacopœia Londonensis shall be printed and published, do not compound,' etc. etc.

Did not extend to Scotland nor to Ireland.

From this extract it will be seen that the province of the London Pharmacopœia did not extend to Scotland and Ireland. Scotland possessed through the Edinburgh College a jurisdiction of its own, and was not bound to recognise the London Pharmacopœia as binding upon it. By its own act the Edinburgh College had freed Scotland from the sway of that of London, and it remained so, as has been said, until the issue of the British Pharmacopœia of the General Medical Council.

The Edinburgh College in later years made another advance, when the directions for compounding the preparations were given in English. From its Early Days the Royal College has adapted itself to the times and even anticipated them.

THE DISPENSARY

The second Effort. The Dispensary.

The second great Effort of the Royal College was much to its credit, and bears evidence that, from its commencement, the spirit of the Fellows was liberal and unselfish. It proposed for itself a grand scheme, in which the chief work was to be done by the members individually, and without fee or reward, except the recognition and development of the Christian spirit, 'I was sick and ye visited me'—the practical expression of a duty to our fellows who are not so well off as ourselves, a paraphrase in action and a manifestation of its legend, 'Non sinit esse feros.' It was

The necessity for it.

not the College's duty to take up this neglected work, but the Fellows were too conscious of the ignorance of sanatory and sanitary matters, of the misery, and of the sacrifice of life around them, and were well aware that nothing was being done to mitigate these evils, nor to lessen the insanitary state of the city, by those in positions of authority.

They did not waste time in calling on the Municipality to act, but first deliberated in the College what should be done, resolved that it should be done, and who of their number should first act, and then, by the force of example, they endeavoured to rouse the Town Council, to see that it too had a duty to perform towards its sick fellow-citizens.

No Medical attendant at Paul's Work till near close of seventeenth century.

It is noteworthy that Paul's Work, a place of detention for inmates of various kinds, seems to have been without Medical attendant till near the close of the century, when Mr. Alexander Monteath and Dr. Pitcairne volunteered to attend the sick inmates without payment, on condition of being allowed to have the bodies for dissection of those who died unclaimed and without friends.

After the lapse of two hundred years the position of matters is unchanged in this, that even now Medical aid to the sick poor, unless so poor as to be on the Pauper Roll, is still the work of Medical men's charity.

Considered at second Sederunt of College. 'Phisitians to the poore' to be appointed next meeting.

The second sederunt of the College was held on 6th February 1682. In addition to Dr. Archibald Stevensone, the President, there were present the Censors, Drs. Balfour and Livingstone,—the Council, Drs. Burnet, Balfour, and Sibbald, who was also Secretary, Livingstone, Stewart, and Cranston,—the Procurator-Fiscal Archibald Pitcairne,—and also Drs. Hutton, William Stevensone, and Trotter; in all eleven Fellows. The words of the Minute are few, the business in amount was not great, but it was very significant in its importance, when we consider that it was the basis upon which our splendid charitable Medical Institutions in this city were to be founded; and from which eventually our noble Infirmary, the charity for the sick poor and the school for instruction of thousands of students of Medicine and Surgery, was to arise; and in which in later years numerous ministering nurses were to be trained. 'Resolved at next meeting to appoint some persons to be Phisitians to the Poore.' Truly a noble resolve in these early days. Accordingly, at the next, the third sederunt, four days later, held on 10th February 1682, when Dr. Archibald Stevensone President, Dr. Thomas Burnet, Dr. Robert Craufurd, Dr. John Learmonth, Dr. Patrick Halyburton, Dr. Robert Sibbald, Dr. James Stewart, Dr. John Hutton, Dr. John M'Gill, and Dr. Archibald Pitcairne, ten in all were present, and in the absence of Drs. Andrew Balfour, James Livingstone, Alexander Cranston, William Stevensone, and Robert Trotter, who were present at the previous meeting, the Minute, without unnecessary words, records that it was resolved that Drs. Burnet and Craufurd 'until nex election serve poore of the Citie and Suburbs.' And so this early charitable undertaking was simply inaugurated, and Thomas Burnet, Physician to the King, was the first to undertake the duties of 'Phisitian to the Poore' of Edinburgh.

10th Feb. 1682. At third sederunt Drs. Burnet and Craufurd to serve poor till next election.

I am anxious to point out that this early stage of a great movement received at the two meetings the approval of fifteen of the nineteen Fellows on the Roll of the College, and from the first appears to have received the hearty support of all the best men amongst the original members. They were all impressed with the necessity for the movement, and the duty pressing upon them to undertake the performance of it. Whilst quite ready to do their professional part of the work, they recognised that the Municipality had also a duty to perform, and should at least bear a share of it. The Minute goes on to state, 'And recommend the President and Censors to acquaint the Provost, and desyre him to acquaint the Council to nominate some persone to be Apothecary, and to give some allowance, by whom accompts are to be only paiable by the Phisitians recepts, who are to put rates yrupon. And that the

Received the approval of fifteen of the nineteen attending Fellows on the Roll.

Provost and Town Council appealed to to help in this great work by nominating an Apothecary, ministers of the several kirksessions be acquainted herewith, who are desyred to give certificates that the poore that are sick are in severe bounds, and this act is to be but prejudice of the Colledge to serve theire poore if they think fitt'; and, as showing how cordially and harmoniously the movement was to be carried on, the Minute further states, 'the doctors named are authorised to depute any of the Colledge, in caice of their necessary abscence, for service.'

and city ministers to certify cases requiring attendance.

All the Fellows may be called on to act in emergency.

It does not appear from the Minutes that the Town Council contributed towards the expenses, and from time to time the question of maintenance crops up. It would seem as if at first the Fellows themselves bore the expense. A fund towards this at a later period was formed by the fines exacted from late and absent Fellows at quarterly meetings, and, later still, by the assessment of intrants. The duties of 'Phisitians to the poore' appear to have been carried on by the two gentlemen first appointed, but from the imperfectness of the Record of the College proceedings it is impossible to say for what number of years they acted, or who succeeded them. It is probable that Burnet and Craufurd acted during all The Early Days of the College.

Sources of revenue. (1) The Fellows. (2) The fine fund. (3) Assessment of intrants.

Duties carried on by two Physicians during all The Early Days.

I should like to continue this subject a little longer. When the Minutes again recommence, on 6th December 1694, Sir Archibald Stevenson is once more President, twelve Fellows are at the meetings, and Archibald Stevenson, Trotter, Cranston, and Pitcairn represent the original Fellows. No mention is made of the Dispensary, nor is there any mention of it, till 5th December 1695, when, as if it was a usual proceeding, 'Drs. St. Clair and Dundas were chosen Physitians for ye poore for ye ensuing year,' and so on in following years.

After 1694.

In November 1704 the College obtained possession from Sir James M'Kenzie of its own premises in the Fountain Close. Dr. Dundas is now President. A committee regarding the management of the Dispensary gave in its report on 30th August

1704. Removes to new premises, Fountain Close.

1705. The Minute bears, 'that it is their opinion that two of the Socii shall attend two or three dayes in the week at their meeting hous in the Fountain Close, for giving their advyce to the poore that are sick gratis. The Colledge agried to the opinion of the Committee, and referred it to be furder considered.' Accordingly in the Minute of October 29th (Halket being President and Sibbald present at these meetings), it is stated, 'Two to attend at ye Colledge Hall and give advice to the sick poore gratis, three days a week from three to four o'clock.'

30 August 1705. Regulation of Dispensary attendance to be three days a week.

That the benefits arising from and the question of expense, must have been before the general public is, I think, proved by the Minute of 27th June 1707, from which it appears that 1250 merks were mortified to the College by Mary Erskine 'for buying druggs to sick poor who have advice gratis from the College.' She was the relict of James Hair, Druggist and Burgess of Edinburgh, and left benefactions to the Trades' Maiden, the Merchant Maidens' Hospitals, and other beneficent objects in the city.

1707. 1250 merks mortified by Mrs. Mary Erskine or Hair, for drugs.

In 1708 a Repository for furnishing medicines to the sick poor was set up, and, from the wording of the Minute, it looks as if the Fellows of the College were following the steps which the London College had taken in order to repress the excessive charges and forwardness of the Apothecaries, although there is no direct evidence of these exactions prevailing in Edinburgh at this time.

Repository for cheap drugs established 1708.

Thus from Bell and Redwood (*op. cit.* p. 14), we learn that in 1694 the increased power and importance of the Apothecaries in London excited the jealousy of the Physicians; and the high charges of the Apothecaries were felt, especially by the poor; and, in order to meet the emergency, 'Some of the Physicians united together in the establishment of Dispensaries, where they supplied Medicines on reasonable terms, employing assistants to dispense them under their own superintendence.' From the same authorities we further learn that the following statement was subscribed by the President, Censors, most of the Elect, senior Fellows, and

Similar to those established by the Physicians in London in 1694.

Candidates, of the London College of Physicians under date 22nd December 1696, relative to the sick poor: 'Whereas the several orders of the College of Physicians, London, for prescribing Medicines gratis to the poor sick of the Cities of London and Westminster and parts adjacent, as also the proposals made by the said College to the Lord Mayor, Court of Aldermen, and Common Council of London in pursuance thereof, have hitherto been ineffectual, for that no method *hath been taken to furnish the poor with Medicines at low and reasonable rates,*' then follows a statement that they oblige themselves to pay the sum of ten pounds apiece, 'which money, when received by the said Dr. Thomas Barwell, is to be by him *expended in preparing and delivering Medicines to the poor at their* intrinsic value,' etc.

London Dispensaries were drug stores.

These Dispensaries evidently were for the *supply of drugs*, rather than for *giving advice* (the one established in 1682 by the Edinburgh College did both); and the Repository established in Edinburgh in 1708 was for the like purpose, and was distinct from the Dispensary at the College Hall. Bell and Redwood continue as regards London, 'Three Dispensaries were established (at College Warwick Lane, St. Martins Lane Westminster, and a third in Cornhill). They came into operation about the beginning of February 1697; and *were soon very generally resorted to for the preparation of Physicians' prescriptions, or bills as they were termed, and also for the sale of Medicines by retail.*'

These London Dispensaries, whatever they may have been originally, ultimately became of no scientific value, being mere drug stores or shops.

And so was the Edinburgh Repository of 1708. Its promoters loaned Mrs. Hair's money.

But to return to the Edinburgh Repository. Mrs. Hair's bequest was lent to its promoters to further its purposes; and, on May 4th, 1708, the Treasurer is instructed 'to get security from such members as subscribed for setting up a Repository for Medicines, and who borrowed the same for that use.'

I have failed to trace the ultimate disposal of this mortification. When I was Treasurer of the Royal College, I did not find any reference to it in any of the cash-books committed to my care.

1712. Scope enlarged so that Licentiates might help.

By the year 1712, the scope of the Dispensary work would seem to have been enlarged so that younger members of the profession might benefit, for on 4th November in this year, 'the College considering the . . . giving attendance on the sick poore, they appoynt that for the future the Licentiats shall give their advice and attendance on the said poore as well as the ordinary members.' The monetary affairs of the Dispensary and the College were by this time, if not previously, kept quite separate, and by distinct Treasurers.

Funds kept separate from those of College.

Fines for non-attendance.

In 1714, the fine for absence on attendance upon the sick poor was 12s. Scots, which was to be paid to the Treasurer for the drug expenses of the Dispensary.

Yearly expenditure £144, 15s. 4d. Scots.

In 1717, it appears that from January 1711 to January 1717, the amount received for the Dispensary was £908, 15s. 4d. Scots, and the discharge £866, 11s. 10d., leaving a creditable balance of £42, 3s. 6d. This would give an average yearly expenditure for drugs of £144, 8s. 8d. Scots, thus implying that a good amount of work had been done yearly.

Necessity arising for Infirmary.

The Dispensary work was steadily continued, but the necessity for greater accommodation became more and more urgent as years went on, and the quieter times allowed the city and suburbs to enlarge, and so the necessity for an Infirmary became clamant.

Originally Dispensary used for Clinical purposes.

The Dispensary from the first had, I judge, been made use of for Clinical Examinations, as I shall shortly afterwards show, and that before the Medical School was established.

The attempt to form Infirmary in 1721 failed.

The teaching in the latter was now becoming systematic; the necessity for an Infirmary for Clinical instruction was pressing, and for the better treatment of serious illness, urgent; and one attempt in 1721 to get up a House for these purposes without the co-operation of the College of Physicians, had been unsuccessful. The question was being spoken about and discussed; and at length, a favourable opportunity presenting itself, the Royal College took it up, and, under the Presidentship of Dr. John Drummond, the following Minute occurs: '1st February 1726.—The President, Dr. J. Drummond, represented to the Colledge that, according to their desire, he and severall of the members had sett on foot a subscription for erecting and maintaining ane Infirmary or Hospital for the sick poor, and had pretty good success, and recommended to all the members of the Colledge to use their best endeavours to procure more subscriptions for accomplishing so good and charitable a work.'

Effort of 1726.

That the Royal College was disinterested and earnest in its desire to promote and carry on the Infirmary, the following extract strongly testifies to: '1st August 1727.—The same day the Colledge agreed that the following advertisement in relation to ye Infirmary now read to ye Colledge be published in ye newspapers, of which the tenor follows.' . . . 'The Royal Colledge of Physitians having always shown such a particular concern for the sick poor, that for several years two of ye number have attended every week in ye Hall to give advice, and also medicine to some proper objects gratis, and now considering that yr is ane Hospital for the sick poor to be erected at Edinburgh; therefore, they for the encouragement of such a pious undertaking oblidge ym selves that ane or more of their number shall attend the said Hospital faithfully and freely, without any prospect of reward or sallary, until the stock of ye sd Hospital shall be so increased that it can afford a reasonable allowance for one or two Physitians for ye proper use, and the Colledge order this advertisement.—Signed in yr name by ye President to be published.'

Minute of 1st August 1727.

Three months afterwards the success of the scheme is assured, and the relation of the College to it is declared in the next Minute.

1727. Relation of College to Royal Infirmary.

'7th November 1727.—Thereafter the President represented to ye Colledge that the first subscription for erecting the Infirmary was compleated in due time, and the money was comeing in, and that it was the members of ye Colledge that had sett this charitable work on foot and had contributed for ym selves and procured contributions from other well disposed persons, and still hoped they would procure more subscriptions for establishing the Infirmary, that might be in some measure suitable to the necessity of the countrey.'

1728. College move to make application to the General Assembly.

As the Church does not appear to have spontaneously assisted in the good work, the College determined to remind it of its duty, and accordingly we read that on '7th May 1728, the Colledge thinking it proper that application should be made to the Generall Assembly for their assistance in procuring contributions for the Infirmary, and ane address for that purpose being read, the Colledge appointed Dr. Rule, and Dr. Riddell, and Dr. Innes to attend ye Committee of Bills yr anent.' (Here follows the address.)

The Assembly, when applied to, graciously granted an act, but with that exception, it did not do much in favour of the erection of the Infirmary as the following extract shows:—

1st Aug. 1728. Report by Drs. Rule, Riddell, and Innes.

'1st Aug. 1728.—Drs. Rule, Riddell, and Innes reported they had attended the Committee of Bills in the Generall Assembly in favour of ye Infirmary. But the Colledge not well knowing the forme of getting qt act made effectuall so as to answer the desyne yr by patented, they yr for impower the President and Dr. Riddell to meet with Mast. Spence, Depute Clerk to Assembly and advise with him what is the proper method of applying to the Presbyterys for getting the act of ye Assembly for the contributions in favour of ye Infirmary putt in execution.'

5th Nov. 1728. Meeting with Nicol Spence.

'5th Novr. 1728.—The President (Dr. Pringle) and Dr. Riddell reported that they had spoke with Nicol Spence anent the way and manner of getting the Act of Assembly in relation to the Infirmary putt in execution and that they were told this was to be done by sending circular letters and copy of the said Act of the Assembly to the Moderators of the severall Presbyterys in Scotland, and that ye samen would accordingly be transmitted to the respective Presbyterys with ye first opportunity, a copy of which act and letter was read.'

4th Feb. 1729. Letters to the Presbyteries.

'4th Feby. 1729.—The President reported that conform to ye minute anent the circular letters to be sent to severall Presbyterys in relation to the Infirmary were signed, and would be transmitted to them.' The Church does not appear to have greatly advanced the cause; and an extract from the first report of the Managers of the Infirmary is not complimentary to the Presbyterian churches throughout Scotland, as will be seen in due course.

Presbyterian Church did not much advance the cause.

The next Minute of the College shows the readiness of the Royal College to aid this charitable work. '5th Aug. 1729.—The Colledge considering that the Infirmary is now in readiness of receiving patients, and that it will be necessary that they attend the same, doe therefore unanimously agrie to attend the Infirmary in yr turns for the space of a fortnight untill some settled method be agried upon anent their attendences and impowered the President till quarterly meeting to appoint any Physicians he thinks fitt to attend for the space of a fortnight and accordingly the President appointed Dr. Drummond to attend the Infirmary for the first fortnight which commences to-morrow.'

Attendance of Physicians at the Infirmary, 5th August 1729.

Each in turn for a fortnight.

'4th Nov. 1729.—Continued the power to the President to name any Physician he thinks fitt, till next quarterly meeting, to attend the Infirmary for the space of a fortnight.' '3rd Feby. 1730.—Recommend the Council to meet and consider the manner of attendance on the sick poor and to report their opinion agt next quarterly meeting.'

President to appoint any Physician he thinks fit.

The usefulness of the Dispensary having been established for nearly fifty years, it is not to be sacrificed when the Infirmary begins, and we must admire the Christian spirit and professional zeal and energy of the College in arranging to carry on *both*

Dispensary to be continued too after fifty years' existence.

Order of attendance of Physicians and Licentiates. 5th May 1730.

charities. Thus '5th May 1730.—The opinion of the Councill in relation to ye attendances on ye Infirmary and sick poor, being reported to the Colledge, the same was approven of, and the Colledge did yr upon order that in place of two Physitians who ordinarilly attend the Hall formerly, only one shall wait on; and, when the present course is over, the eldest Physitian shall begin, and so in course go on as formerly; and furder the Colledge ordered that when all the Fellows and Licentiats have gone through this course at the Infirmary, the senior Physitian shall again begin, and so to go on in order, until the Colledge shall think fitt to alter it; and that all the Fellows and Licentiats shall be obliged to attend, both at the Hall and Infirmary in yr turns or send oyers of ye Colledge number for them; and who does not observe these Rules shall be subject to the censure of ye Colledge.' But here I end these extracts. They prove the early origin of the Infirmary, its relation to the 'Royall Colledge' when opened, and the early method of ministering to the patients and the Dispensary at the Hall.

Licentiates to attend Infirmary also.

First Report of Infirmary Managers to end of 1730.

I submit the following extracts from the Managers' first report of the Infirmary as substantiating the relation of the Royal College to the Infirmary. The first report embraces the period to the end of 1730. It appears from 'an account of the rise and establishment of the Infirmary or Hospital for sick poor, erected at Edinburgh,' that 'among the many objects of charity that daily present themselves to our view, there have been none so entirely destitute hitherto of relief from any publick institution in this country, as the poor when attacked with diseases or disabled by accidents; for this the Royal College of Physicians at Edinburgh have, for many years past, attended in their turns twice a week at their Hall, to give advice to the poor gratis, yet they very often have had the mortification to see their advice and medicines prove unsuccessful, by their patients not having due care taken of them by their wants of proper diet and lodging.' To supply these defects the report continues, 'Some gentlemen, in the year 1721, caused print and dispense a pamphlet setting forth the great necessity and advantages of a Hospital for maintaining and curing the sick poor, and containing proposals for raising a fund for such a Hospital. This scheme did not succeed . . . and there appeared, at that time, so little probability of success that they dropped the prosecution of their scheme.'

Unsuccessful attempt of 1721.

'Notwithstanding this discouragement, in the year 1725, when the copartners of the Fishing Company were about to dissolve themselves, and to divide the remainder of their stock, the College of Physicians thought it a proper opportunity for trying to procure part of this money from the proprietors towards founding a Hospital for sick poor at Edinburgh, and for that end, caused draw up a form of assignation . . . for the purpose above mentioned, and the College also caused prepare a form of a bond by which the subscribers obliged themselves to pay the sums annexed to their names . . . for the same purpose . . . which would be null if £2000 was not made up before a specified day, that being the least sum with which the erection of an Infirmary could be set about. . . . Severall copies of these two papers being sent out on stamped paper, and most of the gentlemen of the Royal College having subscribed to one or other of them, they were delivered to such of their members as were willing to take the trouble of soliciting for subscriptions, who being assisted by several of the Incorporation of Surgeons and other charitable people, did obtain subscriptions for something more than £2000 stg. before the day specified,' etc. etc.

Dissolving of Fishing Company taken advantage of by Physicians.

A favourable opportunity.

£2000 required to begin with.

After mentioning that the College also advertised the above, and at same time would without fee or reward or salary attend the Infirmary faithfully, the report says the College also petitioned 'the General Assembly of the Church for a voluntary contribution in all the parishes of the kingdom, presented in name of the College of Physicians and managed by them. Some ministers complied, but the far greater part have neglected to make

Unsuccessful appeal to Parish Ministers.

Episcopal Clergy more helpful.

these collections,' though 'the Reverend Episcopal Clergy in Edinburgh have assisted by collections at their meeting houses.' . . . 'These gentlemen took from the Treasurer to the University of Edinburgh, with the consent of the Town Council, a lease for nineteen years of a house of a small rent near the College (University), which was made more agreeable and convenient by the Professors of Medicine granting liberty to the patients to walk in a garden adjacent.'

SURGEONS AND MEDICINE SUPPLY

Surgeons and supply of Medicine. Offer of six Surgeon Apothecaries.

'By a generous offer made and subscribed by six Chirurgeon Apothecaries in Edinburgh, viz. Messrs. John M'Gill, Francis Congalton, George Cunninghame, Robt. Hope, Alex. Monro, and John Douglas to attend the Hospital in their turns without any Reward or Sallary, to dispense the Medicines prescribed by the Physicians faithfully from their shops, each in the course of their attendance and to give their advice and assistance jointly in extraordinary cases, mutually to supply each other's absence in case of necessary avocations, and generally perform all the duties of Surgeons and Apothecaries to the Infirmary.' The Rules were agreed to, after two meetings, by the Managers on the 13th January 1728.

Infirmary rules agreed to by Managers, 13th January 1728.

From the foregoing extract it will be seen that the Infirmary at first did not receive the support of the College of Surgeons. It is said that only six Surgeons and Apothecaries voluntarily gave the Infirmary their support, and nobly aided it not only by professional skill but by generously dispensing as well as supplying the necessary medicines. The connection of the Royal College with the institution of the Infirmary was recognised, for by enactment no one can be a Physician to it unless he be first associated with the College, hitherto as a Fellow. This is one of the highly valued prerogatives of the Royal College of Physicians.

Infirmary prerogative granted to Physicians.

THE LICENTIAT'S EXAMINATION, ADMITTING TO PRACTISE IN THE CITY AND PRECINCTS OF EDINBURGH

The third great Effort at professional advancement and reform was the institution of methodical and uniform professional entrance examinations for permission or licence to practise.

Third Effort. Professional Examinations.

At the tenth sederunt of the Royal College eleven Fellows were present, amongst whom were the President Archibald Stevensone, and Drs. Burnet, Balfour, Sibbald, and Pitcairn.

The subject which occupied their attention was the qualification of Practitioners of Medicine within the city and its suburbs.

By the Charter no one could practise Medicine in Edinburgh or its precincts without obtaining the Licence of the College; and if practising without it, he was liable, even although a Scottish University graduate, to be fined. At this meeting it was resolved and agreed 'that hereafter no persone shall be licensed to practise Medicine in the City of Edinburgh or Suburbs thereof except he be first ane graduat Doctor of Physick.'

The Licence of the College necessary to practise in city or suburbs. Graduates only allowed to practise in city.

The College recognised that the practitioner in the country under its jurisdiction need not have the University title, but both the city and the country physician, unless he were a graduate of a Scottish University, must equally be examined by the Royal College Examiners before the College Licence to practise was given. By the Charter the Medical graduates of the Scottish Universities could, of course, on payment of the dues, claim the Licence without any examination. The prohibitory powers of the College did not extend beyond the city and suburbs, but the College was doubtless prepared to give a Licence *after examination* testifying to the qualification of the holder to practise Medicine. This is shown by the following: 'But upon application made to the College by any persone in the Country for Licence to

Licence only required for country. Both for city and country examination necessary before Licence.

College examined for Licence for country Practitioner.

practise in the Country, the College, after examination and tryall of the qualifications of any such persons, may grant a Licence or Certificate to him as a fitt persone sufficiently qualified for practiseing of Medicine in the Country.'

No power to enforce Licence.

Prepared to advance professional status.

Although the College had no power to enforce its licence in the country, it was prepared to advance the professional status as secured by personal and individual examination, and so to ensure that the people were being treated by efficient practitioners.

Further examination necessary if Country Practitioner came to Edinburgh. Must be an M.D.

A barrier, however, was put to the country practitioner encroaching upon the College's sphere of jurisdiction, and we next find that 'if such a persone shall happen to come into Edinburgh, he shall not have allowance to Practise without a New Examinatione and Licence, and be first a graduate Doctor.' Observe the consistency of the College and its honourable allegiance to the Universities! Can we blame it for, in the *first* instance, placing a check on the number of Practitioners of Medicine in the city, which in those days could not with the suburbs have had a population of more than 30,000; and in the *second*, increasing the funds of the College by exacting the fee for liberty to practise as a Physician within the city and its suburbs!

Objects to lessen number of Practitioners in city. To increase funds of College.

Fairness to graduates before the Patent.

The fairness and justness of the College are also shown by its resolving 'that here after any Physitian graduate before the Patent, upon application to the College for a Licence to practise in Edinburgh shall, without any Examination, upon payment to the Treasurer of Fyve Pounds Ster. have a Licence to practise in Edinburgh, he having his ordinary residence in the Country.' Is not the spirit of the 'year of grace' for which the College in recent years has been severely criticised in some quarters, foreshadowed in this early resolution? The graduate was already 'qualified.' A new controlling power had been called into existence. Had these graduates been in the city at the time, they would have had the opportunity to join the College as original Fellows. It was but fair and just that they should have the

Foreshadowing of the 'year of grace' spirit.

opportunity to partake of the benefits and privileges of the College, with as little trouble or annoyance to themselves as possible! The College, however, for its own protection, welfare, and consistency, wisely resolved further that the graduate, and Licentiate without examination, on commencing practice in Edinburgh, shall pay five pounds sterling and 'enter himself Candidat, whenever the College shall require him, and pay all the dues of a Candidat,' and of course, ultimately become 'Socius' of the College.

Fees to be paid by graduates of Scottish Universities without examination.

In the case of any Doctor graduate since the Patent resident in Edinburgh making 'the lyke application, he shall be obliged imediately to consigne into the Thesaurer's hands before the examinatione Five Pounds Star.; and if he be not after examinatione found sufficient, he shall losse Fyftie shillings starling thereof; and if he be found sufficient, shall have Licence as aforesaid allowed to Doctors formerly graduat, upon payment as aforesaid; and when required by the Colledge, shall enter Candidat, and pay uther Ten Pounds Star.; besyd the Ten Pounds formerly payed for his licence, and when advanced to be a Fellow, he shall pay uther Ten Pounds Star.' That would amount to thirty pounds sterling for the whole stages of Licentiat, Candidat, and Socius.

Fees payable by graduates since the Patent.

Share of fee to be returned to unsuccessful examinee.

Total fee for Licentiat, Candidat, and Socius £30 sterling.

During this period, and subsequent to it, various charges of illegal practice were investigated and adjudicated upon, but into the merits of these, I do not intend to enter. One of them, as I already mentioned, was a case from the 'Privie Council' for the sale of poisons, which was referred to Dr. Sibbald to examine and report on. At this date, Sibbald was Secretary and Censor with Balfour, whilst Pitcairn was Procurator-Fiscal.

Charges of illegal practice.

From the consideration of the first examination for admission to the Royal College, one is impressed with the idea that the managers of the College business had determined, as they had no power to teach, that they would stimulate those who had that privilege, by enforcing an examination which, as a test of know-

The first examination for Licence.

A high standard for 1682,

ledge, was undoubtedly of high standard in this country in 1682. It is difficult to determine what knowledge other examining bodies throughout Great Britain and Ireland required from their candidates at this period, but, so far as I can ascertain, after careful investigation, neither the Universities conferring the degree of Doctor of Medicine, nor the Incorporations and Colleges, had so complete and perfectly uniform a standard of examination as that at first instituted by the Royal College of Physicians of Edinburgh. One marked peculiarity of it, from the first, was what would nowadays be termed 'The Clinical Examination,' and the Dispensary, having been established first, was evidently made use of, to supply the two 'severall' or 'practicall caices' upon which the candidate was always examined in the presence of the College in session.

and the most complete in Scotland at the time.

One marked peculiarity, the Clinical Examination.

Use of Dispensary for supplying two practical cases.

Public examination not peculiar to Royal College of Physicians.

This public examination was not peculiar to the Royal College. Mr. Alexander Duncan, in his *Memorials of the Faculty of Physicians and Surgeons of Glasgow*, 1599-1850, at page 49, quotes a Faculty minute of 22nd June 1602, regarding apprentices, from which it appears each was to be examined at the end of three, five, and seven years. At the end of the third year, there was to be an examination possibly as a test of education in writing; and at the end of the seventh, 'qhen he passes Master to be examinat upon the holl particulars of his airt, of the definitions, causses, synes, accidents, and cures of all diseases pertaining to his airt, wt the composition of nature and fit medicaments as shall be requisit.' This reads as if it had been a tolerably thorough examination. It must, however, have had defects arising from defective teaching; and to remedy this, in 1612, the deacon, or visitors, or one of the quartermasters, was obliged to 'teach upon medicine, chirurgeri, or apothecari, the nature of herbs, droges, and such lyk as shall be thought expedient by the brethrene of sd vocation.' Mr. Duncan (at page 51) observes, even the clinical examination . . . was not always awanting in the examinations of

Form of examination Glasgow Faculty Physicians and Surgeons.

Teaching before examination by Deacon, etc.

Occasional Clinical examination.

these early days. It is not a little interesting to note the straits to which the examiners were put to find clinical *matériel*. Thus in 1671, a candidate was licensed on the condition 'that before he be recavit he acquaint the Visitour when any patient did employ him . . . who sould tak two of his number with himself, see his applica^{one},' etc. The foregoing quotations refer to the examination in Surgery. The Faculty also examined Licentiates in Medicine, but the nature of their examination is not given. As regards the eighteenth century, Mr. Duncan writes, page 95: 'Though some considerable modifications were effected in the latter half of the century, the following may be taken as descriptive of its general plan. The test was divided into two parts—the first known as the "Private," and the last as the "Public" trial. The private examination was of the most importance. The candidate was tested on both the theory and the practice of his profession.' If successful at the private examination, 'he was ordered to appear at the next meeting of the Faculty, and then and there to dissect a previously prescribed part, to discourse on a set surgical or medical theme, and finally to make up a complex pharmaceutical preparation.' 'The private equally with the public examination was at first conducted in the presence of the assembled Faculty.' About 1740 this was changed, and 'a committee was appointed on each occasion to conduct the private examination and to report.' Ultimately an annual examining committee was appointed. It will be observed that in this examination of the eighteenth century there is no reference to a *Clinical Examination* for Licentiates, either in Medicine or Surgery, nor is the nature of the medical examination detailed. I cannot but think you will agree with me that the form of examination of the Royal College I am about to describe, instituted in 1682, and modified and improved previously to the beginning of the eighteenth century, is more uniform and superior—in several respects, although it could not possess the 'anatomie' to dissect.

1671. Candidate to supply his own case, when he has one.

Nature of Medical Licentiate examination not given.

Modifications during eighteenth century.

Public and practical examination in Anatomy.

Conducted in presence of Faculty.

1740. A Committee to examine in private.

No Clinical mentioned.

Royal College of Physicians examination of 1682 was more uniform.

The method of admission to the Royal College and its privileges, and the dues to be paid for them being now arranged, the Royal College was prepared to receive an increase to its number. At first applicants were few. The first was Dr. Peter Kello, and to show how thorough, even in The Early Days, the original Examination was, I shall give an account of the proceedings as shortly as possible :—

Dr. Peter Kello first applicant for Licence.

His Bill considered at the fourteenth sederunt.

At the fourteenth sederunt, held on 4th December 1682, it is stated that Dr. Kello had 'addressed a Bill to the College to be received as one of the Society and offering himself to abyde by and conforme to the rules of the Colledge, . . . and the Thesaurer haveing declared that conforme to the Act of the Colledge he had consigned in his hands Fyve Pounds Star: . . . Appoynt him to be examined, and Doctors Balfour and Cranstoun appoynted to doe it, who examined him upon severall materiall questiones, *i.e.* "De purgatione et venisectione," with whose ansers the Colledge were well satisfied, and appoynted him to be examined *pro secundo* upon ane Aphorism, and that Doctors Burnet and Sibbald should be upon his second examination, who are to chose yr own Aphorisms and intimat the samen to him, and Fryday at two o'clock appoynted therefor.' On the 8th December 1682, in the presence of the College, Dr. Kello was examined for the second time. He was examined upon two Aphorisms of Hippocrates, and the Examiners reported they were well satisfied.

Examiners for first part, on several material questions.

For second part, on two Aphorisms of Hippocrates.

For third part, on 'two severall caices of Medicine.'

The College then appointed Drs. Craufurd and Pitcairne 'to examine him for the last tyme upon Monday at two o'clock, upon two severall caices of Medicine, which is to be intimat to him.' Accordingly on the 11th December 1682, in the presence of the sederunt of eleven Fellows, Dr. Kello entered upon his third and last examination, 'and Dr. Pitcairne having told, that he had intimat to him what the caice he was to judge upon was, yr upon he being publickly examined, with whose answers the Colledge being well satisfied, and in regard that Dr. Craufurd was absent, without intimating to Dr. Kello or the President the caice he designed the Doctor should be examined upon, the Colledge finds it not just, that his admission should be delayed, upon Dr. Craufurd's neglect, and thairfore, having now reconsidered the several examinations and Dr. Kello's answers admitted, and admit him to be a Licentiat, and appoynts him to have a warrand therefore under the act and seale of the Colledge conforme to the former acts made yr anent.' Dr. Craufurd's neglect.

At the next meeting, on 5th February 1683, a further advancement was made, and a form of Licentiate's Diploma agreed on. We read: 'The formula of the admission of Doctor Kello to be a Licentiat being drawn up and presented by Dr. Sibbald, secretary, was read and agried to, and the forme yr off to be put upon Record, off which the tenor follows.' Here follows the 'forme' in Latin. Licentiate's Diploma agreed on 5th Feb. 1683. Drawn up by Sibbald. To be put on record.

Hence it is seen that on the first opportunity a form of 'tryall,' for Licentiates was established as early as the commencement of the second year of the College, and that it consisted of three separate examinations, each of which was upon distinct subjects. The first on this the earliest occasion being on Purgation and Venesection, which at this time took the place of what I shall show was soon improved on by the substitution of an examination in the theory of Medicine, under the designation of the 'Institutiones of Medicine.' The second was based on the Hippocratic doctrines as they were defined in his Aphorisms, 'a teacher who never suffered his theory of the humours to supersede his vigilant observation of facts' (Paris, *Pharmacologia*, 9th edition, 1843, page 56). But this examination also bears evidence that the applicant or practitioner undergoing the 'tryall' must have had a sufficient preliminary education, and that he had been instructed in the Latin and Greek languages, otherwise the subjects would not have been entered in the Minutes in Latin by the Clerk, 'Hugh Stevensone,' whom one would judge not to have been a Observations on the 'tryall.'

very highly educated 'wryter.' The most remarkable part, of this interesting original examination, was that of the third day, for it foreshadowed that upon which in the present day so great importance is placed; and in which even now a considerable portion of our present-day students are defective,—The Clinical Examination. I again direct your attention to the words, 'the caice he was to judge upon.' This part of the examination never seems to have been changed so long as under the first Charter the Licentiate's examination continued. All the candidates for the Licence to practise and for admission to the Fellowship of the College, underwent this examination in practical cases. It has occurred to me that, as the 'Dispensary for the Poore' was already in working order, one use of it was to supply those practical cases, two of which were submitted to the candidate 'to judge upon.' The Minutes of The Early Days do not say much upon such matters, but, from the wording of them, I conclude that the 'cases' from the Dispensary were examined. Only on two occasions do I find that 'diseases,' and not 'caices' were the subject of examination; and in the one instance, Dr. Gilbert Rule, on October 2, 1695, was examined on a particular case *de apoplexia,* whilst in the other, Dr. Alexander Dundas, on 4th November 1695, gave two discourses *de pleuritide* and *de febre tertiana* as his practical examination. Whether these were commentaries upon two 'practical caices' examined by him does not appear. These instances differ from all the recorded examinations and trials. ***Possibly the Dispensary could not at the time supply suitable cases.*** As bearing on this point I refer to what has been previously stated that after some years the Intrants contributed to the funds of the Dispensary. Why should they have been called on to pay for its support unless they had an interest in it? and their only interest was that it supplied the practical cases examined upon.

Only two exceptions to 'practical caices.'

Another point deserving of attention is that the examination was conducted by two Examiners specially appointed at the preceding sederunt by the College, and 'yr upon he being publickly examined,' that is in the presence of the assembled College, *it was the Fellows who decided*, for the Minute continues, 'with whose answers the Colledge being well satisfied, and having now reconsidered the several examinations, and Dr. Kello's answers, admitted, and admit him to be a Licentiat.'

For an examination in Medicine instituted and conducted by the recently erected College—it had just completed its first year—two hundred and fifteen years ago, I have been much impressed with the form, the perfectness, the uniformity, and the method of carrying it out. It undoubtedly testifies very strongly to the ability, the practical knowledge, and the perception of what was necessary to test the professional acquirements of petitioners, on the part of the organisers of this early scheme of Medical Examination.

It is comprehensive, and yet when we recall the imperfect means for instruction in this country, we cannot but admire its suitability for testing whether the candidate had made the best use of his opportunities at home or abroad for acquiring information. Whilst so far as the subjects of examination were concerned, it was calculated to develop a better system of giving instruction in them, as well as in diagnosis of practical cases. The classical training of the academic mind found expression in the mastering in Greek of the 'Aphorisms' of Hippocrates. The first examination was the weakest; but that was improved in the course of a few years, by possibly the influence of Pitcairne (as will be more fully expounded in his life), after his return from the University of Leyden, when its subject became 'The Institutions of Medicine.' This included a knowledge of Anatomy, and the foundation of a true Physiology, based on Harveian teaching, whilst the testing of the thoroughness of the instruction imparted by a professional master was exhibited in the examination and

Title of first part changed to the Institutions of Medicine.

'judging' of the Practical cases. The whole examination was suited, while thoroughly comprehensive, to the imperfect teaching of the day. It is little wonder, therefore, that this test of professional knowledge, so well conceived, so thoroughly carried out and so markedly progressive, should have advanced the founding of the Medical School of Edinburgh, and should have stamped the young College of Physicians of that city as being distinctly in advance of the Medical institutions of the day.

Are the examinations of to-day in better form?

Since then Medical Science has made immense progress, and the subjects a student of the present age has to study and master are vastly increased; but I do not know that our examinations at the close of the nineteenth century are conducted in a better form, except in this, that we have a written conjoined with the oral and the clinical, thus giving the youth who is nervous when face to face with his examiner an opportunity to show what he can do, when left with time to collect his thoughts, and when undisturbed to elaborate his ideas. Do not we also show our approval of the public part of it, by a recent vote of the Royal College in favour of our Licentiates' examination being conducted openly? and is not the increasing desire of recent years not only towards teaching but also in rendering our examinations more 'practical'?

The Examiners.

Before leaving this first examination, I must say a word regarding the Examiners. For the first part of it they were Drs. Andrew Balfour and Cranstoun, and the subjects considered, 'severall materiall questiones,' formed part of the public discourse the former presented to the University of Caen, when he graduated there 'de venae sectione.' It is, however, of further interest to note that the examination instituted by the Edinburgh Royal College was not identical in form or subjects with that at Caen. The absence of the practical cases in that University examination is notable, and favours the view that the Edinburgh one was a modification of the form in use at Leyden, and owed its introduction to Sibbald and the other Fellows who had studied or graduated there. And that the first part of the examination assumed an improved form after Pitcairne's return from that University, when the subject of it became the Institutes or Institutions of Medicine, tends to confirm this opinion.

For the second part Drs. Burnet and Sibbald, and for the third part Dr. Pitcairne conducted the examinations. These Examiners were without doubt five of the best men of the College, and I may add that fourteen Fellows were present at the first part and eleven at the last part of this memorable examination.

(May I be pardoned for here parenthetically alluding to another important subject connected with the early College days—the Library—and chiefly with the desire to correct an error the previous historians of the College have perpetuated. I note that at the next sederunt, the eighteenth, 'the Library' engaged the attention of the College. Amongst the first Fellows of the College there were two Dr. Stevensones, viz. Dr. Archibald, the first President, and Dr. William, who was the first Librarian. In this Minute his name is entered as 'Dr. Stevensone yo^{er}'—that is 'younger'—and at this sederunt he was 'appoynted Librarian,' and Dr. Pitcairne was nominated Depute-Librarian. Dr. William Stevensone does not seem to have been related to Dr. Archibald, and died within a few years. I do not however dwell longer on the Library, although it commenced in The Early Days, save to correct this mistake.)

The Library.

At eighteenth sederunt Dr. William Stevensone appointed Librarian.

Dr. Pitcairne Depute-Librarian.

The applications for admission to the College which immediately follow that of Dr. Kello, were from Physicians who had graduated before the establishment of the College, and who according to the Act of the College previously approven were admitted without examination on condition of paying dues and pledging to enter Candidat and thereafter Socius, and 'subscrybing the promissory declarations.'

Next applications from Physicians graduated before Charter.

The next Minute which bears on the subject of examination

Act of Privie Councill anent admission of Intrants to Apothecaries.

is dated 1st February 1684, and is in these terms: 'There being ane Act of His Maties Privie Councill read anent the visiting of Apothecaries Shops and Chambers and admission of intrants—The Colledge is to meet to-morrow in the forenoon to think upon the best way for executing thereof, and for considering the Apothecaries Bill,' and 'Dr. Sibbald is desyred to revise the severall Acts anent the electing and admitting of intrants to the Colledge, and what furder will be necessary to be done yr anent.'

Dr. Sibbald to revise Acts anent admission of Intrants to College.

Apothecaries' examinations.

At the subsequent meeting 'a Petitione from the Apothecaries anent the examination of Intrants, being read to the Colledge' is minuted, but there is no mention of the conclusion to which the College came on the matter. Probably its relations to the Apothecaries led the College to be discreet, and to delay coming to a conclusion at this time.

4th Dec. 1684. Election meeting.

At the meeting held on 4th December 1684 the Elections took place; and at a sederunt of fourteen fellows, Drs. Trotter, St. Clair, M'Gill, and Learmont, with the former President Archibald Stevensone, and the Censors Balfour and Sibbald, were elected the Council, who retired, and 'by pleurality of votes elected Sir Robert Sibbald to be President for the ensueing year.' Dr. Balfour though elected Censor 'by reason of his indispositione of body and for severall other reasons desyred to be excused, and some other personne to be named in his place.' Accordingly, at the meeting held on 11th December, the College admitted his excuse, and the Council appoynted Dr. Learmont in his place, who, with Dr. Trotter, were the Censors of the year. They both were also in the Council.

Sir Robert Sibbald elected President.

Dr. A. Balfour's indisposition of body.

Oath *de fideli* taken. First mention of President swearing and signing the Test.

Dr. Craufurd was elected Theasurer, Dr. Pitcairne Secretary, and Dr. Cranstoun Fiscall. 'The President and his Censors did take the oath *de fideli* and *did swear and signe the Test.* The Thesaurer took the oath *de fideli.*

'Doctors Stevensone, elder' (he is now so designated in the

Minute Book, and it is noteworthy that 'Sir' is never or almost never prefixed to his name), 'Burnet, Balfour, and the President were appoynted as a Committee to inspect the former laws and to reporte.' On the 19th December it appears that—'The draught of ane declaratione anent the sentence of the Lords of Sessione desydeing the calling of Chirurgery and Pharmacy, being unanimously agreed to, by all present, by a vote and signed by all except Drs. Trotter and M'Gill who declared, as they voted to the samen formerly, so they have now agreed to the samen, but have taken some tyme to think upon it before they signe it.'

Committee to inspect Laws and Report.

Lords of Session decide the calling of Chirurgery and Pharmacy.

But to return to the subject of professional education and examination, Sibbald, always true to the high object he had in view, the elevation of the Medical Profession, at this meeting moved, or as the Minute has it, 'Moved by the President that the Colledge take to their consideratione the minimum *quid sit* of the tyme that a Licentiat should study before he be licensed—the same is remitted to the Councill of the Colledge.'

Motion by Sibbald to consider time a Licentiat should study before examination.

As bearing on the Fellowship I may quote the following Minute of the meeting of 22nd December: 'The draught of a Patent to be given to some Honorarie Members desyred to be received by the Colledge and appoynted to be further considered against next meeting.'

Draught of Patent to Honorary Members.

At this date the record of The Early Days of the College comes to a sudden termination, whilst a note on the board of the Minute Book, vol. ii., as previously mentioned, states, 'Minutes from 22 December 1684 to 21st March 1693 not in Mr. Boswell's possession.' It does not appear whether any record of the College proceedings during these eight years and three months was kept or not, only that if kept, the Minutes did not come into the then Clerk's possession; but from the fact that new Fellows were received during that period, it is evident that the College had continued to meet.

Sudden end of Early Days' Minutes.

Eight years and three months interval.

The next preserved Minute is that of the sederunt of

Sederunt of 6th December 1694.

6th December 1694. An unrecorded interval of ten years therefore occurs. The subject of the Examinations is too interesting to be thus suddenly dropped, and, having shown how complete in form the examination originated and conducted in The Early Days was, I beg you will bear with me whilst I continue my inquiry after this date which opens with the commencement of the fourteenth year of the College, just emerging from the years of its childhood, and not yet attained to its manhood.

College now in its fourteenth year.

Effects of Sir Robert Sibbald's sudden withdrawal from Edinburgh.

It is probable that the sudden withdrawal of Sir Robert Sibbald from Edinburgh, necessitated by the too spasmodic change in his religion and church, must have seriously affected the business of the College, and must doubtless have tended to disorganise its procedure; and after his return to Scotland and to Protestantism, a long time elapses before his name is found in the roll of attendance. But the Minutes during the whole of 1685 when he was President are wanting. Pitcairn was then Secretary, and it was that official's duty to see the Minute Book was properly kept.

Minute, 6th December 1694.

During these ten minuteless years the manner of conducting the business of the College had changed, for the Minute of 6th December 1694 opens with the words, 'the qlk day the Colledge according to yr usual custome by billet proceeded to ye electione for the ensueing year'; and after narrating the various office-bearers, continues—'and likewise continued ye Examinators till ye next meeting, qlk is appoynted to be Thursday the third day of Jan[y] next.' The College did not meet till the 17th January 1695, when the Minute of that day begins thus: 'The qlk day ye Colledge continued Drs. Pitcairn, Eccles, and Olyphant, thrie of ye Examinators last chosen and in place of Dr. Trotter now Praeses, and Sir Robert Sibbald, have appoynted and nominate Sir Arch. Stevenson and Dr. Halket qlk five are to continue untill ye next election.'

The Examinators.

Changes in 17th January 1695.

The five Examinators till next election.

On this occasion the only original Fellows present were Sir

Archibald Stevenson, Drs. Trotter, Cranstoun, and Halket. It is clear from this Minute that, during the ten years of which there is no record extant, the system of special Fellows being nominated as the Examinators of the College had found favour with the Fellows, and also that Sibbald had been one of them, but, for some reason not stated, though apparently of his own accord, he had retired.

Special yearly Examinators had been approved of.

Subsequent to this time the following was the procedure for the Examination of intrants:—

Return to old form.

14th September 1695, after minuting that the College met at Dr. Trotter's lodging,—that Dr. Mitchell was unanimously admitted Socius,—and that by a plurality of votes, Dr. Edward Izat having made application to be 'licensed to practise Physick without any previous tryall, he having received his degree before ye erection of the Colledge of Physitians, . . . ye same day it was, by plurality of votes, carried he should be received Candidat, and he was likeways admitted Socius and took place accordingly at ye Colledge table, and gave his vote for receaving Dr. Rule's Bill.' The Minute continues:—'The same day Dr. Gilbert Rule, having given in his Bill to the Colledge desiring to be admitted to examination, the Colledge receaved his petitione, and appoynted Weddensday next at two o'clock in ye afternoon for his examination.'

Meeting in President's lodging, Dr. Mitchell admitted.

Dr. Izat admitted by plurality of votes.

Dr. Rule's application.

'The same day it being putt to ye vote whether ye old law anent ye Examination or ye new law appoynting Examinators for whole year together should be observed in time coming, it was carried by ye plurality yt ye old law should be observed, and ye new abrogated; and adjourned ye meeting till Monday at eleven o'clock in ye forenoon.'

Change in appointing Examinators.

Old law carried.

The Fellows who voted on this occasion were Dr. Trotter the President, Sir Thomas Burnet, Sir Robert Sibbald, and Drs. St. Clair, Cranstoun, Halket, Lauder of the original Fellows; and of the new, Eccles, Dicksone, Olyphant, and Smellum (Smelholm)—eleven in all.

Eleven Fellows voted.

The College met again on 16th September, five of the original Fellows being present (Burnet and Halket absent), and Dicksone and Olyphant of the new (Eccles and Smellum absent) but in addition Eizat and Mitchell which gives a total of thirteen old and new Fellows, when it was 'carried by plurality of votes for ye second time yt ye old law should be ye form and ye new law abrogated.' The College met again on the 21st, and nine of the above-named Fellows being present, it was 'put to vote for third time and carried that the old rule for examination of intrants be revived.' By this vote, only two of the five Examinators appointed on 17th January preceding, did not vote on the question. They were Sir Archibald Stevenson, and his son-in-law Dr. Archibald Pitcairn. It may be surmised, therefore, that the promoters of the yearly Examinators were the Stevenson party in the College. In furtherance of the resolution, the Minute continues: 'accordingly appointed Sir Thomas Burnet and Dr. Eizat for Dr. Rule's first tryal; for ye second, Sir Robert Sibbald and Dr. Dicksone; for ye third, Dr. St. Clare and Dr. Cranstoun.'

Return to old law carried second time.

Old law carried third time.

Examiners appointed for Dr. Rule's examination.

These proceedings delayed Dr. Rule's examination till 25th September 1695, when in presence of the sederunt of the College, thirteen being present, Dr. Rule was 'examined by Sir Thomas Burnet and Dr. Eizat upon ye Institutions of Medicine. The Colledge were satisfied with his answers, and appointed him to be examined, upon ye Aphorisms, upon Monday, and appoint ye same day to examine Dr. Frier for ye first time, and ye Praeses and Dr. Mitchell to examine him,' etc.

Dr. Rule examined on 'ye Institutions of Medicine.'

On September 30th, 1695, the sederunt consisted of ten of the same Fellows. Dr. Rule was examined by Sir Robert Sibbald and Dr. Dicksone upon two of the Aphorisms of Hippocrates, in their presence, and his answers approved. On October 2nd, in presence of ten Fellows, Dr. Rule was examined for the third time, and it is only on this occasion, that the examination is described as being upon a particular case, viz. *de Apoplexia* by

On Aphorisms.

Third time on a particular case, *de Apoplexia.*

Dr. St. Clare. Dr. Cranstoun does not seem to have been present. 'Ye Colledge were well satisfied with and approve of his answers'; and accordingly declare him Licentiat, and after three votes 'admitted him Socius with all ye previledges and immunitys belonging to any member yr of.'

On 4th October, Dr. Alexander Dundas is appointed to be examined by Sir Thomas Burnet and Dr. St. Clare, upon 'ye Institutions,' whilst Dr. Frier is examined by Sir Robert Sibbald and Dr. Blackader upon two Aphorisms of Hippocrates, and is next to be examined 'upon a practical case' by Drs. Cranstoun and Blackader, and on October 7, after three votes was admitted Socius. On the same day, Dr. Dundas was examined upon 'ye Institutes' by Sir Thomas Burnet and Dr. St. Clare, and the College approved his answers.

Dr. Dundas examined upon 'ye Institutions' and Aphorisms,

On 4th November, Dr. Dundas, having been previously examined upon the twenty-first Aphorism of the first section and the twenty-eighth Aphorism of the eleventh section, by Drs. Mitchell and Dicksone, and the College having unanimously approved of his discourses, appeared to-day for his third examination. The form adopted on this occasion seems to have been different from that previously, and subsequently, followed. The Minute states, 'Dr. Dundas was heard on his discourse *de Pleuritide* and yr after his discourse *de febre tertianâ*, declared their satisfaction, and Licentiate him, by a second vote, admitted him Candidate, and by a third vote admitted him Socius.'

for third examination, discoursed *de Pleuritide* and *de febre tertianâ*.

Dr. J. Forrest.

Dr. James Forrest was the next applicant for admission, who, in November 1696, presented his Bill 'desyring to subject himself to tryall in order to be Licentiate to practise Medicine in Edinburgh, the College *nemine contradiscente* granted ye desire of ye Bill and appoynt Dr. St. Clare and Dr. Cranstoun to examine him upon the Institutes'; accordingly, on November 16, in the presence of Dr. Trotter President, Sir Thomas Burnet, Sir Robert Sibbald, Drs. St. Clare, Cranstoun, Rule, Freer,

Examined upon the Institutes.

Dicksone, and Dundas, he was examined upon the Institutes, and the Colledge was well satisfied.'

The Aphorisms.

On the 18th, the College was well satisfied with his answers, on the two prescribed Aphorisms; and on November 20th, in the presence of ten Fellows, 'the qlk day, Dr. Forrest having produced his diploma of ye date ye twelveth of June 1691 at Leiden; and being examined, upon two practicall cases, for ye third time, and having given Bond to satisfie ye ordinary dews, the College was sufficiently satisfied with his answers, and admitted him Licentiat,' etc.

Upon two Practical Cases.

Dr. William Jardyne examined on the Institutes, Aphorisms and Practical Cases.

Dr. William Jardyne, M.D. of Haderwick, was examined on 13th, 15th, and 20th April on the Institutes and Aphorisms, and on two practical cases, the College being fully satisfied with his answers, allow him to practise Medicine.

21st June 1699. Patrick Ford apologises for unwarrantable practice.

On 21st June 1699, Patrick Ford, against whom proceedings for unwarrantable practice had been commenced, but allowed to expire, 'compeared before the Colledge, and declared he was sensible of being in the wrong in standing out and suspending the fyne passed by the Colledge for his not subjecting himself to them, which the Colledge having considered, they passed from their fyne, and he having produced in presence of the Colledge ane Patent from the Universitie of Aberdeen conferring upon him the degrie of Doctor of Medicine, and the Colledge having seen and considered the same, are satisfyed yr with, and allow and admitt him a Licentiat of the Colledge, and ordain there shall be given him ye Licence under the seall of the Colledge, he paying ane hundreth pounds Scots to ye Treasurer of ye Colledge in hand, and giving his Bond to ye Colledge for ane uther hundreth pounds Scots payable within year and day after this date,' etc.

Presents Patent from Aberdeen.

Admitted Licentiat.

Comment on case.

And so this illegal non-qualified practitioner sets the College at defiance, gets a degree at Aberdeen, to which, being a Scotch University, the College cannot object, and with the fine remitted by his submission, without examination, on submitting his Patent, demands, whether properly qualified or not, a Licence to practise in Edinburgh, and the College are obliged to give it to him, on his payment of the usual fees. I have interpolated this flagrant instance to show how the elevation of the standard of Medical proficiency and qualification, which the Edinburgh College of Physicians was honourably striving for, was and could be frustrated by the jealous action of the Universities which should have aided the Royal College by raising the position of their graduates, rather than in helping them to escape the punishment such offenders ought to have received.

On 21st April 1701, another case of similar kind occurred. Dr. Dundas had been ordered to speak to Dr. John Drummond 'anent practising in the place, he not being Licentiat by the College.' Dr. Dundas reported that 'the said Dr. Drummond did require some further time before he should give a determinate answer, that so he might write to the College of Aberdeen from whom he pretends to have a Patent.'

Case of Dr. J. Drummond practising without Licence.

How differently the University of Edinburgh acted with regard to Medical Degrees it will be my privilege subsequently to show.

The next Examination is in November 1702, when 'Dr. John Riddell, Doctor of Medicine, petitions for tryall.' After consideration the College ordains the day of examination, and that the President Dr. Trotter, and Dr. Forrest examine him upon the Institutions, and the same day Dr. John Sinclair having petitioned, is to be examined upon the Institutions by Drs. Eizat and Mitchell.

On 19th November 1702, seven Fellows being present, 'the said day the Colledge having examined Doctor Riddell upon the Institutions, they are satisfied with his answers, and ordain him to attend upon Monday next at three o'clock in the afternoon in order to his second examination, and appoynt Doctor Sinclair and Doctor Jardyne to be his Examinators, to examine him upon two

Dr. J. Riddell examined on the Institutions, the Aphorisms and two Practical Cases.

Dr. John Sinclair examined on the Institutions, Aphorisms and Practical Cases.

Aphorisms of Hippocrates.' Further, 'the same day the College having examined Dr. John Sinclair upon the Institutions, are well satisfied with his answers, and ordain him to attend upon Monday next at thrie o'clock in the afternoon to his second examination, and appoynt Drs. Sinclair and Jardyne to be his Examinators, and to examine him upon the Aphorisms of Hippocrates.'

'23rd November 1702.—The qlk day the Doctor Sinclair and Dr. Jardyne, Examinators appoynted for examination of Dr. John Riddell upon the two Aphorisms of Hippocrates, and they having examined him yr upon in presence of the Colledge upon the 29th Aphorisme of the 2nd sectione, and 43rd Aphorisme of the 17th sectione of the appoynted, the Colledge is well satisfied, and ordain him to attend Thursday nixt att thrie o'clock in the afternoon for his third and last examination, and appoynt Drs. Dundasse and Frier or Forrest to examine him upon two practicall caices. Also Drs. Sinclair and Jardyne examine Dr. John Sinclair, in presence of the Colledge upon two of the 2nd sectione and 47 of the 6th sect. of Aphorisms appoynted. The Colledge is satisfied with his answers, and ordain him to attend upon Thursday nixt at,' etc. etc. 'to the third examination and appoynt Dr. Dundasse and Dr. Frier or Forrest to be his Examinators, and to examine him upon two practicall caices.' Accordingly on 26th November 1702, 'Drs. Dundasse and Forrest examined Dr. John Riddell in presence of the Colledge. . . . Satisfied with examination and ordain him to be Licentiat,' and Dr. John Sinclair was also 'examined on practicall caices,' in presence of the College who admit him Licentiat.

Dr. J. Drummond having now got his Aberdeen Degree of M.D. petitions for admission without examination.

On 11th January 1704, it appears the petition of Dr. John Drummond for Licence without previous examination he being a Doctor of Medicine, University of Aberdeen, was presented and granted. It is the same Drummond who delayed giving answer regarding his practising in Edinburgh, but as soon as he obtains a University Diploma he presents himself. He was afterwards

Secretary to the College in 1706 and 1707, he was elected President in 1725, and was the first Physician who acted when the Infirmary was opened to receive patients.

On 28th July 1704, a Petition for Licence from Dr. William Stewart, graduate of St. Andrews, of 24th July was presented and admitted.

Dr. William Stewart, M.D. St. Andrews: no examination.

A Petition by Dr. Francis Pringle, M.D. Leyden, of 14th July 1702, was presented for Licence on 24th October 1704, and admitted after the usual examinations.

Dr. F. Pringle admitted.

On 15th January 1706, Dr. James Brown, M.D. of Rheymes petitions 'for tryall as Licentiat,' and was examined by Drs. Drummond and Learmont upon the Institutions on the 29th. There were twenty Fellows present, who were well pleased; and, on 12th February, he was examined by Drs. Robertson and Smelholme on two Aphorisms, and being approven, Drs. Dicksone and Stewart are to give him two practical cases, on 25th February, and he was admitted Licentiat.

Dr. J. Brown examined on the Institutions, Aphorisms and Practical Cases.

James Stevenson, a graduate of Rheyms, also applies for 'tryall,' and after passing a like examination in the Institutions, and explaining two Aphorisms, he was given his two practical cases by Sir Robert Sibbald and Dr. Trotter on 16th April. The wording of the Minute is that 'Dr. James Stevensone having been heard explaining his practical cases given him by Sibbald and Trotter, were well satisfied with his performance,' and admitted him Licentiat.

Dr. James Stevenson examined on the Institutions, Aphorisms and Practical Cases.

On 23rd November 1710, Dr. James Crawford petitions for 'tryal' for Licence. He was M.D. of Leyden, and underwent the regular form of examination, being examined for the first by Drs. Dicksone and Lowis, for the second by Drs. Robertson and Forrest, and for the third by Drs. Mitchell and Stewart, and the Minute says that he explained the two practical cases given him, and that 'the Colledge were well satisfied with his explication yr of.'

Dr. James Crawford examined on three subjects.

Dr. John Learmont, M.D. of Rheims, after being as usual

Dr. John Learmont examined on the three subjects.

examined on the Institutions and the Aphorisms, has this Minute: 'The Colledge having heard him explain, and give his opinion of his practicall cases, given him by Dr. Robertson and Dr. Carmichael, conform to the last sederunt yr anent, the Colledge are well satisfyed with the examination and opinion yr of, and sustain the samen,' etc. etc.

Dr. W. Porterfield examined in three subjects.

Under date 25th May 1721, it appears that Dr. William Porterfield, having passed the first and second examinations to-day, 'Dr. Dicksone and Dr. Riddell are appoynted to give him two practicall cases to be solved by him, and to give his opinion yr of,' etc., and on 8th June, 'the College, having heard Dr. William Porterfield explain and give his opinion of the two practical cases, given him by the President in the absence of Dr. Riddell and by Dr. Dicksone, the Colledge are well satisfied with his explanation yr of,' etc. etc.

Dr. John Marshall, M.D. Aberdeen, Dr. C. Austen, M.D. Glasgow, admitted without examination.

On March 21st, 1721, Dr. John Marshall, M.D. Aberdeen, of 22nd October 1719, and Dr. Charles Austen, M.D. Glasgow, of 2nd December 1719 (the first candidate of the University of Glasgow), petition to be Licentiat without previous examination, which desire the College thought reasonable, and therefore admitted them. And on 1st August 1721, both were admitted Fellows after signing promissory engagement and act of the College to maintain decreet, etc.

Dr. James Stewart examined on the three subjects.

On 31st October 1721, there is the following Minute—'The said day forsaid, the Colledge having heard Dr. James Stewart examined upon the Institutions by Doctor Clerk and Doctor Cochrane admitt the samen as his first examination, and Dr. William Stewart and Dr. James Crawford are appoynted, each of them, to give him an Aphorism of Hippocrates to be examined by him this day eight days, being the 7th instant at thrie o'clock in the afternoon,' signed 'Ja. Forrest, P.C.R.M.E.' And on 7th November 1721, 'the same day haveing heard Dr. James Stewart explain the two Aphorisms of Hippocrates given him by Dr.

William Stewart and Dr. James Crawford, admit the samen as his second examination, and Dr. Dicksone and Dr. Smellum are appoynted to give him two practicall cases to give his opinion qr of, and to be solved by him, upon this day eight days,' and on 14th November, 'The said day the Colledge having heard Dr. James Stewart give his opinion and solve the two practicall cases given him by Drs. Dicksone and Smellum, are well satisfied with the opinion and solution yr of, and therefore the Colledge admitt said Dr. James Stewart a Licentiat of the Colledge.'

On 25th March 1723, at the examination of Dr. John Drummond Junior for the Licence, there is the first notice of written examination. The Minute states, 'The said Dr. Drummond is to give in a copy of his explanatione of the two Aphorisms given him as above to the Secretary of the Colledge, to be copied in a book to be prepaired by the Thesaurer for that effect, and the Colledge ordain that for here after all the Candidates and Licentiats of the Colledge shall give in just copies of the severall explanations of their Aphorisms, and of their severall opinions of the practicall cases to be given them at any tyme here after, to the Secretarius for the tyme, and either to wryte the samen in the said book themselves, or if they can not attend or be necessarilie absent, that the Secretary for the tyme wryte the samen there in himself.'

Dr. John Drummond Jr. to give a copy of his explanations of Aphorisms and also of the Practical Cases to be preserved in a book.

Hereafter all Candidates to give in copies.

On 23rd August 1723, Dr. David Kinnear of St. Andrews was admitted Licentiat without examination.

Dr. David Kinnear, M.D. St. Andrews, admitted without examination.

On 21st November 1723, reference to a Doctor of Medicine of the University of Edinburgh is made. Dr. George Oswald was admitted Licentiat on that date. He is stated to be a Doctor of Medicine of the University of Rheims in 1696; 'also that he was admitted *eundem gradum* by the University of Edinburgh on the 16th day of November inst. 1723 years, and craves admission as Licentiat.' His petition was granted and admitted. Also on 4th February 1724, Dr. George Oswald 'admitted Socius, . . . and

21st Nov. 1723. Dr. G. Oswald, M.D. of Edinburgh, admitted.

Twenty shillings to be paid by Intrants for the use of the Dispensary.

payed twenty shillings sterling to the Thesaurer for the use of the Dispensary belonging to the Colledge, and took his seat accordingly.'

This payment to the Dispensary would appear to have been introduced at about this time as a means of increasing the income of that institution, which you may remember I pointed out was kept quite distinct from the income or revenue of the College. Dr. David Kinnear was admitted Socius on the same terms for the Dispensary.

Dr. A. St. Clair and Dr. And. Plummer examined in usual form.

On 4th February 1724, Dr. Andrew St. Clair, M.D. Angers, and Dr. Andrew Plummer, M.D. of Leyden, 'Petition for tryall,' and they are examined in the usual form on 7th, 18th, and 25th February, and Licensed.

Dr. J. Rutherford and Dr. J. Innes examined in usual form.

On the 25th February 1724, Dr. John Rutherford, M.D. of Rheims, and Dr. John Innes, M.D. Padua, 'petition for tryal,' and are examined in usual form on March 3rd, 12th, and 29th, and were then Licensed.

Dr. A. Scott, St. Andrews, admitted without examination. Dr. James Dundas examined in usual form.

Dr. James Dundas, M.D. Rheims, petitions on 2nd February 1725, and Dr. Alexander Scott on 9th February. He was M.D. of Rheims, but also having a Patent from St. Andrews, is admitted without examination. Dr. Dundas goes through the three examinations, but the record of the last is unusual. It reads that on 2nd March 1725, he 'discoursed upon the two practical cases,' and thereafter is admitted Licentiat.

Observations.

But it is needless to report further instances. What I claim for the Royal College of Physicians of Edinburgh is, that it made a distinct and decided progress in the system of Examination for intrants to the Medical profession in this country; and that this change was introduced in The Early Days. Even from the first, it aimed at as perfect an examination as possible at that time. And the same form and the same system, only the title of the first being altered as Physiology on a scientific basis was established, continued, as I have shown by the perhaps too

Claims for College.

ample extracts I have made from the Minutes, from the Early Days of the College, till the succeeding century was far advanced, and the College approaching its fiftieth year. I shall afterwards show that the Edinburgh University graduates were at first examined on the same system, and it was only after the Edinburgh University School was fairly established, and the Hippocratic doctrines were superseded by those of Boerhaave and by advancing Science, that the system was changed.

Edinburgh Graduates were first examined in this form.

The Theory of Medicine, the Aphorisms, and the Practical Cases characterised the Royal College examination from the first, and I do consider that in the past sufficient credit has not been given to it for its adaptation of the Dispensary to the Practical, or as we would now say to the Clinical, part of the examination. As bearing upon this association, I again direct your attention to the fact that the intrants after 1723 were called on to support the Dispensary, as no doubt it was used for their benefit, as well as for that of the sick poor.

Character of the Royal College of Physicians examination.

Another noticeable feature of the examinations is, that they were conducted, not merely in theory, but actually, in the presence of a sederunt of the College, and in illustration, I have stated the number of Fellows present, who could hear the examination, and be a check on both the Examiner and the examinee. Although in the present day we are in favour of fixed Examiners, and that they should be specially qualified for the duty, I cannot but think that in these early days all the Fellows being called on, was the better arrangement. Each Socius was in turn called on to take part, and was, therefore, himself preserved from falling into a state of decrepitude. It was an excellent method for keeping the Fellows up in their knowledge to a level with the progress and acquirements of the day, and those candidates they had to examine were the best of the age. Those who would have been the better of being examined, had obtained a 'Degree' in Medicine from a Scotch University, without exami-

Examinations were public—benefit of.

Fixed Examiners or not.

nation, and apparently sometimes without even presenting themselves to the authorities, and had, by the weakness of the Charter, to be received and admitted without examination if they paid the fees. Whilst those who were examined in the presence of the College were, for the most part, young men who, according to the system on the Continent where they gained their degrees of Doctor of Medicine, were highly and thoroughly preliminarily educated, so that they were each 'Mr.,'—that is, each was in the possession of a Master or Magister of Arts degree—or in many instances, they had laureated at a Scottish University, before going to the Continental Schools, to obtain their Medical education. They had studied in Schools abroad, where, as I have shown, the best—indeed the only Medical education was to be obtained—or at least the only complete training in Medical Science, before the first quarter of the eighteenth century.

The system of Examination introduced in The Early Days of the Royal College was of great benefit to Medicine, for it could not but act as a stimulus to the members of the profession in and around Edinburgh, and through them on the instruction of their apprentices or pupils in the progressive ideas in Medical subjects then rapidly developing. To the College system I consider, in great measure, the distinguished position this city soon after attained, and still maintains amongst the numerous Medical Schools was due. Apart from the teaching, no contumelious term can ever be applied to the Medical Degree of the University of Edinburgh. The robe and hood which clothe a Medical graduate of Edinburgh, have never been soiled by being conferred on any one unworthily, but from the first, the recipient of the Degree only obtained it after a strict, and according to the time, severe examination or 'tryall,' instituted on the form, and conducted by the Fellows, of the Royal College of Physicians, without fee or pecuniary reward.

Medical Degree of University of Edinburgh always above reproach.

To four men I am of opinion are the credit and honour of the creation of the College of Physicians Examination mainly due; for, although probably the originators of the College took the initiative, still it seems as if they all should share the merit, for all the four took active duty in the examination of the first candidate, Dr. Peter Kello.

The College Examination due to four men.

The four who took action chiefly were Andrew Balfour, Thomas Burnet, Archibald Pitcairn, and Robert Sibbald. No doubt Drs. Cranstoun and Craufurd also were appointed to assist in the conduction of that examination, but the subjects for the first stage of the examination, from the evidence I have given, were manifestly selected,—possibly from the remembrance of his own examination at the University of Caen, by Balfour; whilst so little interest in the matter was taken by Craufurd, that he neither appeared at the final part of the examination, nor even troubled himself to indicate the 'caice' he proposed for Dr. Kello to 'judge upon,' so that the severe remark is minuted that 'the Colledge finds it not just, that his (Kello's) admission should be delayed, upon Dr. Craufurd's neglect.' From the position the four at that early time took in the affairs of the College, to them the honour is manifestly due. One feature from the first was noticeable, the importance given to the third part of the examination—'the Practical Caices.'

Claims for Royal College.

At Dr. Kello's examination, just when the College had completed its first year, we learn that, for the first part, Drs. Balfour and Cranstoun, 'who were appoynted to doe it, examined him upon several materiall questions.' They foreshadowed the Theory of Medicine, which gradually developed in the years succeeding into 'The Institutions of Medicine,' sometimes written 'the Institutes'—as has been shown.

For the second examination, 'the Aphorisms of Hippocrates' held their ground, and were not superseded for at least fifty years in the Edinburgh School; and not until the University took upon itself, not only the duty of Examining, but also of Teaching its own

Claims for the Royal College.

graduates, when the views of Bellini and Boerhaave had come to the front through the pupils of the latter being the Professors.

To the third part of the examination, I would once more solicit your attention. Occasionally, in the course of succeeding years, the words employed to describe it undergo modification, but the principle of this being *a practical examination of cases* is unchanged. Dr. Pitcairn had intimated to Dr. Kello 'the caice' (not disease) he was to judge upon. I can come to no other conclusion than this, that the patient or 'caice' was brought into the College Hall, and Dr. Kello had publicly 'to judge upon it,' 'with whose answers the Colledge was well satisfied,' and I claim for the College Examiners the credit of being, in this country, the first to introduce regularly and systematically 'the Clinical Examination' as a part of the 'Tryall' for a Medical Licence, the cases being taken from a suitable source.

But I also go a step further. The Dispensary was in active working order. It was a charitable undertaking conducted by two of the Socii of the College. Those gentlemen were engaged in Dr. Kello's examination. They were Burnet, the author of the *Thesaurus Medicinae Practicae*, and Craufurd his colleague, who failed to be present; but what more likely than that the acting Dispensary Physicians should supply from amongst the patients attending the Dispensary 'a caice' for the practical examination?

Just a word or two are called for on the exceptional examination of Dr. Alexander Dundas. It was after The Early Days of the College, and took place in October 1696. The writers of the Minutes of the College Meetings, though no doubt different individuals, seem to have copied the wording of the preceding scribe, but in Dr. Dundas's examination it would almost seem as if he had made a written discourse or lecture not only upon 'the Aphorisms,' but also on the two diseases Pleurisy and Tertian Fever. On this occasion there is no mention of 'practical cases,' but it is stated he 'was heard on his discourse *de Pleuritide* and yr after his discourse *de febre tertiana,*' and 'that the College declared their satisfaction.' This is not the usual form, and gives colour to the idea that on this occasion it was, or partook of, the nature of a written examination, or of a thesis. An explanation, as already suggested, might be hazarded that possibly there were no practical cases suitable for the purpose then in attendance at the Dispensary.

Claims for the Royal College.

A further change many years after this occurs, when the examination undoubtedly became written in its style, and a book was provided for the enrolment of the candidate's replies—but how long this was continued does not appear.

In concluding this section of my address, I desire to add as creditable to the College, that whilst from its earliest year it endeavoured in the way it chiefly could, to advance medical knowledge by enforcing a three-part examination upon candidates not possessing a Scotch University Degree, it also was always desirous to maintain a high professional tone and good feeling amongst the medical men of whom it consisted, as is shown by the Minutes. Thus under the date 3rd May 1709 the following occurs, a 'Committee appoynted for better regulating the practice of Medicine amongst themselves, viz., Drs. Eccles, Mitchell, Dundas, Dicksone, and Drummond to bring in Notes for that effect.'

THE MEDICAL AND SCIENTIFIC DISCOURSES AND CONFERENCES

I pass now to the fourth Effort of The Early Days of the College, the prototype of the Medical Societies of the present day. For the oldest of these, Edinburgh is noted. The Royal Medical Society of our city is almost coeval with our University Medical School.

The fourth Effort. Medical Society.

Sibbald's fortnightly meetings at his lodging in 1680.

Sibbald, as previously referred to, in his Autobiography says (page 28), that 'In the year 1680, I induced some of the Physitians in town, especially Dr. Burnet, Dr. Steenson, Dr. Balfour, and Dr. Pitcairne, to meet at my lodging once a fourthnight or so, when we had conferences. The matters we discoursed upon, were letters from those abroad, giving account of what was most remarkable adoing by the learned, some rare cases had happened in our practice, and ane account of Bookes, that tended to the improvement of Medicine, or naturall history, or any other curious learning, and were continued till the erection of the Colledge of Physitians. Severall of the Discourses are inserted in a book I call *Acta Medica Edinburgensia.* They were forborne then upon the introducing of such conferences once a moneth in the Colledge.' Also, at page 33, he says, 'We had our conferences in the Colledge frequently. At one of them I had a discourse concerning the *Concha Anatifera*, the surname of which is the Appendix to the *Scotia Illustrata.*' At page 43, he further observes, 'The conferences were kept up lykewyse during my tyme, and the Discourses were made.' So far Sibbald.

His *Acta Medica Edinburgensia.* Conferences introduced by him at the Royal College meetings.

The value and importance of such meetings as Sibbald instituted in Edinburgh are well supported by the results elsewhere. This is what the Hon. G. C. Brodrick, D.C.L., Warden of Merton College, in *A History of the University of Oxford,* relates. Sibbald does not inform us whether his idea was original or not, but it may have been suggested by the following circumstances as related by Brodrick in his reference (page 153, 2nd edit.) to the Sheldonian Theatre:—'Christopher Wren was engaged as the architect, and Streeter as the painter of the pictures which adorn the ceiling; and the building having been commenced in 1664 was completed in 1669. The year in which the Divinity School was restored according to Wren's designs, John Evelyn received a Degree at the first academical festival held in it, and was so much impressed by the grandeur of the spectacle

Hon. G. C. Brodrick's account of commencement of Royal Society at Oxford and London and the learning of the Discourses, as he was shocked by the vulgar ribaldry of the *Terrae Filius.* It is worthy of notice that in the address delivered on this occasion by Dr. Smith, as Public Orator, were "some malicious and indecent reflections" on the Royal Society, as underminers of the University! That Society in fact passed through much of its infancy, if it did not take its birth at Oxford. Among its earliest and most influential Members were Dr. Wilkins, the Warden of Wadham; Dr. Goddard, the Warden of Merton; and Dr. Wallis, a Cambridge man; who afterwards became Savilian Professor of Geometry in Oxford. These and others were in the habit of meeting for scientific discussions at Goddard's lodgings, or Gresham College, in London, before the end of the Civil War, but about 1649 all three of them were settled in Oxford, where they found congenial associates in such men as William Petty, Robert Boyle, and Wren; and resumed their meetings in Petty's or Wilkins' lodgings, while the rest continued to meet in London.'

Earliest Members meet in Dr. Goddard's lodging, Oxford, or Gresham College, London.

It is quite possible, as Sibbald seems to have known Boyle, for at page 40 of his Autobiography he remarks that when he was in London (in 1686), he waited upon the Honourable Sir Robert Boyle, who received him very kindly, and after that sent him such books as he published, and also his picture 'in Taildouce very well done.' Or it may be, as there was more scientific energy on the Continent at this time, that the idea may have been borrowed from France, but if not original—and I do not see why it should not have been—it appears to be more probable that the scheme was suggested by the early days of the Royal Society of London.

Did Sibbald take his idea from Boyle or from the Continent, or was it his own?

On 7th January 1684, the fourth of the great Efforts for medical progress and scientific development of the College commenced.

7th Jan. 1684. The fourth Effort at Royal College commenced.

At a sederunt of eleven Fellows, including Stevensone, Balfour, Sibbald, Craufurd, Trotter, St. Clare, Cranstoun, Pit-

Eleven Fellows present at Sir Archibald Stevenson's Discourse on *Polypus Cordis.*

cairn, and three others, the Minute states: 'The President—Sir Archibald Stevensone—had a discourse which was the first of those ordered to be monthly, on the *Polypus Cordis,* to the great satisfactione of the Colledge, and was desyred to give it in to the Secretarius to be insert in the Register.'

Second Discourse by Dr. Balfour on *Hippocratic Aphorism.*

The next discourse was delivered by Doctor Balfour upon *the Hippocratic Aphorism* 22, sect. 1, which was very satisfactory to them; and he also was 'desyred to give in the samen to the Secretarius.'

Third Discourse, Dr. Sibbald, *de Concha Anatifera.*

'Doctor Sibbald on 3d March 1684 had his discourse *de concha Anatifera* to the Colledge, which gave great satisfactione, and which he was desyred to put upon record.'

Fourth Discourse, Dr. Craufurd, *de Natura et usu Succi Pancreatici.*

'Doctor Craufurd on 7 Aprile 1684 had his discourse *de natura et usu succi pancreatici,* with which the Colledge was satisfyed,' etc.

Fifth Discourse, Dr. Trotter, *de Essentia Febris.*

'Dr. Trotter, 6th May 1684, had his discourse *de essentia febris,* with which the Colledge was well satisfied,' etc.

Sixth Discourse, Dr. Sinclair, *de Diissenteria.*

'Dr. Sinclair on 2d June 1684 had his discourse *de diissenteria,* with which the Colledge were well pleased,' etc.

Seventh Discourse, Dr. Cranstoun, *de alienatione Mentis.*

'Dr. Cranstoun on 7 July 1684 had his discourse *de alienatione Mentis,* with which the Colledge were well pleased,' etc.

Eighth Discourse, Dr. Learmont.

'Dr. Learmont on 8th Sept. 1684 had a discourse in absence of Dr. M'Gill, who being out of town is excused till his returne. The Colledge are well satisfied,' etc.

Ninth Discourse, Dr. Halkett, *de peculiaribus Infantium Morbis.*

'Dr. Halkett, 20 October 1684, had his discourse, *de peculiaribus infantium Morbis,* in absence of Dr. Burnet, with which the Colledge were well satisfied,' etc.

Tenth Discourse, Dr. M'Gill, *de Chiilificatione.*

'Dr. M'Gill, Nov. 30th, 1684, had his discourse *de chiilificatione,* with which the Colledge were well pleased,' etc.

Eleventh Discourse, Dr. Burnet, *de Pleuritide.*

'Dr. Burnet, Decr. 1st, 1684, had a part of his disertatione *ae Pleuritide,* and was desyred to have the rest of it tomorrow.'

'Dr. Halyburton had also a discourse *de Febris intermittationis natura et curatione.*' Twelfth Discourse, Dr. Halyburton, *de Febris intermittationis natura et curatione.*

After this occurs the hiatus of ten years in the Minute Book, but these are the discourses and deliverers of them in The Early Days of the College; and form the record of what I regard as the basis of a Medical Society in Edinburgh for the mutual improvement of the Fellows, under the auspices of the Royal College of Physicians. The hiatus in the Minute Book.

As I have done in the other three Efforts of The Early Days, I submit a subsequent record of the discourses minuted. After The Early Days, 1695.

In 1695, Dr. Trotter is now the President, and on 7th February had a discourse '*de Catarrho suffocativo*, to qlk ye Colledge were very well satisfied, and gave him ye thanks of ye board.' Dr. Trotter, *de Catarrho suffocativo.*

Dr. Cranston (the spelling of names varied in those days) was appointed next to give his discourse on *an Aphorism of Hippocrates.* Dr. Cranston, Hippocratic Aphorism.

Sir Robert Sibbald, on 28th November 1695—at a sederunt of twenty-one Fellows, including the President Dr. Trotter, Sir Archibald Stevenson, Sir Thomas Burnet, Drs. St. Clair, Cranston, Pitcairn, etc.—was the Fellow appointed to give the discourse; and after ten years further consideration, he returns to the old subject: 'The qlk day Colledge having heard Sir Robert Sibbald's discourse *de Concha Anatifera*, were well pleased with it, as curious, eloquent, and new, and returned him ye thanks of ye house.' Dr. Sibbald, *de Concha Anatifera.*

We now come to 7th December 1696. Sir Thomas Burnet has at last been elected President. There must have been a falling off in the regularity with which the discourses were delivered; for at this meeting it is resolved that 'The monthly discourses be revived, and appoynt Sir Robert Sibbald to have a discourse the first meeting in January 1697.' From this may not it be concluded that Sibbald himself was the proposer of this 1696. Resolved the Monthly Discourses be revived. Proposed probably by Sibbald.

revival? He had given the last more than a year before, and with his characteristic zeal and energy, he is ready to come forward to the support of the College and of his schemes when called on.

5th February 1697. Dr. Sibbald, *de Generatione univocâ.*

It was not, however, until 5th February that the discourses were resumed, and under that date is the following Minute:—'Sir Robert Sibbald according to order had a discourse *de Generatione univocâ*, qlk was approven.'

Dr. Trotter was appointed to have the next discourse. This does not appear to have been delivered, for a Minute of December 12th, 1699, states it 'Being the laudable custome of the Colledge to have discourses upon subjects, they appoint Dr. Trotter give one the second Thursday of January.' And accordingly on 9th January 1700, it is minuted: 'Dr. Trotter had a discourse before the Colledge *de Catarrho suffocativo* wherewith the College was very well satisfyed.' And Dr. St. Clair, the President, is to have a discourse in February, but at this period the College being much disturbed by the action of certain of its Fellows, the discourse was not given.

January 1700. Dr. Trotter, *de Catarrho suffocativo.*

Dr. St. Clair's Discourse not given.

On 30th November 1704, Dr. Dundas was the President, and this was Election day. After a long interval Sir Robert Sibbald returns to the meetings. So do Sir Archibald Stevenson and his son-in-law, Dr. Pitcairn; in all twenty-four Fellows are present, Sir Archibald Stevenson and Sir Robert Sibbald are voted Councillors (but not Pitcairn), and Dr. Halket is chosen President.

1705. Discourses revived by Dr. Sibbald. Historical Account of Doctors of Medicine—Scotsmen.

On the following 12th January (1705) Sir Robert Sibbald again revives the discourses, for 'The same day Sir Robert Sibbald had a discourse giving a Historical Account of such Doctors of Medicine as were Scotsmen, and particularlie of those that practised in Scotland, and what they had written in Physic or Philosophie, with which the College were very well satisfied.'

Discourses ordered to be resumed.

The same day the College ordered the monthly discourses to be renewed, and on this occasion Dr. John Drummond was present.

According to Minute of 10th April, Dr. Trotter was appointed to have his discourse next month, and in his absence Dr. Sinclair, elder. Dr. Trotter, however, delivered his 'discourse *de acido et alkali.*'

Dr. Trotter, *de Acido et Alkali.*

On 30th August 1705, at a meeting of eighteen Fellows, Dr. John Drummond being present, Dr. Sinclair, elder, had discourse *de Ileo*, and 'the said day it being proposed that any of the members that please may meet att the Colledge every Monday betwixt thrie and four in the afternoon, to confer about Medicine or other parts of learning. The Colledge relished the proposall very well, and allowed the first voluntary meeting to be upon Monday next.'

Dr. Sinclair, *de Ileo.*

Afternoon Weekly Conference at College instituted 30th August 1705.

5th September 1705 may therefore be regarded as the inauguration day for special meetings for the exchange of views upon medical questions and allied subjects, in addition to listening to discourses; and the completion of what, nowadays, we regard as a Medical Society Meeting, communications, discussions, and cases.

First held 5th September 1705.

On October 29th, 1705, Sibbald again supports his scheme. 'The which day Sir Robert Sibbald had a discourse with which the Colledge was very well pleased,' but the subject of it is not stated.

October 29th, 1705. Dr. Sibbald had a discourse.

On 29th January 1706, Dr. Halket, the Præses, being present, as well as Stevenson, Sibbald, Pitcairn, Drummond, etc., Dr. Lauder had a discourse upon a *Singular case*, and on 12th March, Stevenson, Sibbald, Pitcairn, etc., being present, 'Doctor Halket, Præses, had a discourse, *de cura Volvuli, quartis Medicinae Principibus*,' and 'Dr. Pitcairn was desyred to have his discourse ready as soon as he can conveniently.'

Dr. Lauder on a singular case. Dr. Halket *de cura Volvuli.* 12th March 1706. Dr. Pitcairn desired to have a discourse.

Although distinct from these improvement meetings, and the early ideas of a Medical Society, I think it well to quote the following Minute, as the subject is allied to that under present consideration, and I may also at a later period have to refer to it. 'The said day, 12th March, Sir Robert Sibbald offered to

Sir Robert Sibbald's offer of curiosities accepted by College, and press provided.

give a large parcel of curiosities to the Colledge, provyded he have the power of keeping and ordering them, for which offer he had the thanks of the Colledge; and the Theasaurer was desyred to provyde a convenient press in the Colledge for them.'

The foundation of a Museum.

Sibbald's idea evidently was not only to have the medical discourses and conferences, but also a Museum for purposes of illustration and reference.

Dr. Archibald Pitcairn had not yet taken part in delivering a discourse. He had been requested to have it ready when convenient, but as that time had not come, on 5th August 1706, 'the same day Dr. Pitcairn was desyred to have his discourse the second Tuesday of September next, and in his absence Dr. Eizat or Dr. Eccles.'

5th August 1706. Dr. Pitcairn again desired to have his discourse.

Dr. Eccles, *de Hydrophobia.*

On 26th September 1706, Dr. Eccles gave a discourse *de Hydrophobia.* Sibbald was not present at this meeting; of the old Fellows, Drs. Lauder and Mitchell were.

Dr. Mitchell, *de Diisenteria.*

On 23rd September 1707, Dr. Mitchell had a discourse *de Diisenteria.*

August 1707. Fines for Absent and Sero now to be exacted for benefit of Dispensary.

9th August 1707, Dr. Archibald Pitcairn's name does not appear in the sederunt, nor had it since he was desired on 5th August 1706 to have his discourse, but as fines for 'absents' and 'seros' were now to be exacted, and applied to the benefit of the sick poor of the Dispensary, he amongst others was fined for absence from this meeting. This went on for many meetings, and up to 3rd August 1708 he had not attended the College meetings.

9th December 1708. Day for Weekly Conference changed to Wednesday.

On 9th December 1708, the 'day appoynted for conferences was changed to Wednesdays at three.' At first they were to be held on Mondays. No reason is given for this change of day.

On 3rd May 1709, Dr. Pitcairn has not yet been present, and is still fined for 'absence.' Dr. Robertson was appointed to have his discourse the first Tuesday of June.

On 15th December 1709, Dr. Pitcairn is still fined for absence, and Dr. Dundas was appointed to have his discourse in January 1710.

5th August 1710, Dr. Pitcairn continues to be fined as he has not yet appeared, nor has Dr. Dundas given his discourse. At this meeting he is appointed to have a discourse upon any subject in Physick he pleases.

There is no record either of the subjects or of the days on which Drs. Robertson and Dundas discoursed, but at the various meetings up to 4th November 1712, Dr. Pitcairn continues to be fined for absence, and his name does not appear in any subsequent sederunt. It would almost seem as if his conduct in shirking the delivery of a discourse, for what reasons is not indicated, had a depressing effect upon the movement, for the discourses are not mentioned again. Probably the weekly Wednesday meetings were continued for conference, but it is not stated that any appointed papers were read or discourses delivered. Does not this incident give some insight into the character and disposition of Pitcairn, and lead us to suspect that he, like his father-in-law, Archibald Stevensone, was not persistently influenced by the same high scientific aspirations observed in some of the nobler founders of the College? It also points to some of the difficulties Sibbald and his supporters had to contend against, when a man of the originally intellectual ability of Pitcairn chose rather the meaner part (for he assented to the discourses when first proposed) of abstaining from taking any active share in the work of these meetings, than rouse himself, and put himself to a little trouble and personal inconvenience in preparing the discourse requested. The effect seems to have been to entirely stop the meetings. This appears to have been the only original scheme of The Early Days of the College which did not directly end in a successful development, but doubtless it paved the way for what followed. The College discourses ceased some

Discourses cease.

Insight into Dr. Pitcairn's character.

The only scheme, not ending in a directly successful development.

Conferences were distinct and not minuted.

time in 1710-1712, but as the weekly conferences were distinct from the discourses at the sederunts of the Royal College, they are not referred to in the Minutes, and how long they continued cannot be ascertained. Within the last forty years an attempt was made to have a monthly meeting of the Fellows for the promotion of good feeling and conference on medical or professional subjects, and ending in a convivial supper. They were only partially successful, and after a short trial, were given up. The late Dr. Alexander Wood was the chief promoter. These meetings were held for several years between 1862 and 1870.

Renewed attempt at Conferences in late years.

. . . . .

1712, last reference to Discourses. For twenty-five years no Medical Society.

The last reference to the discourses was in 1712, and for twenty-five years Edinburgh was without a Medical Union or Society. In the interval the University Medical School had been developing, and with the following result.

Rise of Royal Medical Soc. Dr. W. B. Carpenter's account, Centenary Oration, 17th February 1837.

Dr. W. B. Carpenter in his Centenary Oration, delivered before the Members of the Royal Medical Society of Edinburgh on 17th February 1837, quotes from Dr. Fothergill's works (p. 432) his account of the commencement of this Society, and also refers to Dr. Lettsom's account as given in his *Memorial of Fothergill*, and regards it as originating with several students. 'The foremost in application and knowledge, fired by the example of their Masters, who had nothing more at heart than the improvement of those who committed themselves to their tuition, formed themselves into a Society for their mutual instruction and advancement in their studies.' Of the six founders, Dr. Cleghorn subsequently became Professor of Anatomy in the University of Dublin; Dr. Russell, the author of the *Memorial of the Natural History of Aleppo*, afterwards settled in London, and was 'mainly instrumental in the establishment of the London Medical Society' (1773), and this 'the oldest Institution of its kind in England may thus be considered the legitimate offspring of that whose nativity we are now commemorating' (Carpenter,

1773, London Medical Soc., relation to Royal Medical.

p. 15). Dr. Cumming became a great local practitioner, and was the beloved friend of Fothergill, but was not otherwise distinguished. Of 'Dr. Hamilton, Dr. James Kennedy, and Mr. Archibald Taylor history has transmitted us no information.' Fothergill and Cullen were early associated with it. 'It was in the year 1734 that the Association was formed, which may be regarded as having originated the Medical Society; but it was not permanently constituted until three years afterwards' (p. 16). But another Medical Society besides that of London emanated from that of Edinburgh. From *Aberdeen Doctors at Home and Abroad, the Narrative of a Medical School*, by Ella Hill Burton Rodger, 1893, it appears that in 1789 on 15th December, 'twelve young Medical students from Marischal College, from seventeen to twenty years of age, founded under the guise of a youthful debating school, for mutual benefit, the Aberdeen Medical Society.' And it is further stated (p. 52), 'James M'Grigor and his companion were the suggestors and organisers of the Society. They had completed their studies at Marischal College, and, travelling down to Edinburgh together, passed a year at its University, where they studied under the great Monro Secundus, Professor of Anatomy. Attending meetings of the Edinburgh Medico-Chirurgical (*sic*, should be Royal Medical) Society, they thought of a similar Society for Aberdeen.' 'The theories of Dr. Cullen of Edinburgh were admiringly discussed, and the great Boerhaave was looked upon as old-fashioned, it being the popular belief of young men that our forefathers knew little of Medicine.' Nevertheless (p. 57) they followed the example of the College of Physicians of a hundred years before, and the best discourses were ordered by the President to be copied and preserved by an official of the Society.

Founders of Roy. Med. Soc., 1734.

1789, Aberdeen Medico-Chirur. Society.

Relation to Royal Medical.

Started by James M'Grigor and companion.

Intermediate between the stoppage of the College discourses and shortly before the establishment of the Royal Medical Society by students, action had been taken by a number of medical practitioners in the city, and a Society was formed for the *publishing of* papers and communications relating to Medicine and Surgery. In the Minutes of the Royal College, of 4th May 1731, bearing on this Society, it is entered, a proposal by William Monro as to the publishing of a volume of medical essays and observations was submitted, and the 'letter being read, the Colledge resolved to contribute all they can to the promoting so good a designe and undertaking.' The first volume of this Society was printed by T. and W. Ruddiman for Mr. William Monro, bookseller, in 1733, at the price of five shillings; and bears the title, '*Medical Essays and Observations*, revised and published by a Society in Edinburgh.' It was in fact intended to be what we now term 'A Year Book of Medicine.' As this volume contains papers written by Fellows of the Royal College, they must have, or ought to have, been well aware of two things:

Minutes of 4th May 1731.

Royal College approves, and

William Munro publishes *Medical Essays and Observations* in 1733.

Ignores the College Discourses and Weekly Conferences.

1st. That one of the four Efforts, originated and made by Fellows of the Royal College in its Early Days, and carried on sometimes regularly every month, sometimes with intermissions, over a period of upwards of twenty-five years, at the meetings thereof, was having discourses read before it on medical and scientific subjects allied to Medicine; and also that, during a part of those years, weekly conferences for the consideration of similar subjects were appointed, and that it was the intention of the College to preserve these discourses in the Register as the 'Acta Medica' almost fifty years before this volume was published or even thought of.

Also the early efforts to promote Sanitation. Report to Town Council, November 1721.

2nd. That from time to time, the College made early efforts to promote sanitation, and that its report to the Town Council, signed by the President, so lately as 2nd November 1721, was presented in the name of the College by Dr. John Clerk to the committee of the Town Council, to whom had been assigned the duty of taking steps to protect the city from an apprehended attack of the plague.

Nevertheless, not even the slightest allusion is made to the early Efforts of the Royal College to establish the discourses, the medical conferences, or the weekly meetings, nor is reference even made to the College's Report presented only twelve years before, to the Town Council on the sanitary improvement of the city.

In spite of the condemnatory Report by the College on the North Loch and the slaughter-houses, the collectors of this volume of *Medical Essays and Observations* in their first article, 'The Description of Edinburgh,' complacently observe in 1732-3, 'The Lanes' (closes) 'going off from the High Street are narrow and steep, especially those on the north side; on which side the Houses are not continued down to the foot of the Hill, but on the Brow there are Gardens between the Buildings, and the fresh water Lake (the Nore-loch). On the side of this Loch nearest the Town, the Butchers have their Slaughter-houses, and the Tanners and Skinners their pits.'

Most unfairly no mention is made of the College, nor is any reference made regarding its efforts to promote medical advancement, by conferences amongst its members after the manner of a Medical Society, nor is the association of the 'Nore-loch,' the butchers and the tanners, so strongly objected to by the College, regarded as in any way calling for improvement or indeed in any way marring the amenity of the city, whilst the loch is mentioned as a *fresh water Lake,* which, improved as no doubt it may then have been, requires even now an amount of imagination somewhat difficult to attain to.

Indeed, the only reference to the collections of observations 'of this kind, that we know to be continued of late, are the *Acta Medica Berolinensia,* and *Acta Wratislaviensia*'; but it also mentions, 'the last method of communicating observations to the Publick, has been in Collections made by Societies, the most conspicuous of which are the Royal Society in London, the Academic

Royale des Sciences at Paris, the Academia Scientiarum Imperialis at Petersburgh, and the Academia Naturae Curiosorum in Germany; *all instituted by Publick Authority*, for the advancement of natural knowledge, under which the several Branches of Medicine are comprehended.' The Royal College Efforts were totally ignored. Truly a prophet has no honour in his own country!

And yet, among the contributors to this volume are the following Fellows of the Royal College, who must have been aware of the past Efforts which had been made: Dr. John Drummond, senior, late President R.C.P.E., I place first, for I quoted his name in the sederunt of the College at which references were made to the discourses. He, however, does not appear to have ever communicated or delivered one at the College. Alexander Monro, Professor of Anatomy in the University of Edinburgh, and F.R.S.: he was afterwards a Fellow of the College, but not till 1756; Andrew Plummer, M.D., F.R.C.P.E., Professor of Medicine in the University of Edinburgh; Dr. William Porterfield, F.R.C.P.E.; Dr. John Innes, F.R.C.P.E., Professor of Medicine in the University of Edinburgh; and Dr. Robert Lowis, F.R.C.P.E., and formerly Secretary, etc.

Other medical interests arising, tried to obscure Royal College.

It would appear that other medical interests were now arising in Edinburgh. The College had played its part in the past, and the less importance given to it, the better for the new institutions pressing to the front. But was this honest on the part of those whom it had benefited, and who desired their new venture to have the reputation of originality?

1721, Royal College's Report on Sanitary Improvement in the City.

In the Report on the sanitary improvement of the city, presented in 1721 by the Royal College to the Town Council, the immediate draining of the Nor Loch 'with all imaginable expedition' is first insisted on, and that a canal of *running water* should take the place of 'the water that forms the loch which by its stagnating is so offensive.' Next 'that the slaughter-houses should be removed from the town'; that the carrion should be buried, and the dunghills removed to a greater distance; that all nastiness should be removed from all public streets and closes or lands (*i.e.* tenements); that they may be kept clean and sweet and to have them frequently washed, the water being carried off and not allowed to stagnate. In order that the streets and bye places be kept clean that 'houses of office be placed att convenient distances and in convenient places, on the south and north sydes of the Toun.' Also that 'Waggons or Carts be appoynted to call airlie in the morning at certain places, to be appoynted to give attendance to receive . . . what is gathered from families; and, by sounding of a horne or other warning, to give advertisement that the Servants may be ready to bring the refuse to them, and that none be allowed upon severe penalties to throw any kynd of Nastiness over Windows or in the Stairs or Closes,' etc. This Report by the Royal College was very thorough. Its suggested sanitary measures were not entirely carried out by the Town Council, though possibly it led to some improvement in the condition of the city. Whilst the Nor Loch continued in its Lake form, with its border of objectionable trades, there was yet much room for reformation, and the Effort of the Royal College to effect this twelve years previously might have been alluded to in *Medical Essays and Observations.*

Following this volume of medical essays and observations, arose in the following order, the Royal Medical Society formed in 1734, and permanently constituted in 1737. The next record of a Medical Society in Edinburgh appeared in 1754, in the shape of the first volume of '*Essays and Observations, Physical and Literary*, read before a Society in Edinburgh and published by them.'

Following Medical Essays, 1734, Royal Medical Society.

1754, *Essays and Observations, Physical and Literary*, published by a Society.

It was printed by G. Hamilton and J. Balfour, printers to the University, and was the successor of the 'volumes published by the Society in Edinburgh' whose first volume I have just referred to.

The papers it will be observed are stated to have been *first read* before the Society.

The appearance of the essays in this new form had been delayed first by the Rebellion of 1745, and thereafter by the death of Mr. MacCourin, one of the Secretaries. Mr. Alexander Monro, Professor of Anatomy, and Mr. David Hume, Library Keeper to the Faculty of Advocates, were the Secretaries at the date of publication of the first volume, and it contains papers entitled, 'Some Remarks on the Laws of Motion and the Inertia of Matter,' by John Stewart, M.D., F.R.C.P.E., and Professor of Natural Philosophy in the University of Edinburgh; 'A Dissertation on the Sexes of Plants,' by Charles Alston, M.D., King's Botanist in Scotland, F.R.C.P.E., and Professor of Medicine and Botany in the University of Edinburgh; 'Remarks on Chemical Solutions and Precipitations,' by Andrew Plummer, M.D., F.R.C.P.E., Professor of Medicine and Chemistry in the University of Edinburgh; 'Of the Various Strength of Different Lime Waters,' by Robert Whytt, M.D., F.R.S., F.R.C.P.E., and Professor of Medicine in the University of Edinburgh. While Alexander Monro, F.R.S., Professor of Anatomy, and his son Alexander Monro, Student of Medicine, and Dr. Donald Monro, Physician in London, contribute a joint paper 'On the Dissection of a Woman with Child and Remarks on Gravid Uteri.'

Contains papers by Fellows of Royal College.

This Society afterwards developed into the Royal Society of Edinburgh. From the contributions I have quoted from the first volume, it is evident that the old spirit of 'The Early Days' animated some at least of the Fellows of the Royal College in 1754.

This Society after developed into Royal Society of Edinburgh.

As regards what was being done in other parts of Great Britain, I should state that in the Metropolis there was in 1752 the London Medical Society; which, like the Edinburgh volumes issued by Mr. W. Monro, was for publishing papers under the title of *Medical Observations and Inquiries by a Society of Physicians in*

Metropolitan Societies, 1752. London Medical published papers.

London. According to Mr. D'Arcy Power (*Brit. Med. Journal*) a Society of Physicians was started for similar objects in 1764, and the Abernethian Society of St. Bartholomew's Hospital dates from 1795.

1764, Society of Physicians. 1795, Abernethian Society.

The effect of these two publishing societies was to stimulate the Royal College of Physicians of London, with the result that it issued the first volume of '*Medical Transactions*, published by the College of Physicians in London' in 1768. At page five of the preface it is remarked, 'As the art of Physic hath been much improved by this method of communicating observations, the College of Physicians in London are desirous of furthering a design so worthy of their attention, and are ready to receive any medical papers that shall be presented to them, in order to publish the most useful'—and so on—very much after the manner, thirty-five years previously, of the Edinburgh preface to its volume of *Medical Essays and Observations* of 1733.

1768, Royal College of Physicians Transactions.

After this review of the development of Medical Societies, and the preservation and publication of observations and transactions, I conclude that, in the question of priority, the Edinburgh Royal College takes the lead of the Medical Societies in Britain and of the Edinburgh Society for the publication of its Essays and Observations, and that the origination in Edinburgh of these mutual improvement medical periodical meetings, and the preservation of transactions in a volume of Acta Medica, must be assigned to the prefervid genius of Robert Sibbald.

Royal College of Physicians in Edinburgh takes the lead, and the idea was due to Sir Robert Sibbald.

PART IV

THE FIRST KNIGHTS

GENERAL NOTICE OF THE OTHER ORIGINAL FELLOWS

DR. SIR DAVID HAY
DR. MATTHEW BRISBANE
DR. JAMES LIVINGSTONE
DR. ROBERT CRAUFURD
DR. ROBERT TROTTER
DR. MATHEW ST. CLAIR
DR. JAMES STEWART
DR. ALEXANDER CRANSTOUNE
DR. JOHN HUTTOUNE
DR. JOHN M'GILL
DR. JOHN LEARMONTH
DR. WILLIAM STEVENSONE, YOUNGER
DR. JAMES HALKETT
DR. WILLIAM WRIGHT
DR. PATRICK HALYBURTOUNE
DR. WILLIAM LAUDER
DR. ARCHIBALD PITTCAIRNE

AND OF

DR. GEORGE HEPBURN, AN ELECTED FELLOW.

PART IV

THE FIRST KNIGHTS

HAVE now concluded the Retrospect of The Early Days of the Royal College. I have shown how, with the assistance of Sir Charles Scarborough and the Duke of York, the difficulties attending its origination were overcome. I have pointed out that, within three years of its being established, it engaged in four great Efforts. The first for the benefit of the people of the country at large by the preparation of a Pharmacopœia for Scotland. The second for the benefit of the city of Edinburgh by the organisation of a Dispensary for the sick poor. The third for the benefit of the medical profession by inaugurating a uniform tripartite Examination for the Licence of the College to practise. It was not only theoretical but practical, and embraced in its first part a 'tryall' based on the then developing Physiology, towards the foundation of which the labours of Harvey had so largely contributed and those of Bellini advanced. This 'tryall' was shortly afterwards styled upon 'the Institutions of Medicine,' and that before the publication of Boerhaave's or Haller's works, whilst the final 'tryall' was upon what was then termed, 'two practicall caices,' supplied from the Dispensary of the College, which seems to be the basis of 'the Clinical' which is now regarded as so important by the modern organisers of medical study for testing competent knowledge, and by those who aim at the examinations being made practical. The fourth Effort was for the

Résumé of The Early Days.

The four Efforts.

The first for the benefit of the people at large.

The second for the city of Edinburgh.

The third for the Medical Profession.

The fourth for the Fellows themselves.

benefit of the Fellows of the College themselves, by having 'Discourses' at the meetings of the College and 'Conferences' for the interchange of ideas on professional subjects amongst themselves, so soon as the College possessed a Hall of its own, at the foot of Fountain Close, in which to meet, and these Professional Meetings were the precursors of our present day Medical Societies.

To whom were the four important Efforts to be ascribed?

I now proceed to consider to whom these four important Efforts at medical progress must be ascribed. Were they the work of the College as a body, or were they due to a few of the Fellows?

To a few Fellows.

They could not, of course, be adopted and carried out without the approval of the College; but their inception and introduction must be undoubtedly ascribed to a few.

An interest is naturally felt in these early pioneers; and as most of them gained their spurs after a strenuous struggle in a well-fought field, I have introduced them to your notice as 'The First Knights' of the Royal College of Physicians of Edinburgh.

'The First Knights.'

Of the other Fellows some contributed also, to the honour and distinction of the College, though in a less degree; and regarding each of them I shall preliminarily offer some remarks, but outside the College Minutes I have been unable to learn many particulars.

The leading spirits.

The leading spirit, without question, was Sir Robert Sibbald. He was strongly supported and ably aided by Sir Andrew Balfour, Alexander Cranstoune, Archibald Pittcairne, Sir Thomas Burnet, especially at first, and by John M'Gill, Robert Craufurd, and William Stevensone, the first Librarian and second Treasurer. Sir Archibald Stevensone, also, during the very Early Days gave the Efforts his support; but he does not appear to have consistently done so, at least as regards the promotion of the Pharmacopœia.

Progressive Fellows not more than nine.

Of the twenty-one original Fellows who constituted the College, and are named in the Charter, the more enterprising minds were, it may be said, no more than nine.

During the first year, as has been stated, fifteen meetings were held. The Fellows most regular in attendance were, in the order of precedence in the Roll of the College, Drs. Burnett, Archibald Stevensone, Robert Sibbald, Andrew Balfour, Robert Craufurd, Robert Trotter, James Stewart, Alexander Cranstoune, John Huttoune, John M'Gill, John Learmonth, William Stevensone, and Archibald Pittcairne.

First year fifteen meetings held.

Attendance of the Fellows.

Reserving the Knights to be afterwards considered, I have learned the following particulars of the Fellows of the College which may serve as a basis on which to add future information, and I mention them as their names are entered in the Charter of the College and written in the early Minutes.

Dr. David Hay stands foremost in the Charter, and although he was a Knight did not receive that honour in consequence of his connection with the Royal College. I do not therefore rank him with the First Knights of The Early Days.

Dr. David Hay, Knight No. 1 in Charter,

It is with much regret that I am unable to treat him with the same degree of praise as I assign to the four first Knights. Although an offshoot from the House of Erroll, he wanted the noble unselfishness of most of the other Fellows, and whilst a Court Physician, his conduct showed him to be narrow in nature, wanting in generosity, and restricted in his views. He therefore was never received as an Ordinary, but only took rank as an Honorary Fellow, because, after being communicated with, he declined to pay his share of the preliminary expenses of the 'Royall Colledge.' Could it have been that his poverty and not his will consented? I fear not, for reference to the Stent Roll of 1699 shows that he was rated for assessment on the highest rent of any Physician in town. In the Stent Roll of 1681-82, Dr. Hay is entered as residing in the third part of the north-west quarter in the High Street, probably in the neighbourhood of what is now the entrance to Cockburn Street. The amount he

was received only as an Honorary Fellow.

Rated at highest rental of the Edinburgh Physicians.

Sir Robert Sibbald and Sir Archibald Stevensone.

had to pay of Cess was £24 Scots, which was considerably higher than either Sir Robert Sibbald or Sir Archibald Stevensone paid. In 1696 he still resided in the same district, and he is Stented on a rental value of £430, whilst Sibbald is rated on £300, and Stevensone on £130. In the Roll of 1699 'the airs of Sir David Hay' are still rated on £430, whilst Sibbald's rental is at £350 and Stevensone at £160. It does not seem therefore that his poverty could have been, unless he were occupying a residence out of proportion to his means, the reason for his declining to pay his share of the preliminary expenses of the College.

Rents of Physicians in Edinburgh in 1699.

It may be of interest to state the rents of the other Physicians named in the Stent Roll of 1699, as possibly showing their respective social if not professional importance. The city was divided into four quarters—north-west, north-east, south-east and south-west—and each quarter was sub-divided into three parts.

Dr. Stirling resided in second part of north-west quarter at yearly rent of £200 Scots.

Dr. Oliphant resided in third part of north-west quarter at yearly rent of £140 Scots.

George Preston, Apothecarie, in third part of north-east quarter and paid tax of 8s. for watching.

Heirs of Andrew Balfour on property in third part of north-east quarter at rent of £270 Scots.

Dr. Smellum (Smelholme) resided in first part of south-east quarter at yearly rent of £80 Scots.

Dr. Pitcairne resided in second part of south-east quarter at yearly rent of £80 Scots.

Heirs Dr. Balfour resided in second part of south-east quarter at yearly rent of £300 Scots.

Dr. Eccles resided in first part of south-west quarter at yearly rent of £150 Scots.

Dr. Trotter resided in first part of south-west quarter at yearly rent of £100 Scots.

Dr. Robertson resided in second part of south-west quarter at yearly rent of £280 Scots.

Hugh Stevenson, of Mongreenan, the Clerk, resided in first part of south-west quarter at yearly rent of £300 Scots.

Sir David Hay occupied, therefore, the most valuable property.

Nor could it have been age which was his excuse for not paying, for he died in 1699, and therefore survived the founding of the College no less than eighteen years.

That Sir David occupied a leading and prominent position amongst the Physicians in the city is indicated by his being the first named of the four selected by the Court of Session to guide the Court regarding the Union of Surgeons and Apothecaries, which you may remember was the occasion of the steps being taken for the erection of the College when proposed by Sibbald.

Name was never on roll of Ordinary Fellows.

From Sibbald's Autobiography we learn that, although from his professional status, his name is the first in the Patent, yet he declined to bear his share of the cost of preliminary expenses, and was in consequence never on the roll of attendance; and he and Dr. M. Brisbane, who also declined to share the expenses, were both ranked as Honorary Socii or Fellows. Dr. Brisbane probably lived to regret his parsimony, for he in after years applied to have his name put on the Roll; and was refused. Hay, however, never appears to have applied for admission as an Ordinary Fellow. Bearing upon the position of Drs. David Hay and Matthew Brisbane in the College, I may state that there was presented in the year 1707, 'An Historical Account of the Rights and Privileges of the Royal College of Physicians and of the Incorporation of Chirurgeons in Edinburgh,' which concludes with the recital of the 'Promissorie Declaration' subscribed by every member of the College at his admission. Neither of these two original Fellows' names appear as having signed it, which confirms what has been previously stated that neither of them was admitted as

He never signed the Promissory Declaration.

an Ordinary Fellow. To neither of these gentlemen is any share of merit due, for they contributed to the good name and enlightened Acts of the new College in no way, either by their money or their presence. The date of Dr. David Hay's knighthood I have been unable to ascertain, but from the Stent Rolls, I learned that in that of 1681-82, he is entered as 'Doctor Hay.' In that of 1696 he is styled Sir David Hay, and in that for 1699 his 'airs' pay the assessment. He is however designated in the Town Council Records Sir David as early as 1684.

As I have said, his name stands first of the four leading Physicians of the city consulted by the Court of Session. He must at that time have occupied no mean position, but I surmise he took precedence by seniority, and from being King's Physician, rather than from professional merit, or he would not have been rated before Burnet or Balfour. From the extracts of the Town Council Records of Edinburgh, 1606-1726, quoted in the Introduction to Brown's *Greyfriars' Epitaphs*, the following particulars may be learned concerning Dr. David Hay; and as the dates correspond to The Early Days of the College, I conclude they refer to the same Physician. I quote from p. lxxii of the Introduction: '1684, December 3rd. Grants to Sir David Hay, one of His Majesty's Physicians in Ordinary, permission to erect a monument or tomb, betwixt Ravelston's tomb and Ballantyne's tomb, which are erected upon the west side of Greyfriars' Kirkyard.' Vol. xxxi. fol. 108.

1684, Town Council Records show he got permission to erect a Monument in Greyfriars' Kirkyard.

And later, at page lxxv: '1696, Sept. 4th, a lengthened Petition is here inserted from Sir Wm. Hope of Craighall and Sir Arch. Hope of Rankeillor, regarding the grounds granted in 1688 or 82, to Sir David Hay, M.D. The boundary of the Doctor's ground is removed northward, and a piece is appropriated to the family of the Hopes lying upon the west side of the Greyfriars, near to Ravelston's tomb, extending in breadth ten feet from the said tomb towards the north, alongst the yard dyking, and extending in length from the dyke towards the east upon the yard fourteen feet.' Vol. xxxv. fol. 382.

The Hays of Mountblairie would seem to have been related to Dr. Sir David Hay, for some of that family are buried near to or at this spot. Amongst the first subscribers to the Infirmary was a Hay of Mountblairie.

Buried in Foulis' tomb, 9th June 1699.

The monument was never erected; but alas for human vanity! although an *Eques Auratus* and a Court Physician, the Burial Records of Greyfriars' Kirkyard show, that on the 9th of June 1699, Sir David Hay, Doctor, was buried in a tomb belonging to another, by warrant, and that the cause of his death was 'decay.' He lies in 'Fouls Tom,' and no monumental stone, recording his dignity, his courtly honours or his name, now marks the spot. But he was buried with the pomp of a hearse, and had fresh 'turf' over his grave. At that time in Greyfriars' Kirkyard these were the indications of respectability.

Dr. Matthew Brisbane, No. 3 in Charter.

Dr. Matthew Brisbane, No. 3 on the Charter, was one of the two original Fellows who declined to pay their share of the preliminary expenses, which were heavy, incurred in connection with the formation of the College. He was in consequence never admitted as an Ordinary Fellow. He and Dr. Sir David Hay were considered to be 'Honorarie Socii.' Dr. Brisbane's name only appears once in the Minutes, on 7th February 1695, when he applies to be placed on the Roll of Ordinary Fellows; but his application was not granted, and on 4th November he is declared to be an Honorary Fellow. He must be the same Matthew Brisbane that is entered in the Roll of Members of the Faculty of Physicians and Surgeons of Glasgow in Mr. Duncan's *Memorials*, p. 245. If so, a probable reason for his not paying his fees and not joining the College as an Ordinary Fellow at first, is found in his being then settled in Glasgow. In the Faculty Roll he is stated to have entered as Physician about 1684, and that he graduated

was a Fellow of Faculty of Physicians and Surgeons of Glasgow, and settled in Glasgow.

Family History.

M.D. at Utrecht in 1661, the subject of his Thesis being *De Catalepsi.* He is further stated to have been the son of the Rev. Matthew Brisbane, parson of Erskine, a scion of the House of Brisbane of Bishopton. From Anderson's *Scottish Nation*, vol. ii. p. 879, it is learned that the surname belongs to an ancient family, the possessors of Bishoptoun in Renfrewshire, with Lands in Stirling and Ayr shires, prior to the dates of any personal charters, and now represented by Brisbane of Brisbane in Ayrshire and Makerstoun in Roxburghshire. The same authority states that Matthew Brisbane, the fifth proprietor of Bishoptoun, fell at Flodden, 9th September 1513, and that his nephew, John Brisbane, was slain at the battle of Pinkie in 1547. Dr. Matthew Brisbane held office in the University of Glasgow as Dean of Faculty in 1675 and 1676, and Rector in 1677-81. He was also Glasgow's Town Physician in 1682. 'He gave a professional opinion in the famous Bargarran witchcraft case in 1696,' which would be just after his application to be entered on the Roll of Ordinary Fellows of the Edinburgh College. 'In the latter half of the century the name of Dr. Matthew Brisbane stands out prominently as a Glasgow Physician of note.' He had a son, Dr. Thomas Brisbane, who also entered the Glasgow Faculty as Physician, and who, the same authority (Faculty *Memorials*) states was the first Professor of Anatomy and Botany in the University of Glasgow, from 1720 to 1742; but he does not appear to have taught either of the subjects. He died in 1742. His son, John, was M.D. of Edinburgh, 1750, and is enrolled as an Honorary Fellow of the Glasgow Faculty in 1768. He settled in London, was admitted Licentiate of the Royal College of Physicians, London, on 24th March 1766, and was Physician to Middlesex Hospital from 4th May 1758 to 1st June 1773. He was the author of *The Anatomy of Painting*, London, 1769, and died about 1776 (see Munk's *Roll of R.C.P.L.*, vol. ii. p. 275).

His son, Dr. Thomas, first Professor of Anatomy and Botany in University of Glasgow.

Grandson, John, Physician to Middlesex Hospital, London.

Dr. James Livingstone, whose name is sixth in the Charter, died in May 1682. He was Councillor and Censor of the Royal College, but was not present at more than one meeting. He must have been a man of mark to have been the original holder of these two honourable and important offices. If in ill health when the College was erected, from his being appointed Censor, one would infer that his illness in December 1681 was regarded favourably and likely to terminate in recovery, whilst the importance of the office of Censor is shown by the fact that his successor in it was Dr. Robert Sibbald.

Dr. James Livingstone, No. 6 in Charter.

Died May 1682.

Dr. Robert Craufurd, the eighth in the Charter. I have failed to find of what University he was a graduate. Robertus Craffort, aged 24, was a student of Medicine at Leyden in 1668. During the first year of the Royal College, he was present at only half of the minuted meetings; but he must have been interested in the Pharmacopœia, for he was a member of the Committee of 8th March 1682. He also took interest in the Dispensary, and was one of the first 'Phisitians to the Poore.' His absence, without explanation, from Dr. Kello's third and final examination, might almost be taken to indicate an indifference which would not have been expected in one otherwise so attentive to duty, for in 1683 he was present at three of the six meetings held, and in 1684 was present at twelve of the nineteen minuted sederunts. On 7th April he had a Discourse upon the nature and use of the Pancreatic Juice; and at the Election meeting in December, was elected Treasurer *vice* Cranstoune. This is the last mention of him in the Minutes. When they are again recorded in 1694, and in subsequent years, his name is not again met with.

Dr. Robert Craufurd, No. 8 in Charter.

One of the first 'Phisitians to the Poore.'

Dr. Robert Trotter, the ninth name in the Charter, was the son of an advocate; and a graduate of the University of Leyden in 1672. His Thesis was on *De Lethargo*, 4to, Lugd. Bat. He entered as student there at the age of twenty-two in

Dr. Robert Trotter, No. 9 in Charter.

1670. Though present at about half the meetings, he does not seem to have taken a prominent part in the Efforts of the College, although on 8th March 1682, he was appointed one of the Pharmacopœia Committee. He gave one of the Discourses on 7th April 1684, *De Essentiâ Febris*, and on 7th February 1695, and also on 9th January 1700, he discoursed on *De Catarrho Suffocativo*. On the death of Dr. James Livingstone in May 1682, he was elected his successor in the Council; and on 4th December 1684, was also elected to the important office of Censor. Of the forty-four meetings of The Early Days, he was present at twenty-eight; but he was not always in the sederunt when the consideration of the four Efforts formed the chief business. It is noticeable in subsequent years that he was always present at the Election meetings, and that he was kept in office till 1725, a period of upwards of forty years. He was elected President in December 1694, re-elected in December 1695, and was again President from December 1700 to December 1702. He died on 16th September 1727.

Kept in office upwards of forty years.

Three times President.

Died 16th September 1727.

The most remarkable event in his College career was that, whilst he was President, on the 14th September 1695, Sir Archibald Stevenson, who preceded him in the Chair, and who also occupied part of the building or house in which the College held its meetings, 'denyed ye keyes of the Colledge,' and 'the meeting was held in Dr. Trotter ye President's lodging.' This was at the beginning of the unfortunate misunderstandings amongst the Fellows, which led to the suspension, by the majority of the College, for contumacy, of Sir Archibald Stevenson, and Drs. William Eccles, John Robertson, Charles Oliphant, Andrew Melville, and John Smelholme; and which was not rescinded until after January 1700. Dr. Pitcairn was also suspended about this time for his protest.

1695, when President Stevenson denied the keys.

It has been supposed that the College occupied a room in Sir Archibald Stevenson's house; but, from the Minute of 29th

September 1696, it would appear as if he had been the tenant of the College, for on that date the Treasurer is instructed to take steps to make him pay the money due for that part of the house possessed by him; and at meeting of 5th November, he is again instructed to demand the discharge Dr. Stevenson pretends he has.

Did the College occupy room in Stevensone's house?

Hoping to obtain some information regarding the position of the College in, and subsequent to The Early Days, on application, I was courteously permitted by Mr. Paton, the City Chamberlain, to inspect the Stent Rolls of the City of Edinburgh for the year 1681-82. In it, after careful revision, I find no reference to the College of Physicians; nor did I find mention of the Surgeons' Hall. On mentioning this to Mr. Paton, he thought it unlikely that Corporations would be then assessed. I found, however, the names of Dr. Stevenson and Dr. Sibbald, the former assessed for 15 and the latter 16 pounds Scots. The city for Stent purposes, was divided, as previously mentioned, into four quarters, and these into three north-west parts, three north-east parts, three south-east, and three south-west parts. Dr. Stevenson occupied a house in the second part of the south-east quarter, and Dr. Sibbald's house was in the second part of the north-east quarter. I presume that would be the situation of the Bishop's Land, for one of his neighbours is William Menteith of Carribber. No information as regards the position of the College or its relations to these Fellows' houses is obtained. In the Stent Roll for 1696, Sir Archibald Stevenson is still stented in the south-east quarter on a rental of 130 pounds Scots, and also on property in the second part of the north-west quarter, 100 pounds Scots. Where Dr. Trotter resided I could not ascertain, as his name is not entered for that year. In the Stent Scroll Book for 1699-1700, Sir Archibald Stevenson is still in the same position, but his rental increased to 160 pounds, and Sir Robert Sibbald's to 350 pounds Scots. Dr. Trotter's name is entered in the south-west quarter first part, and he is rented at 100 pounds; but at that

Stent Rolls throw no light on the question.

Information from Stent Rolls.

date the College rented a chamber from Mr. William Livingston, and that name is found in the third part of the north-west quarter. I was greatly disappointed to find I could learn nothing more definite from these old records of the city. From the fact that Sir Archibald Stevenson resided in the second part of the south-east quarter, it would be more probable that the College occupied a chamber in his lodging, for after he locked out the College in 1695 he still lived in the same quarter in 1696 and was still there in 1699-1700, whilst the College had changed its location. As the eastern end of the city was divided into north and south quarters, and each again into three parts, and it is known that Sibbald occupied that portion of the Bishop's Land entering from Carribber's Close, it is probable that Stevenson occupied a lodging just opposite on the south side of the High Street.

Position of Dr. Trotter's, Stevenson's, and Sibbald's houses.

Information regarding family from Dr. James Trotter of Bedlington, a descendant.

Dr. James Trotter of Bedlington, Northumberland, is a descendant, and from him I have learned that Dr. Robert Trotter was a member of the old family of Trotter of Printonan, Berwickshire. He had two sons, one the Rev. Alexander, A.M., the Minister of Edrom, and the other Robert Trotter, A.M., who settled in Galloway. He was the author of a Latin Grammar and other works. His eldest son, Dr. John, was a Surgeon in Nithsdale; and in 1746, narrowly escaped the vengeance of the Hanoverian side, for having concealed and protected one of Prince Charles's wounded officers. His (John's) eldest son, Dr. Robert, gained considerable celebrity in his day for his successful treatment of the disease known as Sivens, or 'the Yaws,' which was then prevalent in his neighbourhood; and is in consequence mentioned by Professor Adams of London, in his work, on 'Morbid Poisons.' His (Dr. Robert's) eldest son was also a medical man, and the author of *Derwent Water, or the adherent of King James.* He left six sons, all medical men in practice. At present there are five Trotters living descendants of the College Dr. Robert, practising Medicine, whilst six of their sons are in training as medical students. Every generation for the last two hundred years has furnished medical men in unbroken succession.

Dr. Mathew St. Clare or Clair or Sinclare was the tenth in the original Charter. At the age of twenty he matriculated Student of Medicine at Leyden in October 1674. He did not attend the College meetings till the 13th and 14th in November and December 1682; but being present again in January 1684, he was elected in place of Dr. Stewart to the Council; and in June of that year gave a Discourse *On Dysentery*. He was re-elected Councillor in December 1684, and after 1694, was regular in attendance and was a member of the Council. He was repeatedly nominated Pro-præses, after that office was determined on by the College, and ultimately was elected President in December 1698 and 1699, and also from 2nd December 1708 to 6th December 1716. On 3rd November 1724, after a considerable absence from the College meetings the venerable past President was present, when his son, Dr. Andrew, who became in 1726 Professor of the Institutes of Medicine in the University, was admitted Socius of the Royal College. He died in 1728, the last survivor of the twenty-one original Fellows.

Dr. Mathew St. Clare or Clair or Sinclare, No. 10 in Charter.

Died in 1728, last survivor of original Fellows.

Dr. James Stewart, number eleven in Charter, was one of the first Councillors. He died after being able to be present at only fifteen of the early meetings. He was re-elected to the Council on 30th November 1682, and also in December 1683; and at the next meeting, on 7th January 1684, his death is intimated. He evidently would have done good work for the Royal College, had his health been better. He was one of those interested in the Pharmacopœia; and on 21st March 1682, he was appointed a member of the additional Pharmacopœia Committee 'to revise the severall parts.' Was he related to Sir James Stewart of Coltness, Lord Provost of Edinburgh in 1648-49 and 1658-59? He was a

Dr. James Stewart, No. 11 in Charter, died January 1684.

Medical Student at Leyden in 1674, and was then in his twenty-second year.

Dr. Alexander Cranstoune or Cranston, No. 12 in Charter.

DR. ALEXANDER CRANSTOUNE or CRANSTON was one of the original Councillors, and was regular in his attendance at the College meetings during the first year, being present on fourteen occasions. He was re-elected to the Council on Election day 1682, and in August 1683, when Dr. William Stevensone retired from the Treasurership, he was appointed his successor. He was again elected Councillor and Treasurer at the December meeting, and during 1684 with one exception only, was present at all the meetings. He took interest therefore in all the four Efforts. His name stands twelfth on the Charter list of original Fellows. In July 1684, he gave a Discourse on 'Mental Alienation'; and in December resigned the Treasurership and Council, and was elected one of the Censors. After 1694, he attended regularly, and in that year, when it is resolved by the College to have a Pro-præses to act in the absence of the President, he was nominated to be the first Vice-President of the Royal College. At election meeting of 1695 he was elected Councillor, and in December 1696 one of the 'Physitians to the Poore.' The following year he was again in the Council, and also appointed Pro-præses, and once again in 1698, but afterwards his name appears no more in the record of the meetings, and the place which knew him so well was now no longer gladdened by his presence.

In 1696 one of the 'Physitians to the Poore.'

Not mentioned in Minutes after 1698.

Dr. John Huttoune or Hutton, No. 13 in Charter, the first Treasurer.

DR. JOHN HUTTOUNE or HUTTON was thirteenth in the Charter, and was the first Treasurer of the Royal College. He held office till 1st May 1682. Previously he had attended the meetings regularly except on the 5th April 1682, when it was resolved that the Fellows pay 'two dollars quarterly for College Public expenses.' This being a matter of finance, it might have been expected that the Treasurer would have been present. A probable reason for his absence appears in the Minute of 1st May; he might have been in an unsettled state, and consequently prevented, for on that day he resigned office as Treasurer, because as the Minute records, he was 'going furth the Kingdome.' Dr. William Stevenson is named in his place, and Drs. Cranstoune and Pitcairne to revise his accounts. He was present at the next meeting, also in May, but thereafter his name is never again entered in the Minutes of the Sederunts of the Royal College. He took part in the Pharmacopœia and Dispensary Efforts.

Resigned May 1682, 'going furth the Kingdome.'

He must have been regarded by the original Fellows as a man of ability and business capacity, or they would not have elected him to the responsible and honourable office of first Treasurer. The information regarding him is scanty, but it occurs to me that he was the same 'John Hutton' who joined the Royal College of Physicians of London at a later period. If I am correct in my surmise, previously to his being admitted to the London College, he was Physician to King William the Third. After accompanying him to Limerick and the Boyne he ultimately settled in London, and joined the Royal College of Physicians therein, and if my surmise regarding his identity with the Dr. John Hutton of London be correct, then according to Dr. Munk (*Roll of Roy. College of Phys. London*, vol. i. p. 481), he was a Doctor of Medicine of Padua, and as first Physician to King William the Third, was admitted a Fellow of that College, 3rd September 1690. He was also incorporated Doctor of Medicine at Oxford, 9th November 1695, and became a Fellow of the Royal Society in 1697. He seems to have been a man of liberal spirit and genial nature.

Supposed to be Dr. John Hutton, Fellow of the Royal College of Physicians, London, and Physician to King William the Third.

Dr. John M'Gill is fourteenth in the Charter. He was present at ten meetings of the College in 1682, and with one exception, at all those of 1683. During 1684, his attendance was not quite so regular. In August he was to have given a Discourse, but is excused on account of 'being out of town.' He, however,

Dr. John M'Gill, No. 14 in Charter.

gave it on 30th November. The subject was *De Chilificatione*. In December he was elected to the Council, and after The Early Days, his name does not again appear in the Minutes. He took interest in all the four Efforts, and was a member of the Pharmacopœia Committee of 1682. Whether he was related to John M'Gill, who entered the College of Surgeons of Edinburgh in December 1710, and was 'an early Professor of Anatomy to the Surgeons and to the University' (*List of Fellows*, p. 23), I have failed to discover.

After December 1684 not again mentioned in Minutes.

DR. JOHN LEARMONTH, whose name is fifteenth in the Charter, was present at twenty-seven of The Early Days' meetings; but was often absent when the Efforts were being considered, although a member of the Pharmacopœia Committee of 1682. He formed one of the Council elected in December 1684, and at next meeting, when Dr. Andrew Balfour declined to accept office on account of his health, was elected a Censor in his place. When Minutes were once more kept, after the ten years' interval, his name is not again entered. He had been a Student at Leyden in 1675.

Dr. John Learmonth, No. 15 in Charter.

Censor in December 1684, name not afterwards mentioned.

DR. WILLIAM STEVENSONE, or Dr. Stevensone younger, as his name sometimes occurs in the Minutes, was the sixteenth in the Roll of Original Fellows. His name appears in the Minutes for the last time on 4th December 1684. He was present at twenty-four meetings of The Early Days; and during the first year was tolerably regular in his attendance, and took interest in all the Efforts. He was the first Librarian of the College, being appointed on 7th May 1683; but had previously held office as Treasurer, having succeeded Dr. Hutton when he retired on 1st May 1682. He resigned the Treasurership on 20th August 1683, after he was appointed Librarian, the reason assigned being in the following words:—'Upon a motion made in behalf of

Dr. William Stevensone, or Stevensone younger, No. 16 in Charter.

First Librarian and second Treasurer.

Doctor Stevensone yor Theasaurer to the College, and that in regard of his indispositione of body, some fit persoune might be named as Thesaurer, which place and his accompts taken off his hands, grant his desyre; and appoynts Doctors Stewart and Cranstoune to consider the accompts and to report, and in the mean tyme elects Doctor Cranstoune to be Thesaurer, until the next electione at St. Andrew's day.' After this, his attendance was irregular; and from March to 30th November 1684 he was not present at any meeting. ' He was present on the 1st and 4th December; and after that date his name is not again entered in the Minutes. 4th December 1684 was the day on which Sibbald was elected President, but Dr. William Stevensone is not named as being elected to any office. From the similarity of names it might be supposed he was connected with the President, Sir Archibald Stevensone, but I have been unable to find out who he was, though he certainly was not brother, son, nor nephew of the President's. The Stent Rolls show that the name of Stevenson was a common one in Edinburgh about this time. He apparently resided in the first part of the south-east quarter of the city. He must have been a young man of merit and distinction, as he was called on so early to fill two such honourable positions as the first Librarian and the second Thesaurer. According to the chronological notes of Lord Fountainhall, the Physitians got an order from Court out of pique to Stevenson younger, and two others, that no Physitian should practise without taking 'the Test.' The date of this being 24th September 1684.

Not mentioned after 4th December 1684.

24th September 1684, through pique to him, no Physician to practise without taking the Test.

Dr. James Halkett, the seventeenth name in the Charter, was present at one only of the early meetings before 6th December 1683. Sixteen meetings were held in 1684, and he was present at eleven of them. He also give a Discourse on 'The Peculiarities of Children's Diseases.' In 1695 he attended seven meetings, and was not again present till the Election meeting

Dr. James Halkett, No. 17 in Charter.

of 1703, when he was put in the Council. On the 30th November 1704 he was elected President, demitted office 6th December 1706, and his name last appears in the Minutes of 5th August 1710. He was appointed a Professor of Medicine in the University with Dr. Pitcairne on 9th September 1685, 'to be joyned with Sir Robert Sibbald, his Majestie's Physitian in Ordinary, to be Professors of Medicine.' Rooms were to be provided in the College for teaching the airt, but he was to have no salary 'from ye good toun nor from ye sd University.' It is little wonder, therefore, that 'neither Halkett nor Pitcairne ever delivered any medical lectures in Edinburgh' (Bower's *History*, vol. i. p. 209). He was a Medical Student at the Leyden University in 1675, and was then aged twenty years. He was therefore in his thirty-first year when appointed Professor.

One of the Professors of Medicine appointed in 9th September 1685.

Dr. William Wright, No. 18 in Charter, not mentioned in Minutes after 11th December 1683.

DR. WILLIAM WRIGHT, the eighteenth on original Roll, was present at six meetings of The Early Days, viz. the fifth, tenth, eleventh, thirteenth, fourteenth, and sixteenth; and after 11th December 1683, his name is not again mentioned. I have been unable to learn any particulars regarding this Fellow, but he was still alive in 1721, as his name is entered in the College copy of the Pharmacopœia published in that year.

Dr. Patrick Hallyburton, No. 19 in Charter, not mentioned after 30th November 1684.

DR. PATRICK HALLYBURTON or HALYBURTOUNE, nineteenth on original Roll, was present at four only of the early meetings—the first, third, and fourth, and was not again present till the thirty-fifth sederunt of the College, on 30th November 1684. After this his name is not entered in any meeting of the Royal College. He was appointed in March 8th, 1682, a member of the Pharmacopœia Committee, but does not appear to have been of much use. His name is not in the Stent Rolls, but Hallyburton was a common name in the city at this time; and a Patrick Hallyburton was one of the Merchant Stent-masters in 1681-82, and seems to

DR. ARCHIBALD PITCAIRN.

have been a man of municipal importance. He and the Doctor may have been related!

Dr. William Lauder, No. 20 in Charter.

DR. WILLIAM LAUDER, whose name is the twentieth in the Charter, attended on only one of The Early Days, 5th April 1682, and his name is not again met with till September 1695. He attended till 3rd December. He was present twice in 1696, and was elected a member of Council in December 1699. He attended a few meetings in 1704, and was regular at the meetings in 1705-6. He was present once in 1708, but after this he ceases to be mentioned. He was alive in 1721. He is entered in the Leyden *Album* as having matriculated there at the age of twenty-two years, on 8th October 1674.

last mentioned in 1708.

Dr. Archibald Pittcairne or Pitcairne, No. 21 and last in Charter,

DR. ARCHIBALD PITTCAIRNE or PITCAIRNE was the last and therefore probably one of the youngest, on the Charter Roll of the original Fellows; but, although occupying this position, he was from the first one of the active spirits of the newly formed Institution. From the position he was called on to occupy requiring forensic qualifications, his ability, legal knowledge, and power must, even in The Early Days, have been recognised; and from the fact that, for a considerable time, he had studied law, with the idea of becoming an Advocate, this possibly led to his being the original Procurator-Fiscal of the Royal College. He was in his twenty-ninth year when the College was erected, and had graduated in Medicine in the preceding year.

was the first Procurator-Fiscal.

Regarding Pitcairne there is not so much difficulty in obtaining information, although it must be confessed the accounts are not always accurately given as to dates. According to the political or religious views of the writer he may be described in the most laudatory terms by one, such as 'not only the first Physician but the greatest wit of his time,' and by another in terms equally condemnatory. The fact was, he did not always speak, or write, in well-weighed words. He was not a perfect character, was highly versatile, and did not confine himself to his professional pursuits. A man of means, in easy circumstances, and of brilliant ability, he allowed his social and convivial inclinations to take too prominent a place in his daily life.

Had his poetic genius been tempered with discretion, rather than been made the medium of his pungent wit at the expense of his contemporaries, it would not only have raised him to a position of greater dignity, and preserved him from giving way to his grosser predilections, but have offered some pieces for preservation, of higher standard than those posthumously published. Possessed of an ample form, a pleasing expression, a genial manner, and generous impulses, he was bound to make his mark; especially as he was also gifted with a naturally powerful mind, a clear insight, and acute perceptions; but if he is to be judged by the record borne to his character in the Courts of Law or by the Minutes of the College of Physicians, there is much evidence of defective discretion and that there must have been an influence within, which depreciated his worth and debased his nature.

As it is his influence upon the medical progress of his age in Edinburgh that I have to deal with, it appears to bear out these preliminary observations, for whilst at first this influence was for good, it ultimately became one for evil.

Born 25th December 1652.

Archibald Pitcairne was born at Edinburgh on Christmas Day, 1652. His father, Mr. Alexander Pitcairne, was a Bailie of the city, and a merchant, but also the proprietor of Pitcairn, near Leslie, in Fife, an estate to which Dr. Archibald ultimately succeeded. The family of Pitcairne was an old one, with an honourable history. He was descended from Andrew Pitcairne, who was born after his father had been slain at Flodden field, and where also his seven sons sacrificed their lives for Scotland and their King. Could the attachment of the Pitcairne family to the House of Stewart be more strongly shown? Is it to be wondered at

Family History.

that Dr. Archibald inherited the loyalty to the Jacobite cause, which was transmitted to his only surviving son? His mother was a Sydserff of Rucklaw in East Lothian. In his early life, after being educated at Dalkeith School and in Edinburgh, he was uncertain as to which profession he would ally himself. He thought of Divinity, but found it not congenial, and he took to Law. On going to study at Paris, he found the means of tuition in this department to be deficient there; and associating with those who were studying Medicine, he threw over Law, and took to it. He had also been attracted by the study of Mathematics, and seems to have associated, at this early period of his career, Medicine and Mathematics. It may be recalled that Sir Charles Scarborough, in his early days, had a congenial taste, considering it the best training for a Physician. Pitcairne after four years' attendance laureated (M.A.) at Edinburgh University in 1671, and returned in 1675 to France to prosecute the study of Medicine in Paris, with which school Andrew Balfour (also connected with Fife it may be remembered) had previously been associated. He graduated on 13th August 1680 as Doctor of Medicine, at Rheims. As a result of his previous mathematical training, he not only supported the views and claims to discovery of the great Harvey, but also adopted the physiological views of Bellini, and was afterwards instrumental as his teacher in influencing Boerhaave at Leyden to adopt them.

M.A. Edinburgh 1671. Studied Medicine at Paris, and graduated August 1680 at Rheims.

Supported views of Harvey, and was a teacher of Boerhaave.

In 1681, Pitcairne became one of the youngest original Fellows of the Royal College—being then in his twenty-ninth year, and a graduate in Medicine of little more than a year.

In 1685, a few months after (in September) the appointment of Sibbald to the first Medical Professorship—the Chair of Practice of Physick—in the University of Edinburgh, he, a graduate of less than five years, was also appointed a Professor of Medicine by the Town Council, the patrons. He never taught in the

Appointed in September 1685 Professor of Medicine in University of Edinburgh.

University, and it is questionable if he was intended to do so; but as I have at a later stage of this address to consider the formation of the Medical Faculty in King James' College, I reserve further remarks upon this matter in the meantime.

1688, published *Solutio Problematis*, etc. 1692, Professor of Medicine at Leyden.

Shortly after the publication of the *Solutio Problematis de Historicis et Inventoribus* (1688), he was offered the Professorship of Medicine in the University of Leyden in 1692.

1680, first marriage.

Soon after he returned from Paris to Edinburgh towards the end of 1680, he married Margaret Hay, the daughter of Colonel James Hay, by whom he had a son and daughter. According to Dr. J. Gairdner (College of Surgeons, List of Fellows), she died before he went to Leyden. The children also died in infancy. One reason alleged for his going to Leyden was the difficulty, after the Revolution, of his advancement on account of his political views and opinions.

1693, returned to Edinburgh. Second marriage, and resigned Leyden in consequence.

In 1693 he returned to Edinburgh, and whilst here he married Elizabeth, eldest daughter of Sir Archibald Stevenson, and her friends being opposed to his again going to Leyden, greatly to the regret of the University authorities there, he resigned his Professorship, settled once more in Edinburgh, and, as we have seen, became very closely identified with his father-in-law in the affairs of the Royal College. By this second marriage he had one son and four daughters.

1699, M.D. Aberdeen, *ad eundem*.

In 1699, he was received to the *ad eundem* degree of Doctor of Medicine in the University of Aberdeen.

After the recapitulation of these details of Pitcairn's history, we are in a better position to understand his relation to the Royal College and the subsequent events in which he played a very important part.

4th December 1684, elected Secretary.

The Early Days close with the Minute of 22nd December 1684, when Pitcairne was present. On the 4th of the same month, when Sir Robert Sibbald was elected President, Pitcairne was present, and in The Early Days he and Sibbald appear to have been on friendly terms. He was elected the second Secretary, as is learned from the Minute of the next meeting held on 11th December, and his place of Fiscal was taken by Dr. Cranstoune. The business was conducted quite harmoniously. Taken in connection with the sudden stoppage of recorded Minutes, that of the election meeting is noticeable: 'Hugh Stevenson, continued Clerk, who declared that he will be ready to attend all the generall meetings of the Colledge, or when there is any use of him in any acts of jurisdiction; but that at privat meetings the Secretary might officiat.' This would almost imply that the Secretary, besides being responsible for the general business of the College, had also a share in the recording of the Minutes. If so, then Pitcairne was in some measure blameable for the Minutes ceasing to be recorded or seeing that they were. But otherwise before he went to Leyden he was helpful in the advance of the College Efforts. He was then uninfluenced by his relation to Stevenson, but at the first meeting recorded on 6th December 1694, he was present. He is now the son-in-law of Sir Archibald Stevenson. It was the Election day when Dr. Trotter was elected President in place of Stevenson. Pitcairne is not elected to any office, but he holds the position of one of the yearly Examinators, and it is subsequent to this date that his action became antagonistic, whilst it was to his inaction or apathy that the Efforts at mutual improvement amongst the Fellows were brought to a close. Ultimately his relation with the College ceased entirely (although there is no record that he resigned his Fellowship), so far as *he* was concerned, but so far as the College Minutes show on *its* part, he was still regarded as a Fellow, for he was repeatedly fined for his persistent absence from its meetings.

Hugh Stevenson continues as Clerk.

Pitcairne blameable for not seeing Minutes of meetings kept.

Subsequent to 6th December 1694 became antagonistic to College.

One point in his favour it is right to mention. It is, that it was possibly due to him that the alteration, in the title at least, of the subject of the first 'tryall' was made. For whilst the

Change in title at second Examination probably due to Pitcairn.

subject of it, previous to 1684, was described as being 'upon severall materiall questions,' after December 1694, when the Minutes are again recorded, the title is changed to the Institutiones or Institutes of Medicine.

It was not until 14th September 1695 that the admission of a candidate for Licence by examination is mentioned. It is important to note this, because during the unrecorded years at least nine Fellows were added to the Roll of the College. During these years, as I have previously indicated, five Fellows were nominated for the year to act as 'Examinators,' when first, cannot be ascertained, but there is no mention of the subject of the first examination being changed; and on this date, 14th September 1695, the proceedings are minuted as follows:—'The same day Dr. Gilbert Rule having given in his Bill to ye Colledge desiring to be admitted to Examination, the Colledge receaved his Petitione, and appoynted Weddensday next at two o'clock in ye afternoon for his Examinatione.' This is according to the original form and custom, and the Minute continues—'The same day it being put to ye vote, whether ye old law anent ye examinatione of intrants as it was at ye first creation or ye new law appoynting Examinators for a whole year together, should be observed in time coming, it was carried by ye pleurality y^t ye old law should be observed, and ye new abrogated; and adjourned ye meeting, till Monday at eleven o'clock in ye forenoon.'

Five Examinators appointed for the year.

Dr. Gilbert Rule's application for Examination.

Motion to revert to old system, appointing Examinators for each trial.

Now, it is noteworthy that this being the day on which Sir Archibald Stevenson 'denyed ye keyes of the Colledge,' and the meeting was held in Dr. Trotter 'ye President's Lodging,' neither Pitcairne nor Sir Archibald was present, and that the sederunt consisted of Dr. Trotter, Sir Thomas Burnet, Sir Robert Sibbald, Drs. St. Clare, Cranstoune, Halket, and Lauder, seven original Fellows (there were now only nine on the Roll); and four elected Fellows, viz. Drs. Eccles, Dicksone, Olyphant, and

Sir Archibald Stevenson 'deny'd ye Keyes of the Colledge.'

Meeting at Dr. Trotter's lodging.

Smelholm. Of these four the Minutes show that three were supporters of Stevenson, as they were afterwards suspended.

Two parties—Stevenson's and Trotter's.

From this action, it occurs to me that Stevenson and his party, consisting of only one other original Fellow, Pitcairn, and the others, recently elected Fellows, were in favour of yearly nominated Examinators, whilst the large majority of the old Fellows being favourable to the old custom as at 'ye first creation,' the appointment of Examinators as each candidate presented himself, Stevenson by his high-handed and unwarrantable action attempted to coerce the College, by preventing the meeting voting upon the matter, in the usual premises, and that his overbearing behaviour and the resoluteness of the majority had a great deal to do with the split which afterwards occurred. At this meeting, held in the President's (Trotter's) lodging on 16th September, it was 'carried by pleurality of votes for ye second tyme y^t ye old law should be ye forn and ye new law abrogated.' Neither Stevenson nor Pitcairn, as I have said, was present at this sederunt. They were aware they were in the minority.

Form of Examination taken from Leyden.

The form of Examination, originally followed, was that of the University of Leyden, of which nine of the Fellows had been matriculated students. At Leyden the Examinators, being the Professors, would be permanent; but Pitcairn, approving of fixed Examiners, with the support of his father-in-law, evidently endeavoured to force this arrangement upon the College against the feeling of Sibbald, Burnet, Trotter, and their party. Stevenson had been a student of that University; and apparently in 1682 approved of *pro re nata* Examiners, but now, influenced by Pitcairn, supported his view of their being appointed for a year. Whilst Sibbald, who had also studied at Leyden upwards of thirty years previously, was supported by Trotter, who had studied and graduated there, and by St. Clair, Halket, and Lauder, who had all been matriculated students of the University of Leyden. No doubt, during that time, the details and methods of conducting the Examinations had undergone change; but when the College Examination was organised fifteen years before this dispute, the system of varying Examinators was considered the best, and after a trial of the innovation, the majority, for reasons not stated, preferred the original form. Probably the number of candidates influenced the decision.

In 1688 Pitcairn's *Solutio Problematis de Historicis et de Inventoribus* was published. In it he supports 'Harvey's right to the discovery of the circulation of the blood,' and 'shows that Hippocrates was not acquainted with it' (Bower's *History*, p. 128). Subsequently to this his reputation had so extended that although a graduate of scarcely twelve years' standing, then in his fortieth year, he was invited to Leyden to fill the Chair of Physick in the University. His introductory Lecture on the 'Method of the Improvement in Medicine' increased his reputation. Returning to Edinburgh in 1693, he married Miss Stevenson as his second wife, and resigned his Professorship at Leyden. According to the *Album*, he was elected Professor there in 1692, so that he held the position for only one year or a little more. I suggest, therefore, that it was to Pitcairn probably that the change in the old law regarding Examinators was due, and also the improvement in the title of the subject of Examination, as is shown by what occurred in Dr. Gilbert Rule's notable examination. It is in accordance, too, with human nature that the proud father-in-law would support the recently made son-in-law, who had given up his Professorial Chair at the request of his new wife's family.

Dr. Pitcairn invited to Leyden.

Change in the appointment of Examinators probably due to Pitcairn, also improved title of second Examination.

1695, 21st September, carried for third time that the old rule for Examination be revived.

On 21st September 1695, the College again met. The President, Dr. Trotter, Sir Thomas Burnet, Sir Robert Sibbald, Drs. Cranstoune, St. Clare, Lauder, Dicksone, Eizat, Blackader, and Mitchell, were present, all the active followers of Stevenson as well as himself being absent. It was put to the vote for the third time and carried, that the old rule for Examination of intrants be revived—'according appoints Sir Thomas Burnet and Dr. Eizat for Dr. Rule's first tryal; for ye second, Sir Robert Sibbald and Dr. Dicksone; for ye third, Dr. St. Clare and Dr. Cranstoune.'

Upon the 25th September 1695, in the presence of Dr. Trotter the President, Sir Robert Sibbald, Drs. St. Clare, Cranstoune, Lauder, Blackader, Eccles, Olyphant, Dicksone, Robertsone, and Mitchell, Dr. Gilbert Rule 'was examined by Sir Thomas Burnet, and Dr. Eizat upon ye Institutions of Medicine. Colledge were well satisfied with his answers and appoynt him to be examined upon ye Aphorisms upon Monday,' etc.

Dr. G. Rule's first Examination, 25th September 1695.

The term 'Institutions' is used here just as if it were use and wont. The question is when was it first used, before or after Pitcairn's return from Leyden? It certainly was not used previously to 1685, and I do not think it would be incorrect to say that it was not used before Pitcairn went there as Professor.

'Institutions' here used as if it were use and wont.

From the presumed share he and Stevenson had in the introduction of Examinators appointed for a year, I incline to the opinion that the 'Institutions of Medicine' as the subject of the first Examination was introduced by Pitcairn. Against this it may be urged that he does not use the words in his writings.

In the sale catalogue of Dr. Sir Andrew Balfour's Library, I observe that Gilbert Jacchæus has a work published at Leyden in 1653, entitled *Institutiones Medicæ*. This book is not in the R. C. P. Library, but there is a work of his, also published at Leyden, in 1615, which bears the title of *Institutiones Physicæ*. Gerard Blasius published at Amsterdam, in 1667, a work also in Balfour's catalogue, *Medicinæ Institutiones*. The College Library does not possess a copy of it, and neither of these writers is quoted by Pitcairn, but it is evident that the word in these days was used in Holland; and as Balfour possessed these books, the term must have been known to some of, if not all, the Fellows. Boer-

Early use of term *Institutiones Medicæ*.

haave, the pupil of Pitcairn when at Leyden, published in that city, in 1720, his work upon the *Institutiones Medicæ*, but however closely the Edinburgh School subsequently became identified with Boerhaave's views, it is clear that in the College of Physicians the 'Institutions of Medicine' as the subject of the first Examination for their Licence, did not take origin with Boerhaave, and long preceded the *Elementa Physiologica*, and the *Methodus*, etc., by more than half a century. I may also note, as of interest in connection with the relation between the early medical days of the University of Edinburgh and the College of Physicians to be afterwards referred to, that the class of Physiology said to have been founded in 1685 bears the title of 'The Institutions or Institutes of Medicine.'

Early use of in Edinburgh University.

1685 was the year in which Sibbald, Halket, and Pitcairne were appointed by the Town Council, Professors of Physick and Medicine in the University of Edinburgh ; but none of them lectured therein, and the title of the Physiology class certainly does not occur at this date. Sir Alexander Grant in *The Story of the University*, vol. ii. p. 401, after alluding to the holders of the appointments made in 1685, observes, 'By the arrangements made in 1726, when four Professors then appointed divided the medical teaching among themselves, the Chair of the Institutes of Medicine was allotted to Andrew Sinclair, a Physician who had graduated at Angers. In lecturing, he took for his text-book the *Institutiones Medicæ* of Boerhaave, and did not go beyond what was therein contained.' But the Royal College's use of the title in its examination preceded this by at least thirty-one years. Whilst the University apparently adopted the title of the Chair from Boerhaave, the Royal College used it whilst Boerhaave was yet a pupil or just 'qualified.'

Bower, vol. ii. p. 193, shows us, that the title was used by the Town Council first in 1724, when Dr. William Porterfield was appointed by it, *on the recommendation of the Royal College of*

Physicians in Edinburgh, 'a person well fitted and qualified for teaching Medicine in all its parts.' The Council Minute of 12th August 1724 continues, 'Therefore, they hereby institute and establish the foresaid Profession of the Institutes and Practice of Medicine in their said College' (the University), etc. It will be observed, the words used imply that this Professorship was new and then established for the first time, for the words are 'hereby institute and establish.' I shall later refer to the Royal College Minute of the 21st November 1723. On that day the recommendation to the Town Council in Dr. W. Porterfield's favour was subscribed by the President and Fellows. The words used are:— 'Wee being informed by Dr. William Porterfield, one of our Members, that he designes to give Colledges upon the Instituts and Practice of Medicine . . . doe applaud his designe,' from which it would appear that the Royal College first used the title Institutes of Medicine in Edinburgh.

Institutes and Practice of Medicine first used by Town Council in 1724.

Institutes first used in Edinburgh by Royal College.

I have dwelt, perhaps, too long on the presumed, and to me it seems, with good reason, beneficial influence of Pitcairn on the progress of the Royal College Examinations; but as much consideration has been given to the evil influence he exercised in the College, in the Preface to the Catalogue of the College Library, published in 1863 (and also in 1898), I can scarcely pass on without alluding to it. As it has been issued with the approval of the Royal College, my best course will be to give the substance of that statement, and thereafter my comments regarding it, even although there will be some unavoidable repetition.

Pitcairn's evil influence in the College mentioned in Preface to Catalogue of College Library.

In my preceding remarks, I have shown the keen feeling existing between the Stevenson-Pitcairn party on the one hand, and the Burnet-Sibbald party on the other. The former supported largely by the elected, the latter by the majority of the original Fellows. The subject of dispute being the appointment of Examiners.

There must, when the rupture occurred on 14th September

1695, have been some reason for Sir Archibald Stevenson trying to prevent the meeting on that day being held, though apart from the Examination question, the Minutes do not throw much light on the matter, but some points may be submitted.

Account as given in the Library Catalogue Preface.

The account given in the Library Catalogue Preface is to the following effect. It was first issued on 31st January 1863. In the year 1691, ten years after the establishment of the College, the subject of the treatment of Fever became a source of rather warm controversy among the Edinburgh Physicians. At this time, Dr. Andrew Brown, a friend and pupil of Sydenham, but an Aberdeen graduate, and not a Fellow of the College, published in 1691, at Edinburgh, *A Vindicatory Schedule concerning the New Cure of Fevers*, in which he advocated, 'in strong terms, the employment of evacuant remedies, especially blood letting, the use of active purgatives, and occasionally emetics.' From the absence of the Minutes it is impossible to know whether or not he was setting the College at defiance, and practising without having obtained Licence. I think this was probable, for there is no subsequent reference in the Minutes to him, as either applying for the Licence or the Fellowship. Living at Dolphinton, he was there beyond the College's jurisdiction, and it could only interfere with him when practising within the city or its suburbs. The controversy lasted for about eight years, and had introduced 'various elements of discord,' not only among the general profession, but also between the Fellows of the College. 'In this state of matters the return of Dr. Pitcairn to Edinburgh about 1693 became an additional source of discord.' In 1695 Dr. Pitcairn published a '*Disputatio de curatione Febrium, quæ per Evacuationes instituitur*; Edita Edinburgi Anno 1695,' in which, without reference to Sydenham, he advocated the treatment 'chiefly by evacuant remedies.' A number of opponents to Pitcairn's views soon appeared. Dr. Edward Eizat anonymously attacked his views, in a pamphlet entitled *Apollo Mathematicus, or the Art of curing diseases by the Mathematicks, etc., according to the principles of Dr. Pitcairn.* This was answered by a supporter of Pitcairn, Dr. George Hepburn, a recently elected Fellow of the College, in another pamphlet, bearing the title *Tarugo Unmasked, or an Answer to a late Pamphlet, entitled Apollo Mathematicus.* In this Dr. Hepburn 'endeavoured to expose the cunning and address of Sir Edward Eizat in studying to attain his objects as a Medical Practitioner.' It was also published in 1695.

According to my reading of the Minutes, the writer of the 'Preface' is not quite correct in his enumeration of the respective supporters of the Stevenson-Pitcairn party and their opponents. The first are tolerably correctly named—Dr. Pitcairn, Sir Archibald Stevenson, Drs. Hepburn, Olyphant, Eccles, Robertson, Smellholm, and Melville; and of the enumerated Burnet-Sibbald and Trotter party, Dr. David Hay never attended a meeting of the Royal College at this time, whilst Dr. Mathew Brisbane was present only once, on the 7th of February 1695. Sir Andrew Balfour was dead. The correct names were—Dr. Trotter the President, Sir Thomas Burnet, Sir Robert Sibbald, Sir (then Dr.) Edward Eizat, and Drs. Cranstone, St. Clare, Halket, Lauder, Dicksone, Mitchell, Dundas, Blackader, Rule, Frier, and Forrest. Dr. Melville was at first a doubtful supporter of Pitcairn.

The supporters of the two sides, according to the Minutes.

In reference to the other causes which aggravated the bad feeling amongst the Fellows, the Preface especially notes 'the conduct and manner of Dr. Pitcairn and his friends'; and Pitcairn is described as 'a Physician of great and deserved celebrity, a man of eminent genius, great learning, and acuteness, but of a fearless and haughty disposition, with a strong tendency to sarcasm and satire. . . . With his powerful genius and extensive knowledge, he not only felt but never hesitated to manifest a large amount of scorn for many of his contemporaries, especially for those who happened to be inferior to him in learning, and were opposed to the mathematical doctrines of Physiology and

Dr. Pitcairn's conduct and manner.

Effects of.

Pathology.' His shafts of satirical criticism were also often directed against Sir Robert Sibbald, and 'all those who were adherents of Sir Robert were of course enemies more or less decided to Dr. Pitcairn, whose manners were far from conciliatory, and he generally succeeded in turning indifferent and neutral parties into positive enemies.'

7th November 1695, *Tarugo Unmasked* before the College.

At the meeting on 7th November, the pamphlet *Tarugo Unmasked* came before the College, and a Committee which consisted of Sir Thomas Burnet, Drs. Cranstone, Mitchell, Dundas, and Olyphant, with the President, was appointed to examine it.

14th November, report of Committee on it.

They reported, on the 14th, that several positions in the pamphlet were censurable. These were read in the presence of the College, put to the vote, and by plurality of votes were found to be censurable, and 'appoint the Author to be cited to appear before the College on the 22nd November to answer what is libelled against him.'

Author cited for 22nd November.

Meeting of College of 18th November.

On the 18th November a meeting was held. The sederunt consisted of twenty-one Fellows; and Stevenson and Pitcairn were present. Pitcairn attempted to stay these violent proceedings by presenting a Protestation against the President (Trotter) and the other Fellows of the College, in name of himself and other Members whose names are entered in this sederunt. 'They have remitted ye s[d] protestation ag[t] ye President and several Members of ye Societie to a Committee to consider it, and give in yr report to ye Colledge. The Committee are ye President (Trotter), Drs. Sibbald, Cranstone, S[t] Clair, Dicksone, and Mitchell,' etc.

Pitcairn's protest against the President, etc., remitted to a Committee.

22nd November, Dr. Hepburn served with libel as author of *Tarugo Unmasked*.

On the 22nd Dr. Hepburn was present, and acknowledged before the College 'y[t] he was the author of *Tarugo Unmasked*,' and he was ordained to be served with a libel to be answered on the following 6th December.

The Committee on Dr. Pitcairn's Protestation, reported it to be 'a calumnious, scandalous, false, and arrogant paper, refusing the authority of the President and Colledge, and contrair to the promissory engagement with ye reasons given in by the Committee, lying in ye President's hand, the Colledge unanimously approve of the same, yrfore suspend Dr. Pitcairn from voting in ye Colledge, or sitting in any meeting thereof, till he give satisfaction to ye Colledge.' At this sederunt fifteen Fellows voted, and one of the objects of Pitcairn's protest was to impugn the validity of Dr. Trotter and other Fellows, to prevent them voting at the ensuing annual Election; but this was prevented by the majority pronouncing on Pitcairn and some of his adherents a vote of suspension.

Report on Pitcairn's Protest approved of by College.

Pitcairn suspended.

Meantime, on 5th December 1695, the 'pleurality' representing the College met, and carried through the annual elections. Dr. Trotter was re-elected President. According to the 'Preface,' Pitcairn and his friends 'appeared to exercise their privilege of voting,' but 'one of the Bailies, and one or more of the Town Officers' being present, they were removed, and proceeding to the house of Sir Archibald Stevenson, elected him President; and this affair is afterwards (6th November 1699) designated as 'a riot in the Colledge.'

5th December 1695, plurality of College carried through the elections.

After several years' litigation, and spending a considerable sum of money to establish the rights of the College, it occurred to the majority that this state of matters should be brought to a termination. A vote of amnesty was passed on the 6th of November 1699, and the suspended Fellows were restored to their previous position.

Such is the statement in the 'Preface' condensed, but from my reading of the Minutes there are some slight variations. For instance, the meeting last named reads in the Minute Book, 'Sir Archibald Stevensone, and Masters William Eccles, John Robertson, John Smelholme, Andrew Melville, Doctors of Medicine, . . . as they have not been sensible of the goodness of the Colledge, but have from tyme to tyme slighted and

Variances of the author from foregoing Preface Statement.

abandoned the meetings of the Colledge doe hereby suspend during pleasure the said . . . as Members of the s[d] Colledge, and from sitting and voting in the s[d] Colledge upon any account whatsomever, and ordain the Colledge Officer to make intimation hereof to ilk ane of them.' It was not till 31st January 1700, that the suspension was removed.

Question of the treatment of fever not the chief cause of discord.

I cannot but conclude, from a careful perusal of the Minutes, something more is learned than that the chief element of discord was the general question of the treatment of fever. There were evidently questions and personalities existing amongst the Fellows. The upsetting by the majority of yearly Examinators, the scheme of Stevenson and Pitcairn, was undoubtedly resented by them and their party. The existing laws also formed a point of controversy, and a third matter was personal opposition to the President, Dr. Trotter; for it was resistance to the President's authority which led to charges of contumacy being laid against Dr. Olyphant the Treasurer, and the late President Sir Archibald Stevenson. Dr. Hepburn was suspended for his attack on Eizat, whilst Pitcairn's protest appears to have been directed against Dr. Trotter the President, and the election of Dr. Eizat. The following extracts from the Minutes support this view.

Opposition to President led to contumacy.

Dr. Hepburn suspended for attack on Dr. Eizat.
Dr. Pitcairn for his protest.

A meeting was held on 9th July 1695, Dr. Trotter the President, and Stevenson, Pitcairn, and five other Fellows were present. The subject of the meeting was to appoint Dr. Dicksone to meet the Chirurgeon Apothecaries to conclude all differences between the College and them, and adjourned 'till *the first Thursday of August next*.' (The italics are mine.) But that meeting was *not held*—why, is not stated. Does it not look as if Stevenson's opposition to the proposed change in the appointment of Examinators was beginning? For some reason there was no meeting till a month later, the 14th September, when 'eleven Fellows mett att ye President's lodging, being denyed ye keys of

Adjourned College meeting in August not held.

ye Colledge by Dr. Stevensone.' It was at this meeting that 'the same day it was carried by a pleurality of votes, y^t Dr. Edward Izat having made application to ye Colledge by his petitione should be licensed to practice Physick without any previous tryall, he having received his degree before ye erection of ye Colledge of Physitians, providing he satisfies ye ordinary dews.' And the same day is received Candidat and admitted Socius. His opinion of the views of Pitcairn had been previously expressed in the *Apollo Mathematicus*.

College locked out on 14th September, and met at Dr. Trotter's, the President's, lodging.

Two days later, on 16th September, a meeting of the College was again held. Dr. Blackader was licensed, received Candidat, and admitted Socius. The change in the Examinators was carried for the second time, and the question was put, whether or not 'ye Patent, Seales, and papers belonging to ye Colledge should be left in ye Colledge, or put in ye President's custody.' It was carried that they should be put in the President's custody. This was a question in which Dr. Stevenson was concerned, for they were locked up in the College of which he held the key, and ought before this to have been passed on to his successor when he resigned the Chair nine months before. At the next meeting, on 21st September, as the papers, seals, and books had not been delivered to the President Trotter, according to the order of the College, it was voted at this meeting that they be required legally from Dr. Stevenson and Dr. Olyphant the Treasurer.

Patent and Seals to be placed in President's custody.

To be required legally from Dr. Stevenson, and the Treasurer, Dr. Olyphant.

The College met again on 24th September, when it was unanimously carried that the Treasurer should be required by an instrument to be present to give receipts to the College for the Bonds he has in his own name. On 25th September the Treasurer, Dr. Olyphant, was present, and it was voted that 'he give a declaration under his hand what Bonds or Money or other effects belonging to the College he hath in his hands, and y^t he shall make y^m furthcoming for ye Colledge behove.' It is evident that the majority desired to act fairly in the Harveian spirit with

Committee appointed to consider the laws and papers.

Stevenson; for this Minute continues, 'the same day appoynt Drs. Stevenson, Sibbald, and Cranstone, or any two of them, with the President, to consider ye laws and papers, referring to ye laws; and ye papers to be delivered to ye President y^t q^{en} they meett, they maybe written over, and putt in order and Inventor made of y^m: and every Member y^t hath any papers, give them up to the President.' Does not it appear from these words that there was a dispute not only about the possession of the papers but also about the laws? and to clear this up fairly, Sir Archibald Stevenson, previously chiefly responsible, was nominated with others to be present at the deliberation. But he does not appear to have availed himself of the courteous attention paid to him by the College.

The College met for Examinations on the 30th September; and on 2nd October, having obtained possession of the books and papers, 'with ye two Seals belonging to the Colledge,' they were all delivered to the President 'by order of the Colledge.' Meetings for Examinations were held on October 4th, 7th, and 30th. On 1st November the meeting deliberated on Honorary and Ordinary Fellows, and on the number present to make a quorum, and on 4th November, ten is fixed as the number for a sederunt for law making and repealing. After these transactions indicative of a contumacious spirit on the part of Drs. Stevenson and Olyphant, the affairs of the College assumed another phase. On 7th November, 'It was represented to ye Colledge y^t y^r was a Pamphlet written by a Fellow of y^r Colledge without a licence from ye Colledge,' and the matter was held to be of such importance that the President appointed a Committee to examine the pamphlet and report. This was accordingly done; and on 14th November, the Committee report on the pamphlet written by a Fellow of the College, and entitled *Tarugo Unmasked.* Certain passages of it the College, by plurality of votes, found to be censurable, and appointed the author to be cited to appear

After these indications of contumacious spirit of Stevenson and Olyphant,

the question of authorship of *Tarugo Unmasked* arises.

Found to be censurable.

before them on the 22nd, to answer to what is libelled against him. At next meeting, on 18th November, Stevenson for the first time since 9th July, and also Pitcairn, were present. The sederunt consisted of twenty-one Fellows. The proceedings commenced by Sir Robert Sibbald giving a Discourse, and then the College considered the Protestation given in by Dr. Pitcairn in name of himself and other Members who were present, against the President and several Members of the Society. It was remitted to a Committee to consider and to report to the College.

Pitcairn's Protestation against the President and others remitted to a Committee.

On 22nd November, Dr. Hepburn appeared before the College, and acknowledged he was the author of *Tarugo Unmasked*, and the Committee report that Dr. Pitcairn's Protestation 'was a calumnious, scandalous, false, and arrogant paper refusing ye authority of ye President and Colledge,' and so on in the terms quoted at length at page 173. So that Dr. Pitcairn was suspended quite independently of the riot in the College; it was for his attempt to save his friend Dr. Hepburn from suffering for his indiscreet pamphlet. Those who signed the Protestation with him were not included in the suspension.

Dr. Hepburn acknowledges the authorship.

Pitcairn's Protest found to be calumnious, and he is suspended.

At the next meeting, on 3rd December 1695, 'ane advocatione was presented by Dr. Eccles for himself and several others,' which the President received and will answer; but Dr. Pitcairn, having been previously suspended, is found to be not comprehended in it; and 'so can have no benefit by it.' Dr. Olyphant, the Treasurer, is also called by the College to give the President what money he calls for, and that he get no money but by the President's orders; and he is appointed to appear the next day before the College in the ordinary place of meeting, and to give in his accounts, and also meantime to give the President forty dollars, for defraying the necessary affairs of the College. The same day the libel against Dr. Hepburn was found censurable. 'The Colledge y[r] upon did remove him as *ipso facto* suspended

Dr. Eccles presents 'ane advocatione' for self and others.

Pitcairn not comprehended in it.

Dr. Hepburn found censurable and suspended.

from sitting or voting, and so is to continue untill he satisfy ye Colledge.'

Dr. Olyphant suspended for contumacy.

On 4th December, Dr. Olyphant, the Treasurer, was called for three times, and did not appear, nor send excuse. He was therefore suspended for his contumacy, and 'no one is to have liberty to vote until they own the authority of the President.' All this clearly shows that *the spirit of discourtesy to the President of the College largely existed, and was the cause of more than one Fellow being suspended.*

The 5th of December was the election day. Dr. Trotter was re-elected President, and Dr. Frier was Treasurer in place of Dr. Olyphant.

Pitcairn's anonymous criticism of Sibbald.

To add to the personal feeling which these extracts show was playing so important a part in disturbing the harmony of the College, and apart from the controversy on the treatment of fever, Pitcairn in the following year, 1696, published anonymously a 'most unreasonably severe' criticism of Sibbald's *Prodromus Historiae Naturalis Scotiae.* This, it is to be presumed, was in retaliation for Sibbald's previously having ridiculed Pitcairn's application of Geometry to Physic. And, as I have said, it was not until after several years' litigation and the expenditure of a considerable sum of money to establish the rights of the College, that it occurred to the majority that this unseemly state of discord should be brought to a termination. A vote of amnesty was passed, but it was not until 1704, Dr. Dundas being President, that Pitcairn and those supporting him were reinstated in the College. And before leaving this record of these discreditable proceedings, I desire to direct your attention to the terms in which the majority strove to restore their erring and contumacious brethren, for they are in harmony with Harvey's spirit of love and good-will. The attempt at reconciliation was made at a meeting held on 31st January 1700. In the Library Catalogue Preface it is said to have been on 6th November 1699, but the Minute of

Vote of amnesty, but Pitcairn and his supporters not reinstated in College till 1704.

that day's proceedings I have already given at page 173. It will be noted that Pitcairn and Olyphant are excempted from this suspension. They had not taken part in 'the Ryot,' being both already suspended, the first for his scandalous protestation, the other for his contumacy as Treasurer.

First attempt at reconcilia-tion, January 1700.

Dr. Matthew St. Clair was now President, and on 29th November 1699, the Treasurer Dr. Forrest is authorised to pay the expenses of the pleas and defences out of the College funds. But a happier frame of mind was forming, the old kindly feelings towards each other were once more asserting themselves, and the spirit of brotherly love was returning. On 31st January 1700, the Harveian spirit comes to the surface, and the Minute states—Dr. St. Clair being President, and Drs. Trotter, Eizat, Mitchell, Lauder, Frier, Dundas, Forrest, and Jardyne being present,—'The which day the Colledge of Physitians taking into consideration how desyrable it is for the Members of the Societie to live in peace and unitie, and being willing to goe all the lenth that may be, to bring in their Members that have so long absented themselves from the Colledge, and for which and several other reasons they were suspended, firstly. . . . Therefore the Colledge ordains the several acts of suspensione previously pronounced against Sir Archibald Stevensone, Messrs. Archibald Pitcairn, William Eccles, John Robertson, Charles Olyphant, Andrew Melville, and John Smelholme, Doctors of Medicine, and Members of the said Colledge, to be taken off, and by these presents take off the same, provyded always the said persons compear, and acknowledge the Authoritie of the said Colledge att any Meeting yroff Betwixt and the first day of May next to come, and the Colledge declairs that y^r^on, these, the said persones, shall have the freedom to sitt and vote and elect in the said Colledge, as freely as any other Member thereof.' Signed, 'Mathew St. Claire, President.' But they would not then come in, and in December 1702, the Court proceedings are still going on, for the Minute says, 'The Colledge

1699, 29th November, Dr. Matthew St. Clair, President.

Conciliatory Minute of 31st January 1700.

allows the President to consult more advocates, in the action —in Defence of the Reduction and Declarator by Dr. Stevensone against the Colledge.'

1703, 7th January, Dr. Dundas, President. Another attempt at reconciliation made.

Still the state of unseemly enmity continued, and the College, under the Presidency of Dr. Dundas, on 7th January 1703, once more tried to be conciliatory as this Minute bears testimony to— 'The which day the Colledge of Physitians considering how desyrable a thing it is for the Members thereof to leave (live) in peace and unity, and being sensible of the prejudice the Society has sustained by the late unhappy divisions, notwithstanding of the repeated offences committed against the said Colledge by the suspended Members after named, whereby the Colledge has been put to a vaste charge to assert its own priviledges, yet to show to the world the Colledge's readiness to forgive injuries, and that nothing may be wanting on their part to restore the peace of the Societie, and in hopes the said suspended members by there after deportment will be ready upon all occasions to show their selves more sensible of the obligationes they lye under, from the Promissory Engadgement signed by all of them, Thairfore the Colledge in consideratione of the premises Doe hereby repeall the former acts of Suspensione made against Sir Archibald Stevensone, Masters Archibald Pittcairne, John Robertsone, William Eccles, Charles Olyphant, John Smelholme, and Andrew Melvill, Doctors of Medicine and Members of the said Colledge; and the Colledge declaires that the saide persones shall have the same freedome to sitt, vote, and elect, in the said Colledge as any other Member there of has, and ordained this act to be intimat to the afore named persones. Signed. ALEX[R.] DUNDAS, P.C.R.M.'

1703, Election day.

The effect of this Rescinding of Suspension did not show itself until the following December. The Election of 1703 was on the 2nd of that month. The Minute Book of the College has either been very imperfectly kept, or the meetings of the College greatly interfered with, for during this year 1703, with the exception of a meeting held on 24th November, no other is reported from January, till the Election one held on 2nd December. Drs. Eccles, Olyphant, and Smelholm were present. Drs. Eccles and Smelholm were elected Councillors. The former was also elected Censor and the latter Treasurer.

2nd December 1703, Eccles, Olyphant, and Smelholm returned.

On 4th January 1704, an Act of Oblivion to delete Minutes having reference to these quarrels was read for the first time by the President, and carried unanimously. At this meeting, Eccles, Olyphant, Robertson, and Smelholm were present.

4th January 1704, Act of Oblivion passed. Robertson returned.

The Minute of 12th January still further testifies to the desire for peace, and the Act was confirmed.

The absence of Dr. Hepburn's name from the Minutes of 31st January 1700 and 7th January 1703 is very noticeable. Could his premature death have taken place before the first-mentioned date?

Dr. Hepburn not mentioned in the Repeall Minutes.

The first reunion of the Royal College took place on 30th November 1704. It was on St. Andrew's Day, twenty-four Fellows assembled. Amongst them after a long absence were Sir Archibald Stevenson and Dr. Pitcairn. Sir Robert Sibbald and Drs. Eccles, Olyphant, Smelholm, and Robertson, were also present. The only suspended Fellows absent were Melville and Hepburn. The latter's name never appears in the Minutes after he was suspended, 3rd December 1695, and Monteith does not give the date of his death. The elections were proceeded with. Dr. Halket was elected President, Stevenson and Eccles Councillors, as well as Sibbald. Dr. Eccles was also one of the Censors, and Smelholm Treasurer; but Pitcairn is appointed to no office.

30th November 1704, the reunion.

Stevenson and Pitcairn returned.

At the meeting of 1st December Dr. Melville was present, and peace and unity were restored, but only to be soon again disturbed by Pitcairn.

1st December, Dr. Melville returned.

On 12th January 1705, the monthly Discourses were ordered to

1705, 12th January, discourses resumed.

be resumed. On 12th March 1706, it came to Dr. Pitcairn's turn to have his ready. He had never given one before the College, and on this day the President, Dr. Halket, had delivered his, upon the treatment of *Volvulus*; and 'Dr. Pitcairne was desyred to have his Discourse ready as soon as he can conveniently.' This was the last occasion upon which Dr. Pitcairn's name appears in the Sederunt Roll. The request for a Discourse was as effectual in silencing him as if he had been again suspended, and although doubtless quite capable of giving a discourse, his time for doing it 'conveniently' never occurred; and although repeatedly fined for absence from the quarterly meetings, he seems to have died without paying them, *and without giving an Address.* It was mentioned that he was elected to the Fellowship of the College of Surgeons of Edinburgh, on 16th October 1701. After the contemptuous way in which he mentions in his letter to Dr. Gray of London, the Fellows of that College, when he returned from Leyden, and was endeavouring to promote the study of Anatomy, it is rather remarkable that they so graciously received him. I have already under the Medical Institutions of Scotland referred to what Chambers in his *Domestic Annals of Scotland* stated as to his action regarding the teaching of Anatomy in 1694. Pitcairn at that time was in full Fellowship with the Royal College, and did not join the College of Surgeons till 1701, when he had been suspended for about six years. The College of Physicians by its Charter was unable to teach, but there was nothing to prevent one of its Fellows taking part therein. One of the features of the application for a Charter for the College was the desire to extend the knowledge of Anatomy, and in this scheme (see *ante*, p. 26) for which Pitcairn agitated, it will be seen that he was only endeavouring to carry out the desire of the originators of the College of Physicians, and therefore in founding the Edinburgh Medical School the College through him participated. There can be no doubt that this forward action of Pitcairn

Pitcairn desired to give discourse when convenient. This is the last occasion his name appears in the Sederunt.

He continues to be fined for absence.

Elected Fellow of College of Surgeons, 16th October 1701,

when he had been suspended about six years.

His connection with the improvement in teaching Anatomy.

was the stimulus that led the College of Surgeons to promote the study of Anatomy, in a way which previously it had not been doing, by the systematic teaching by a recognised or authorised Teacher or Lecturer, with a better supply of subjects than had ever before been obtained from the hands of the Executioner.

As has been said, the College of Physicians has the merit of one of their number having given the impulse to the study of Anatomy in Edinburgh, and thereby having very materially contributed to the origin of the Medical School here, with the result with which you are all so well acquainted.

Through him College of Physicians contributed to origin of Medical School.

I cannot but feel that, in spite of his turbulent behaviour, one would have had a greater respect for Dr. Archibald Pitcairn if he had acted differently, and made a better and more manly defence, when he was politically charged in consequence of one of his letters to Dr. R. Gray in London falling into the hands of the Scottish Secretary. Dr. Pitcairn was apprehended and lodged in the Tolbooth. To quote again from Chambers (*Domestic Annals*, vol. iii. p. 223): 'On the 25th of January 1700, Pitcairn was brought before the (Privy) Council on a charge of contravening various statutes against *Leasing Making*, that is venting and circulating reproaches or false reports against the Government. He was accused of having, on a certain day in December, written a letter to Dr. Gray in reference to an address which was in course of signature regarding the meeting of Parliament.' The remarks he made I need not give, but the charge was, that as he had 'foolishly and wickedly meddled in the affairs of his Majesty and his Estate, he ought to be severely punished in his person and goods to the terror of others to do the like in time coming.' 'Dr. Pitcairn knowing well the kind of men he had to deal with, made no attempt at defence; neither did he utter any complaint as to the violation of his private correspondence. He pleaded *that he had written in his cups*, with no evil design against the Government, and threw himself entirely on the mercy of the Council.

His answer to the charge of Leasing Making.

His submission was accepted, and he got off with a reprimand from the Lord Chancellor, after giving bond with his friend Sir Archibald Stevenson under two hundred Pounds sterling, to live peacefully under the Government, and consult and contrive nothing against it.' This story unfortunately gives colour to the charges of his opponents as to his intemperate habits—*for he condemns himself*; and the prosecution took place whilst he and the Royal College were at variance for his contumacious behaviour to it, and when he was suspended for his scandalous protestation. The view taken of his prosecution by the Government and his miserable defence could not have been regarded very seriously by the 'profession' in Edinburgh, for he was received into the College of Surgeons in the following year.

His marriage with Miss Elizabeth Stevenson.

By his marriage with Miss Elizabeth Stevenson, Dr. Archibald Pitcairn had one son and four daughters. A strong adherent himself to the Jacobite cause, it was only natural that his son supported the cause of the Chevalier in 1715. He had the misfortune to fall into the Royalists' hands; and being taken prisoner, was lodged in the Tower of London, from which Dr. R. Mead of London, a former pupil of his father at Leyden, by his influence, obtained his release and pardon. His argument in pleading with Sir Robert Walpole for young Pitcairn's life was irresistible, and at the same time a high compliment to the talent and teaching capability of Dr. Archibald Pitcairn. 'If I have been able to save your or any other man's life, I owe the power to this young man's father,' were the words used by Mead.

The career of his son.

Saved by Dr. Mead.

Pitcairn's Jacobite tendencies.

Of the Jacobite tendencies of Pitcairn, there could be no more decided indication than the dedication of his writings collected shortly before his death. It was, 'To God and his Prince, this work is humbly dedicated by Archibald Pitcairne, June 20th, 1713.' The date was the anniversary of the birthday of the Chevalier St. George.

DR. ARCHIBALD PITCAIRN'S MONUMENT, AND GRAVE OF SIR ARCHIBALD STEVENSONE.

His second daughter Janet, eighteen years after her father's deccase, became, by her marriage, the Countess of Kellie in 1731, on 12th October, according to Dr. John Gairdiner. She had three sons and three daughters. Two of her sons were the sixth and seventh Earls of Kellie. They all three died unmarried. Janet Pitcairn, Countess of Kellie, survived her husband for many years, and died 7th June 1776.

His daughter Janet married Earl of Kellie.

Dr. Archibald Pitcairn died on 23rd October 1713, aged sixty-one years. In the Leyden *Album* the date is 20th October, and on his Tombstone it is the 26th, but according to the *Greyfriars' Records* that was the day of his burial. He was buried near Sir Archibald Stevenson in the Greyfriars Churchyard, in the third division of tombs, on the west side of the stone walk, and close to the walk at the lower part of the grounds on the north side of the churchyard. In the course of the year 1800, Dr. Andrew Duncan senior, the Secretary, issued, on behalf of the Æsculapian Society of Edinburgh, a circular to the effect that 'Pitcairn's tombstone lies flat upon the ground and is now almost covered with earth,' and that the Club had resolved to get it repaired by subscriptions amongst the members of the Royal Colleges of Physicians and Surgeons, and to make addition to the inscription which, according to the report of the proceedings, was written by the learned Mr. Thomas Ruddiman, who had been in his early life indebted to the protection and patronage of Pitcairn.

His death.

Restoration of his tomb by Æsculapians.

Dr. Andrew Duncan also records that 'a meeting of the subscribers is to be held at the tombstone on Thursday, 25th December 1800, on business of very great importance; and that immediately after the meeting an adjournment shall take place to the Grapine *alias* Grape-Wine Office, at Keggie's under the Pillars, in the entrance to the Parliament Square, where those who attend will have an opportunity of partaking of a *Jeroboam* left by Dr. Pitcairn, with directions that it should be opened at

Proceedings on the occasion.

the Restoration.' *He* intended it for the Restoration of the House of Stewart; but, on the 148th anniversary of his birth, it was consumed to his memory on the restoration of his monumental tomb. But it was too good liquor evidently to be wasted by being poured out as a libation. There were in all forty-nine medical subscribers, Fellows of the Æsculapian Society, the Colleges of Physicians and Surgeons, and other medical men. The chief promoter of this restoration was Dr. Andrew Duncan senior, a Fellow and President of the Royal College of Physicians of Edinburgh, and founder of the Royal Dispensary, the Royal Asylum, the Æsculapian, this Harveian, and other Societies, and Professor of the Institutes of Medicine in the University. Lady Ann Erskine, Pitcairn's granddaughter, was at the time living, and had graciously given her consent to the repairs being conducted by the gentlemen who had subscribed, as 'She would neither rob her grandfather of the singular mark of respect which was intended to be paid to his memory, nor deprive the Medical Practitioners of Edinburgh of the pleasure which she was convinced they would derive from paying the tribute of gratitude to departed worth.'

His grand-daughter, Lady Ann Erskine.

Inscription on tomb.

The inscription on the repaired or restored tombstone, a flat slab, supported on pedestals, is (*Greyfriars' Epitaphs and Monumental Inscriptions*, by James Brown), as follows:—

'Here lyes Doctor Archibald Pitcairn, who died 26th day of October 1713, aged 61; also Elizabeth Pitcairn, his daughter, who died the 18th day of March 1718; Elizabeth Stevenson, his widow, died 5th October 1734; Margaret Pitcairn, his daughter, died August 1777; Janet Pitcairn, Countess of Kellie, his daughter, died 7th June 1776; Lady Ann Erskine, his last surviving grandchild, one of the best of women, died 18th March 1803.

'Ecce mathematicum, vatem, medicumque, sophumque,
Pitcairnum magnum hæc urnula parva tenet.
Ergo, vale, lux Scotigenum, princepsque medentium.
Musarum columen deliciæque, vale.

[Behold, this little urn contains the great Pitcairn, a Mathematician, Poet, Physician, and Sage. Farewell then light of Scotland, and Prince of Physicians! O Pillar and darling of the Muses, farewell.]

'Sodalitas Edinburgena filiorum Æsculapii, anno 1773 instituta, hoc monumentum reficiendum curabat, Prid. Non. Junii 1800: præside Alex. Wood, col. reg. chir. dec. emer. Andrea Duncan, M.D. et P. a Secretis.'

[The Edinburgh Æsculapian Club, instituted in 1773, caused this monument to be restored on the 12th June 1800, etc.]

Note of his daughter in 1784.

When Dr. Charles Webster delivered the Harveian Oration upon Dr. Archibald Pitcairn, in 1781, his fourth daughter was then alive. She it was of whom Chambers (in his *Traditions of Edinburgh*, new edition, p. 364) tells the story of the Edinburgh Theatre being in the Tennis Court, Canongate. When Mrs. Siddons came to Edinburgh in 1784, Mr. Alexander Campbell, author of the *History of Scottish Poetry*, asked Miss Pitcairn, daughter of Dr. Pitcairn, to accompany him to one of the representations. The old lady refused, saying with coquettish vivacity, 'Laddie, wad ye hae an auld lass like me to be running after the playactors, me that hasna been at a theatre since I gaed wi' papa to the Canongate in the year ten.'

Fate of his son.

When his son, through Dr. Mead's intercession with Sir Robert Walpole, afterwards Earl of Orford, was pardoned after the 1715 rising, he entered the service of the States of Holland, and soon after died.

Death of Lady Ann Erskine.

By the death of his granddaughter, Lady Ann Erskine, in 1803, the descendants of Dr. Archibald Pitcairn of that ilk and Elizabeth Stevenson, the daughter of the first President of the Royal College, came to an end. It is a pleasing privilege to perpetuate this memorial of Lady Ann, his last descendant, that 'she was one of the best of women.'

Dr. George Hepburn, and connection with the Royal College.

Dr. George Hepburn.—On account of the important part Dr. George Hepburn took in the disturbances of the harmony of the College, I have thought it of sufficient interest to add a reference to him, although he was not one of The Early Days' Fellows, but was an elected member of the Royal College. Soon after his admission he asserted himself, though not as a defender of Pitcairn, to be an opponent of Dr. Edward Izatt, the author of *Apollo Mathematicus*. It may be recalled that, on 7th November 1695, the pamphlet *Tarugo Unmasked* came before the College for consideration. The result was, that a Committee was appointed to examine it and report. On the 14th, they reported that several positions in it were censurable, and after being read before the College, they were found to be censurable by plurality of votes, and the author was appointed to appear before the College on the 22nd to answer the libel against him. Pitcairn, on the 18th, stepped into the breach with his protestation against the President, but only with the result that he was himself suspended. On the 22nd Dr. Hepburn was present, and made no effort to prevaricate, but openly and frankly acknowledged that he was the author of the objectionable pamphlet; and the College ordained that he is to be served with a libel, to be answered on the 6th December following, and meantime he is suspended. This closed his appearances in the meetings of the Royal College.

The name of Dr. George Hepburn first appears in the Minutes of the Sederunt of Election Meeting, 6th December 1694, and also in the records of 17th January and 7th February 1695, and not again till 22nd November, when he appears to honestly acknowledge his authorship, is suspended, and his name never thereafter appears. He had as regards the College a brief career, but it lacked discretion. His name is No. 36 on the official Roll of Fellows. He was therefore the fifteenth new Fellow to join, and is stated to have been licensed on

November 15th, 1694, and admitted Fellow on the same day. At what University he obtained his degree has not been ascertained.

The only further particulars regarding Dr. George Hepburn are as follows. In Monteith's *Theater of Mortality* (page 143), in the second part, 'a further collection,' etc., I find that in the churchyard at Haddington there is a monument apparently erected to this Fellow of the College. The inscription is in Latin :— Monument to him in Haddington Churchyard.

'George Hepburn of Monkrig, his Monument. D. Georgii Hepburnii, a *Monachagrio*, Ingenio, Doctrina et Morum elegantia eximii viri vero imprimis celeberrimi, tam in vita quam in morte, omnibus bonis carissimi desideratissimiq: Tumulus,' etc. Then follow six Latin verses, Englished thus by Monteith—'The Tomb of Mr. George Hepburn of Monkrig, a Man notable for his Wit, Learning, and Elegance of Manners, but chiefly a most famous Physician, most dear and most beloved by all good persons, as well in his Life, as at his Death.

'Spread Roses, Passenger: below this Stone
Lies Doctor Hepburn, second unto none!
The Fates envy'd his skill, snatched him away,
Long ere the Ev'ning came of his short day.
Sad case of Mortals! when so small a time
Cuts down rare gifts and vertues, ere the Prime.'

No dates are given, but as the second part of the *Theater* was printed in Edinburgh by the heirs of Andrew Anderson in 1713, he must have died some time previous to that year. At page 181 I suggested from the absence of his name from the Minutes of 31st January 1700, that it occurred before that date. He joined the College during the lost Minutes' period. From the foregoing inscription he must have died prematurely, and have been a man of distinguished ability and worth ; but, viewed from the College record, he must be pronounced to have been a youth possessed of zeal and courageous honesty, but sadly wanting in discretion.

THE FOUR FIRST KNIGHTS

SIR ARCHIBALD STEVENSONE

SIR ANDREW BALFOUR

SIR THOMAS BURNET

SIR ROBERT SIBBALD OF KIPPS

The four first Knights.

Of all the Fellows I have named Drs. Archibald Stevensone, Thomas Burnet, Andrew Balfour, Robert Sibbald, and Archibald Pitcairne were the most important in furthering the greatness of The Early College; and, with the exception of the last, they were the four first Knights of the College.

SIR ARCHIBALD STEVENSONE, M.D.

When I was admitted to the Fellowship of the Royal College in 1861, I could learn no particulars regarding the first President. Although he repeatedly occupied that position, and from so doing conveyed the impression that he loved power and desired to rule, he had done nothing outside the College to perpetuate his name. After much searching I have been able to trace to him only two literary efforts. They were the inscription in Latin on his father's tomb, erected by himself and sister, the only members of the family alive at the time of its erection, and the Discourse I have already mentioned which he gave as the Introductory one to those delivered at the College meetings, upon *Polypus of the Heart*, but which, although handed to the Secretary for preservation, was never published.

Sir Archibald Stevensone, born about end of 1629, died 16th February 1710.

After many unsuccessful inquiries, I accidentally got a clue one day at the Lyon Office, when making search regarding Sir Robert Sibbald. Of the latter I at that time got no trace, but on the page where I looked for 'Sibbald' I observed the name of 'Archibald Stevensone.' His arms had been registered in 1674, before he was knighted, and before the College originated. He must therefore even then have been a man of aspirations and of promise. According to '*An Ordinary of Arms contained in the Public Register of all Arms and Bearings in Scotland*, by James Balfour Paul, King of Arms, Edinburgh 1893,' they are 'Arg. a chevron between three fleurs de lys az., on a chief of the second three mullets of the first.—Archibald Stevensone, M.D' Dr. Archibald Stevensone must have been born about the end of the year 1629, or beginning of 1630, judging from the date of the Registration of Baptism which was solemnised on

Tracing his history at Lyon Office.

His arms registered in 1674.

Description of arms.

Baptized 21st March 1630. Born and died in Edinburgh.

21st March 1630. He was born in Edinburgh, and lived and died therein. The date of his death was 16th February 1710.

It may interest you to know how I traced this out. Two of the early Apothecaries of the College Dispensary were of the name of 'Masterton.' In the *Miscellany* of the Scottish History Society, vol. i. 1893, are 'The Masterton Papers,' and on page 483 are the words, '1710 old Doctor Steinson dyed February ye 9th.' I followed up the hint, and as the 'Greyfriars'' was at that period the burial-place of the city, I obtained permission from the City Chamberlain, Robert Adam, Esq., to inspect the 'Records of Interments in Greyfriars' Churchyard,' and with the kindly assistance of Mr. Ferguson, the Recorder, looked over the books, with the result that I found the following entry, and that Masterton's date was wrong by a week. 'Sir Archibald Steinvenson, Doctor of Medicine, dyed 16, aged 81 years, lyes three d. pac. [double paces] the east Mortons Stone—hearse a turf,' 'was buried on the 18th February 1710.' He lies therefore quite near the grave of his son-in-law, Dr. Archibald Pitcairn.

Death noticed in 'Masterton Papers.'

Greyfriars' Records of Interments.

Place of his burial.

Who was he?

Who was Sir Archibald 'Steinvenson,' otherwise Stevensone, Steinson or Stevenson? The Archibaldus Stephanides of the Leyden *Album*.

Family history.

To obtain that information gave much trouble, but having found his arms registered at the Lyon Office, and learned that he was a son of the manse, the Rev. Hew Scott's *Fasti Ecclesiae Scoticanae*, and Crawford's *History of the University of Edinburgh*, enabled me to trace his parentage. At the Lyon Office, Sir J. W. Mitchell, the Lyon Clerk, further informed me that Colonel the Honourable Robert E. Boyle, who was interested in tracing the collateral family history, could give me particulars regarding him. Colonel Boyle most courteously favoured me with the perusal of the Scheme of family history he had been able to draw out, and from this, with the account of his father given in the *Fasti*, I have been able to find out a little about Dr. Stevenson's family.

Scott's *Fasti*.

Sir J. W. Mitchell.

Colonel the Hon. R. E. Boyle.

Scheme of family history.

Whilst from '*The History of the University of Edinburgh from 1580 to 1646*, by Thomas Crawford, A.M., Professor of Philosophy and Mathematics in the College of Edinburgh in 1646,' the University record of his father may be learned.

Crawford's *History of the University of Edinburgh.*

Sir Archibald was the fifth son of the Reverend Andro Stevinson (who was born on 29th October 1588), 'ane of the Regentis of Kyng James his Colledge,' and who was admitted Burgess and Gild brother of the Burgh of Edinburgh, 10th November 1624, as eldest son to 'Umquhill Andro Stevinsonn, Merchant.' According to Scott he became minister of Dunbar, 19th December 1639, and according to R. Monteith's *Theater of Mortality* died on 13th December 1664, and was buried at Dunbar. The inscription on his tomb at the old church of Dunbar, quoted by Monteith in *An Theater of Mortality*, is the only printed literary production of his son, Sir Archibald, I have been able to learn of; and the original has long been lost or destroyed, for the result of my inquiry at Dunbar is, that no trace of the original monumental stone can now be found. This etching of old Dunbar Church shows its position on the wall to the east of the side door of the church. It was erected by Sir Archibald and his sister Agnes, Mrs. Robertson, the only surviving members of the family.

Was the fifth son of Rev. Andro Stevinson, Regent in Philosophy and Humanity.

Buried at Dunbar. Inscription tomb by Dr. Archibald.

The Rev. Andro was married first to Agnes Cathkin, daughter of James Cathkin, bookseller of Edinburgh, and afterwards to Bethia Cathkin, relict of Cuthbert Miller, Writer to the Signet.

Rev. Andro's wives.

With the exception of Sir Archibald, and Agnes, who married the Rev. David Robertson, at one time assistant to her father at Dunbar, and afterwards appointed minister of Lennell (now Coldstream), the rest of his children, four sons and two daughters, predeceased their father, and they all seem to have died unmarried. They all were the children of Agnes Cathkin, his first wife.

From Crawford's *History*, to illustrate the career and kind of man the father of Sir Archibald was, I make the following extracts.

Rev. Andro's University History. Succeeds Mr. Andrew Young.

Page 73: '1611. The beginning of this year appeared dismal to the Maisters of the Colledge, for Mr. Andrew Young, for many months before, had been afflicted with an lingering and scarcely known disease, and so weakened thereby, that he was forced to entrust the attendance of his scholars to Mr. Andrew Stevenson, who had been laureat under his charge at Lambmas 1609.' (He would then be in his twenty-first year.) 'In the end of the year 1610 the disease seeming to be desparate, programs were set forth, to invite such as aimed at the profession of Philosophy, to give their names for tryal. At the appointed day, appeared three: Mr. Andrew Stevenson, spoken of before (son to Andrew Stevenson, an honest Burges, of an Senatorian family), Mr. Robert Burnet, son to —— Burnet of Barns, in Tweddale, both laureat at Lambmas 1609; and Mr. James Ker, son to the Laird of Linton, Laureat *anno* 1610. The youngnes of their faces at first procured some delay, and a new program, in expectation of more competitors, but none other appearing (except some who did not please the Council and Judges), the disputation and other tryals went on. Mr. Andrew Stevenson was most approven by the Judges, and elected by the Council, with *proviso* that if Mr. Andrew Young should recover, he should recede, and suffer him to enter again to his charge.'

And afterwards Mr. Blase Colt, Professor of Humanity.

Page 74.—'Scarcely was Mr. Andrew Stevenson entered the Chair, when another fell to vake by the untimely death of Mr. Blase Colt, Professor of Humanity, a young man of rich endowments in that Facultie, and of a very debonaire inclination.' Again at page 75, the year 1611 is continued: 'In the vacance following (27th July 1611), Mr. Andrew Young recovering of his long illness, was reponed to his former charge of his own Class, Mr. Andrew Stevenson returning to his private studies for a time. In the end of November, Mr. Olivar Colt demitted his Regency, being called to the Ministry at Holyrood House, whence he was transplanted shortly thereafter to the Kirk of Foulden in the

Mers, where he died . . . with much commendation.' 'Programs being sent abroad to invite young men to tryal, compeared competitors; Mr. Robert Burnet, named before; Mr. Galbreath, son to Valentine Galbreath, burges of the city,' and both being equally favoured, 'the matter being referred to the determination of an lot,' Mr. Robert Burnet was preferred.

As Mr. Andrew Stevenson did not compete, it is probable that he had found another Regency. It may have been as successor to Mr. Blase Colt, Professor of Humanity. In 1617, King James Sixt visited Scotland, and on the 29th day of July, he honoured the College by having a 'publick disputation in Philosophy by the maisters' before him, in the Royal Chapel at Stirling. As Stevenson is not named as taking part, he was not then one of the Regents in Philosophy. This is confirmed by a reference to him in 1623 when he is in his thirty-fifth year. In July of that year, there being no Principal, 'Mr. Andrew Young, Eldest Regent, and Professor of Mathematicks,' discharged the duty of graduating the Maisters of Arts; and at page 95, we are told 'this was his last act, and immediately thereafter he sickened and shortly deceased.' At page 96, the position of Mr. Stevenson is declared: 'Mr. Andrew Stevenson, Professor of Humanity, who had been elected his (Young's) successor in first illness, 1611, after twelve years' space was the second time substitute in his room. There were thereby two charges vakaing in the Colledge; the Primariat by removal of Mr. Robert Boyd, and the Professor of Humanity by Mr. Andrew Stevenson ascending to Mr. Young's charge.' He was succeeded by Mr. Samuel Rutherford.

Stevenson not mentioned in Public Disputation in Philosophy before King James, 1617.

On death of Mr. Andrew Young, again succeeds him in Philosophy.

We now approach the resignation of Mr. Andrew's Professorial position; but before he resigned, there is the following indication of the kind of man he was, and of the force of character transmitted to his son, Sir Archibald. Under the year 1635, at page 126, Crawford says: 'The Prelats and Ministers of their way, after many years labour, at length, this year prevailed so far with the

In 1635 protests against the Masters of the College laying the Covenant aside.

Maisters of the Colledge (only Mr. Andrew Stevenson protesting to the contrary), that the Short Confession of Faith, called the Covenant (which purposely had been drawn up and sworn in the year 1581, to close the door against the re-entry, as well of Episcopacie as Popisme, and all the branches of both), should be laid aside, and instead there of the candidats, yearly, should subscrive ane short oath against Papistrie. But the Lord shortly overturned their power.' And at page 137, in the year 1639: 'The same month (December) also Mr. Andrew Stevenson being called to the Ministry of the Gospel at Dunbar,' Mr. Duncan Forester was elected his successor.

December 1639, called to be minister at Dunbar.

Mr. Andrew Stevenson ceased to be connected with the University when Archibald was in his tenth year. Continuing the Rev. Mr. Andro's history, we learn from Mr. James Miller's *History of Dunbar*, published in 1830 at Dunbar, that 'Mr. Andrew Stevenson appears to have succeeded the Rev. Mr. William Maxwell; on the authority of his Epitaph which is printed in Monteith's *Theater of Mortality*, he was for thirty years a most famous Professor of Philology and Philosophy in the College of Edinburgh, and thereafter for the space of twenty-five years most faithful Minister at the Church at Dunbar.'

Miller's *History of Dunbar*.

The monumental tablet, according to Miller, was placed in the wall of the old church, 'on the right of the door leading into a roofed aisle, on the south-east side of the Collegiate Church.'

Monumental tablet to the Rev. Andro Stevenson on old church wall.

The following is the epitaph, and as translated by Monteith:—

'Ἐγείρεται Πνευματικόν.

Sacris hic reconditis Exuviis clarissimi & charissimi Patris sui, Magistri *Andreæ Stephanide*, primum per Annos 30, in Academia *Edinensi*, Philologiae & Philosophiae Professoris celeberrimi; Annos dein 25. Ecclesiae *Barodunensis* Pastoris fidelissimi (cui micare incepit Diluculum nostrum breve *Octob.* 29, 1588, Lux vero meridiana æterna affulgere *Decemb.* 13, 1664). *Archibaldus Stephanides*,

DUNBAR COLLEGIATE CHURCH. *South-East View.*

Medicinae Doctor, Liberorum octo (quorum M. *Thomas*, *Jacobus*, *Joneta*, a Pedibus Patris requiescunt) solus cum Sorore *Agnesia* superstes, Cippum hunc qualencunque L.L.M.D.C.Q.

The epitaph by Dr. Archibald Stevensone.

'Ecce satus Στεφανω situs hic; qui Lustra peregit
Undena, officiis verna Corona suis;
Spineta hic tetrici perruperat aspra *Lycaei*
Junior; Ast Vegetum Suada suprema senem
Extulit. Æternam adspiras quicunque Coronam,
Vita hujus Vitae Norma sit apta tuæ.'

'To the Sacred Dust, here reposed, of his most famous and most dear Father, Mr. Andrew Stevenson, first for thirty Years a most famous Professor of Philology and Philosophy in the College of Edinburgh; thereafter, for the Space of twenty-five Years, most faithful Minister at the Church of Dunbar (to whom the short dawning of a Natural Life began to appear, or he was born, October 29, 1588, and the Noonday of Eternal Light began to shine, or who died, December 13, 1664). Mr. Archibald Stevenson, Doctor of Medicine, of the Defunct's Eight Children (where of Mr. Thomas, James, and Jonet, rest here at their Father's Feet) only surviving with his Sister Agnes, drenched in Tears, have dedicate, and consecrate, this homely Tomb.

'Here Mr. Stevenson lies, of high renown;
To learning a great Ornament and Crown;
Full five and fifty years, he was in charge,
And wisely did all offices discharge;
In Youth, the School difficulties he broke,
And, in his fresh old age, himself betook
To Divine Eloquence; which did extoll
His reputation, and enrich his soul.
Who seeks a Crown of Life, let this man be,
For his good life, a pattern unto thee.'

Such was the father of the first President of the College of Physicians, and such the superlative esteem in which he was held by his only surviving son and daughter. His mother, too, came of a firm and resolute (probably the Government of the day would have said an obstinate and contumacious) stock. In illustration I may give this extract. In the *Domestic Annals of Scotland*, by

Dr. Archibald Stevenson's mother.

Robert Chambers, 1858, the following passage occurs under the date 'March 30th, 1620':—'While the struggle was going on between the Episcopalian and the Presbyterian principles, there was a small group of Edinburgh citizens, including the booksellers *Cathkin and Lawson*, who took a lead in opposing the new practices, and standing up against the dictates of the High Commission. Deeply impressed with Evangelical doctrine, and viewing all ceremonies as tending to the corruption of pure religion, they were disposed to venture a good way in the course they entered upon. Their wranglings in the Kirk Session against ministers of the Court fashion, and their earnest, private exercises were fully known to the King; but he bore with them, till they began to lend countenance and active help to the few refractory ministers who fell under the ban of the Bishops. He then, at the date noted, ordered them to be removed as "evil weeds" from Edinburgh—William Rig, merchant, and *James Cathkin*, bookseller, to Caithness, Richard Lawson to Aberdeen,' etc. etc. Mr. James Cathkin, as previously mentioned, was the father of Mrs. Andrew Stevenson, and grandfather, therefore, of the first President of the Royal College of Physicians.

His grandfather, Mr. James Cathkin, Bookseller.

Dr. Archibald Stevenson's character.

It was from such an origin that Sir Archibald was descended, and from which he inherited doubtless his determined and strong-willed nature, which when thwarted about the yearly Examinators led to his locking the door of the College meeting-place, and refusing to give up the key, or restore certain papers in his possession, amongst which was the completed manuscript of the Pharmacopœia, until the aid of the law was called in by the President of the time and majority of the Fellows to compel his obedience. As has been previously stated, this led to mutual actions in the Court of Session for 'contumaciousness' on the part of the College, and for 'restitution of rights' of himself and others, on his side. A decision in favour of the College was given in 1699. Another instance of his obstinate disposition was his delaying the publication of the Pharmacopœia for so many (sixteen) years after it had been completed, and its issue authorised by the College.

Sir Archibald married when in his thirty-second year, on the 14th August 1662, Elizabeth Ramsay, daughter of Umquhill John Ramsay of Idingtoun, and Egidia Kellie. The result of the marriage was four sons—George, a Surgeon, who married Elizabeth Kennedy, William, Archibald, and Andrew, who all seem to have died unmarried. There were also four daughters—Elizabeth, Margaret, Jean, and Agnes. Of these, two died unmarried. Elizabeth is thus described (Colonel Boyle's Scheme) in a sasine dated 21st June 1695, as 'eldest daughter to Sir Archibald, now sp. to Mr. Archibald Pitcairn, younger of that Ilk.' She was, as previously mentioned, Dr. Archibald Pitcairn's second wife, and one of their daughters became the second wife of Alexander, fifth Earl of Kellie, and the mother of the sixth and seventh earls.

Married in 1662 Elizabeth Ramsay of Idingtoun. His family—four sons and four daughters.

Agnes, the fourth daughter, married Colin Arthur, a Chirurgeon Apothecary in Fife.

The only living descendants of Sir Archibald Stevenson are those of George, his eldest son, the Surgeon. He appears to have had one son, George, also a Surgeon, who was served heir to his father, 14th March 1747. He married, and had two daughters, Agnes and Christian. Agnes married a Mr. Jackson. They had one daughter, Agnes, who married Mr. George Chordter Cram, Lavelle, Illinois, U.S.A.; and from them descend four sons, the eldest of whom, William Frederick Cram, Oregon, Illinois, U.S.A., was alive in 1879, and may be still. Regarding his brothers, George, Thomas, and Lewis, I have no information.

Descendants of his eldest son, George, the Surgeon.

William Frederick Cram, U.S.A.

In The Early Days of the Royal College, Sir Archibald was a most devoted President, and although he does not appear to have originated any of the great Efforts, he seems to have aided in carrying out those suggested—except the Pharmacopœia. I have already shown that he was instrumental in delaying, not its preparation, but its publication, for sixteen years. His reason for so

Dr. Archibald as President in The Early Days.

acting is not clearly shown in the Minutes. Its publication had been sanctioned by the College, and no objection by him is stated. As, at a later period, his antagonistic attitude to Sibbald is clearly shown, it occurs to me that this might have been the first decided manifestation of it; and that, taking advantage of Sibbald's retirement to London in 1686, he had exercised his influence to prevent its publication for reasons of his own. The Minutes ceasing just at the end of 1684, no light is thrown upon the proceedings by them. With his hereditary bias in favour of Presbyterianism, and his opposition to Episcopacy and especially to Popery, a further reason for his opposition to Sibbald, the pervert, can be understood; and to a man of his nature and jealous temperament, the opposition would indeed be strong.

His opposition to Sibbald.

The relation of the College to his house.

The relation in which his house stood to the Royal College is peculiar. From an entry in the Minutes after the 'Ryot,' the majority of the College evidently regarded him as occupying part of *their* house, and demanded arrears of rent due by him. This he objected to, but there is no evidence of a contrary action on his part, nor is there any Minute that he paid the rent demanded. I have given the fuller reference to this in my notice of Dr. Trotter.

His knighthood in 1682.

Dr. Archibald Stevenson was a Royal Physician, and was Knighted in March 1682, at Holyrood, by the Duke of York at the same time as Sibbald and Balfour, at the combined suggestion of Sir Charles Scarborough and the Earl of Perth.

There is no record of where he obtained his Degree in Medicine, but in the *Album Studiosorum Academiae Lugdano Batavae* in the year 1659, on October 7, Archibaldus Stephanides, aged twenty-nine, is enrolled as a Student of Medicine and as coming from *Lothianensis, Scotus.* This entry is in favour of his having been born in 1630. He may have been a graduate of Leyden.

From the *History of George Heriot's Hospital*, by William

GRAVE OF SIR ARCHIBALD STEVENSONE

Steven, D.D., new edition, 1859, it is learned that he was the earliest recorded (if not the first) Physician of that Institution. He was appointed on 26th August 1666, and held office till 4th June 1705, a period of nearly thirty-nine years, and was succeeded by Dr. George Mackenzie, author of the *Lives and Characters of the Most Eminent Writers of the Scots Nation.* He owed his appointment to Sir Archibald, who agreed to cancel a claim he had against the Hospital for £200 sterling, provided the Governors would confer the office on Dr. Mackenzie. He, however, acted imprudently, and was a violent Jacobite. After holding the office for six years, he was deprived of it 'in respect that the Act in his favour did bear to be during pleasure allenarly,' and was succeeded by Dr. Gilbert Rule, a Fellow of the Royal College.

His death and burial-place.

Sir Archibald Stevenson died on 16th February 1710, in Edinburgh, at the age of eighty-one years, and was buried on the 18th February, on the south side of the north walk, at the position I have already mentioned. No stone marks the spot where the first President of the Royal College lies.

SIR ANDREW BALFOUR, M.D.

Sir Andrew Balfour, M.D. Caen.

THE Morning Star of Science in Scotland,—so he is designated in one of the accounts of his life (M. F. Conolly, *Biographical Dictionary of Eminent Men of Fife*, Cupar-Fife, 1866). He was the fifth and youngest son of Sir Michael Balfour of Denmiln, in the east of Fife, and was born at that place on the 18th January 1630. He was therefore younger than Stevensone by only a month or two.

Born 18th January 1630, died 9th January 1694.

His brother, Sir James, the Lyon King-at-Arms.

He was many years younger than his brother, Sir James Balfour, the Lyon King-at-Arms, who assisted him in his education. He was an Arts student at St. Andrews, and laureated there. About 1650 he proceeded to London, where he is said to have been the pupil of Harvey and other Physicians; and he made the acquaintance of Charles Scarborough and many other distinguished men, such as Mayerne, Glisson, Charleton, etc.

Laureated at St. Andrews, and studied under Harvey in London.

His attachment to Botany. Studies in France.

His 'early attachment to Botany' induced him to study Medicine, and influenced his choice of residences abroad. He first went to Blois, and afterwards studied at Paris. After a short visit to England, he ultimately graduated as Bachelor, and then Doctor of Medicine at the University of Caen, in September 1661, when he was in his thirty-first year, and after eleven of these had been spent in the study of Medicine!

Graduated at Caen in 1661.

Presented to Charles II. Travels with the Earl of Rochester.

Soon after he returned to England he was presented to Charles the Second, and was nominated by him to travel abroad with the Earl of Rochester. This occupied the next four years, and he returned in 1666 from Italy with Rochester, improved by their association.

Professor Walker (*Essays on Natural History*, Edinburgh, 1808), referring to his travels and observations at this time, remarks (p. 352): 'Being previous to Mr. Ray, he appears in fine to have set the first example of a literary and scientific traveller in modern times.' Upon his return to Scotland, he located himself at St. Andrews; and there practised as a Physician, and according to the same authority, employed his leisure hours in the study of Anatomy and Natural History. 'Here,' Walker states, 'he first introduced into Scotland the dissection of the human body; and may thereby be considered as having laid the foundation of any honour that this country may have since acquired in Medicine.' In the course of his dissections he found a four months' fœtus lodged in the Fallopian tube, which was for many years afterwards preserved in his museum.

Professor Walker's Observations upon Dr. Balfour.

First located at St. Andrews.

There first introduced into Scotland the dissection of the human body.

About 1668 he removed to Edinburgh, and resumed the intimacy with his kinsman, Robert Sibbald, which had been formed on the Continent, and he then for some years practised as a Physician in the Metropolis. With the co-operation of Patrick Murray, the Laird of Livingstone, the Botanick or Physick Garden was commenced, and at length established. Sibbald, with whom the idea originated, introduced Balfour to Murray, and with their co-operation the garden took its practical form, at first in the North Yardes, Holyrood, and its success was assured when James Sutherland became its first 'intendent,' and, patronised by the municipal authorities, it was transferred to the Trinity College grounds.

Removes to Edinburgh.

Sibbald introduces him to Laird of Livingstone.

Origin of Physick Garden.

Dr. Balfour, after his removal to Edinburgh, obtained a large and lucrative practice, and the fact of his being one of the four Physicians selected a few years afterwards to advise the Court of Session in the Chirurgeon-Apothecary dispute, indicates the position in the profession he then held, and the respect and esteem with which he was generally regarded.

When the establishment of a College of Physicians was suggested and proposed by Sibbald at the Physicians' congress

Joins with Sibbald to form College of Physicians.

or meeting, Balfour joined heartily with him in the idea, and it seems to me that, as the Physick Garden resulted from their united action, so it was with the College. He helped in planning its constitution, and assisted in the great work of raising the professional status, and promoting all the Efforts in that direction. He was in his forty-first year when he settled in Edinburgh; and therefore, when the Charter was obtained in 1681, he would be in his fifty-second year.

Succeeds Sibbald in President's Chair, December 1685.

From Sibbald's *Autobiography* it is learned that Balfour succeeded him in December 1685 in the Presidential Chair; for the former states that, although the Pharmacopœia was not then published, he, at his own expense, had two copies prepared, one of which he presented to Balfour *when he became President*. He was not one of the Presidents during The Early Days, but immediately followed. His name does not appear in the list of Presidents officially published by the Royal College, but I see no reason to doubt Sibbald's statement. The official list is formed from the records in the Minutes; and, as there is no record of the 1685 Election, the College has not claimed him as a President. It would have been rather discreditable had so distinguished a Fellow never filled the Presidential office. His previous positions in the Early College were distinguished. He was one of the first Council, and, along with Dr. Livingstone, one of the first Censors—indeed, it may be said, as his colleague was never able to attend, the first Censor. It rested therefore with him to organise the method of discharging the duties of an office, which was then not only new, but of much importance, and requiring not only firmness and determination, but also the exercise of suavity, to avoid giving offence towards those acting and practising contrarily to the powers of a recently established authority, or as the offenders would regard it, an objectionable innovation. For this duty Balfour, from his judiciousness, combined with the polished manners acquired by his long Continental travelling and residence, and association with good

But no record of this in the Minutes.

Was one of the first Censors.

society, was eminently fitted. From the Minutes it is learned that, on March 21st, 1682, he was nominated to be one of the additional Pharmacopœia Committee appointed to revise the several parts, and at the election in November he was re-elected Councillor and Censor. During the past year, as several cases of discipline, or of illegal practice, had been dealt with by him as Censor, he participated in the Vote of Confidence with the other office-bearers proposed and passed by the College: 'The College having considered the procedure of the President (Stevensone), Censors (Balfour and Sibbald), and other officials in the affairs of the College for the year preceding, do approve yr of.'

One of the Pharmacopœia Committee of 1682.

Participates in Vote of Confidence.

To Balfour and Cranstoune was assigned the duty of conducting the first Examination of the first candidate for the Licence, Dr. Peter Kello, M.D. of Leyden. I may remind you that it had been previously resolved that the examination was to consist of three parts, and the first part was assigned to these two Fellows, to examine him 'upon severall materiall questions.' Those selected were *de Purgatione et Venesectione*, and it is added: 'The Colledge were well satisfied with Dr. Kello's answers.' From the subjects of examination being in Latin in the Minute, it is probable that the first examination was conducted in that language. Dr. Balfour, as well as ten other Fellows, were present at the Final Examination. The following extracts show the active part he took in the Pharmacopœia. Thus on 13th August 1683 it is 'recommended to Doctor Balfour to bring in his part of the Pharmacopea, the next meeting being this day seventh night.' On 20th August 1683 he is appointed one of a committee consisting of the President (Stevensone), Sibbald, Pitcairne, and himself, to revise the 'haill of the Pharmacopea,' regarding the printing of which Sibbald had arranged with David Lindsay, and that he, the President and Sibbald, are to 'enter into a contract with the Printer.'

One of the first Examiners.

His interest in the Pharmacopœia.

On 6th December, the election day, he was re-elected to the Council and Censorship.

Discourse before the College, February 4th, 1684.

On 4th February 1684, Dr. Balfour had a Discourse before the College upon the *Aphorism* 22, *Sect.* 1, which was very satisfying to them, and he was 'desyred to give in the same to Secretarius,' so that within The Early Days Balfour participated in the four great schemes. He voted for the Dispensary, he assisted in the preparation of the Pharmacopœia, he took part in the first examination, and he contributed a discourse. That he also interested himself in the other business details of the College is shown by this, that on 30th November 1684, he was appointed along with the President and Secretary (Stevensone and Sibbald) to meet 'for revising all former Acts, and to order the booking of such as they shall think fit in the great Register.'

Participates in all the four Efforts.

His interest in other College business.

His health at this time had evidently not been good, for he had not been present at any meeting of the College since 20th October; and on 4th December, when his friend Sibbald was elected President, he by plurality of votes was re-elected Censor along with Dr. Trotter. The Minute further records: 'Doctor Balfour, by reason of his indisposition of body, and for severall other reasons, desyres to be excused, and some other persone to be named in his place.' At the next meeting, on 11th December, he was present, and the Minute states: 'Doctor Balfour his excuse for being Censor for the year being considered by the Colledge, they admit thereof, and the Council appoynted to elect another in his place.'

December 1684, declines on account of his health being re-elected Censor.

One of the first acts of Sibbald when raised to the Chair was to move that the College take into consideration the minimum of time a Licentiate should study before being licensed; and in this he was supported by Balfour. He also was present on 22nd December when the Patent to be given to some Honorary Members was exhibited.

Supports Sibbald's motion of inquiry regarding time a Licentiate should study.

And here closes the record of his work during The Early Days. From Sibbald's *Autobiography* it is learned that Dr. Andrew Balfour succeeded him in the Chair, December 1685, but of his

Presidency there is no existing information. We know, however, that the College business must have been greatly disturbed by the flight of the previous President, without any preparation for such a contingency having been made; and the general state of Scotland, and of Edinburgh especially, must have disarranged the business of the city to a very considerable degree, whilst the rising of Argyle in the west, and his trial and execution in the city, could not but exercise a depressing influence on all supporters of the Protestant cause.

When Minutes again kept, 6th December 1694, his name is wanting.

The Minutes reopen on the 6th December 1694, being the first Thursday after St. Andrew's Day, and Dr. Trotter is elevated to the Presidential Chair. But the honoured name of Balfour is wanting, for he died at the beginning of that year, ere he had completed the age of sixty-four.

His illness and death.

Towards the end of 1693, Sir Andrew Balfour was on his death-bed, displaying 'those virtues and that equanimity which had all along been so remarkable in his life.' He yielded at last to the repeated attacks of arthritic pains, now complicated by hæmorrhages from the bowels, and rejection of food; and, with all his powers exhausted, he passed quietly away, 'Cum vixisset annos 64 et menses undecim, et dies decem.' There is error in this date. It makes the date of Balfour's death 28th December 1694. In one of the inscriptions and epitaphs which are printed at the end of Sibbald's Memorial of him, the date of his death is given as '4 id. Januarii anno æræ Christi, MIƆCXƆIIII. Ætat. LXIII.' But it would be more correctly stated that Sir Andrew Balfour died at Edinburgh, in the High Street, 'e regione Templi Cathedralis,' on 9th January 1694, having all but completed the sixty-fourth year of his age, less nine days, and was buried on the 13th day of January 1694, 'in Tods Tom, with a Trof' (Greyfriars' Records). Tod's Tomb is on the west side of Greyfriars' Kirkyard. He was born on 18th January 1630, and died on 9th January 1694.

In his sixty-fourth year.

Buried on 13th January 1694 in Tod's Tomb.

Knighted in 1682.

In March 1682 he was Knighted by the Duke of York at Holyrood, at the same time as Stevensone and Sibbald, and was subsequently appointed Physician to Charles the Second.

His Guide Book written to Patrick Murray.

The only written volume associated with his name is the interesting Continental Guide-Book he prepared for his friend, 'The Laird of Levingstone,' Patrick Murray. It is in the form of three letters: the first 'containing an account of what is remarkable in and about London, etc., and in and about Paris, etc.'; the second 'containing Advice for making the grand Toure of France, with an account of what is most observable, relating especially to the Natural History and Antiquities of that Kingdom'; and the third, 'Advice for travelling into Italy.' They were published after his death by his son, Michael Balfour of Denmiln, in 1700; and on the title, are said to be written, 'By the learned and judicious Sir Andrew Balfour, M.D.,' from the author's original MS. The reason for publishing the letters is somewhat peculiar: 'My Father's MSS. with all his books being committed to a certain Person, he, without my Privity, gave out Copies to Knowing and Inquisitive Persons, as of late I came to understand; and now these Copies abounding abroad, and most (if not all) being defective or incorrect, (to prevent my Father's being abused) I now send a True Copy abroad unto the world, and let it see the Light,' etc. An address to the reader, written by Sir Robert Sibbald, precedes the Letters, in which he writes of Sir Andrew: 'He was a man of an excellent wit, and of a ripe judgment, and of a most taking behaviour. He had improven himself to the best advantage, with all the learning taught in the most famous Universities of these Countries, had acquired their Languages and conversed with the most famous men then alive. . . . When he wrote these Letters he had settled his abode at Edinburgh, where he Practised Physick, with great Success, so deservedly gained the Reputation of the best Qualified Physitian in the Place, and accordingly was employed by those of the best Rank.' Such

Published after his death by his son in 1700.

Reason for publishing them.

Sir Robert Sibbald's estimate of Dr. Andrew Balfour.

was the testimony of Sibbald, borne to his deceased friend, six years after his death. After paying a high tribute to the character of Patrick Murray, Sibbald states that 'He began his Voyage the 2nd of September 1668, and dyed in August or September 1671.' He 'had travelled through a great part of France, when he was surprised with a Feaver, that he contracted at Avignion, of which he dyed.' From this it is learned that the letters were written during these years, and not published for more than thirty years thereafter; and such was Sir Andrew's 'modesty, that he never showed them to any but his most intimate friends, and could not be persuaded to give a copie of them.'

Patrick Murray died in 1671 during his travels.

It is of interest to note that Andrew Balfour, after studying in London under the guidance of Dr. John Wedderburn, Knight and King's Physician, who also practised Medicine with great credit in London, afterwards frequented the more celebrated Universities, Oxford in England, and in France those of Paris, Montpelier, and Caen, and in Italy that of Padua. He chiefly studied in Paris, and for many years, because Medicine was best taught there, because there the opportunity was greatest of frequent teaching, and because he had opportunities in abundance of anatomical dissections, numerous companions, the most instructive Royal Garden of Plants, and the best instruction in simple and safe treatment of diseases. In the University of Paris there then flourished the great lights, Joannes Riolanus filius, Renatus Moreau, Guenetius, de la Chambre, Guido Patinus, and his son Carolus (*Memoria Balfouriana*, p. 49-50).

His studies in London and elsewhere.

Advantages of Paris to students.

The teachers of the time.

Balfour afterwards graduated at *Cadomum*, Caen, and for comparison with the system of Examination adopted by the College of Physicians, I extract the form as given by Sibbald at p. 53: 'Postea *Cadomum* profectus est, ibique antegressis publicis *Disputationibus*, de venae sectione in *Dysenteria* celebrandâ, et Privatis *Examinibus* a singulis Professoribus, per *Statuta* imperatis, *Baccalauratus* primum, deinde *Licentiatus* gradum consecutus est, demum

Examination at Caen—as given by Sibbald.

vero *Præside*, ac *Laureante* nobili viro, Magistro *Stephano Cathagnesto*, Medicinae *Professore* ordinario, in Academiâ *Cadomensi*, in Medicinâ *Doctoratus* summum gradum est adeptus, *Cadomi* Anno Domini 1661 die *Septembris* 20.'

Compared with that of the Royal College of Physicians.

There is not much resemblance between the foregoing form at the University of Caen and the more perfect form of Examination adopted by the Edinburgh College of Physicians.

Another point of interest is (what I previously alluded to), that the subject of the first Medical Examination introduced by Balfour was the one on which he had given his Public Discourse at Caen, *de Venae Sectione*.

His Museum presented to the University of Edinburgh.

The Record of the Proceedings of the College of Physicians during Balfour's Presidency being lost, we have no trace of his work, but this we know, that the labour of forty years in collecting one of the best Museums of the age resulted in his presenting it to the University of Edinburgh. In the introductory address to his *Letters*, Sibbald tells us that about a year or two after his settlement in Edinburgh, 'He took the resolution of erecting a Publick Garden for Plants, and a Cabinet of Curiosities. He had begun the last in his own Lodging, and was projecting how he might establish the other,' when Sibbald made him acquainted with 'that worthie gentleman Patrick Murray, Baron of Livingstone,' to whom the Letters were addressed. Professor Walker (*Scots Magazine*, 1812, *Memoir of Balfour*, and also in his *Essays on Natural History*) writes of this Museum: 'It was then the most considerable that was in the possession of any University in Europe. There it remained for many years, useless and neglected, some parts of it going to inevitable decay, and others abstracted.' 'Soon after that period (1750), it was dislodged from the Hall where it had been long kept, was thrown aside, and exposed as lumber, was further and further dilapidated, and at length, almost compleatly demolished' (p. 365). Sibbald having also presented his own Museum and a joint Catalogue published, would doubtless

Walker's estimate of the Museum.

Ultimately demolished by neglect.

Sibbald's interest in it and his own—the neglect must have been after 1722.

as a Professor be interested in looking after the collection till the time of his death; and had not it been cared for till then, it is not likely that he would have gifted to the University the portraits he valued so highly. The neglect must therefore have occurred subsequently to his death. Walker further observes: 'These (specimens, saved by Walker) I hope, may now remain long in this place, and be considered as so many precious relics of the first naturalist, and of one of the best and greatest men this country has produced.' Sir Robert Sibbald's contribution, '*Auctarium Musæi Balfouriana e Musæo Sibbaldiano . . . quas Robertus Sibbaldus M.D., Eques Auratus, Academiæ Edinburgenæ donavit,*' was included in the destruction described by Professor Walker.

His Library, can it be said, came to a better end? It was sold by auction in June 1699. Individually the volumes might be preserved, but where? The selling price of the *Catalogus* of it, is in the present day, about twelve shillings.

SIR THOMAS BURNET, M.D.

Sir Thomas Burnet, M.D. Montpelier.

ALTHOUGH Dr. Thomas Burnet was a distinguished author of Medical Works, the correct information regarding his life is but scanty. He was descended from the old family of Leys.

Born 1638, died 25th March 1704.

His descent.

Alexander Burnet, the eleventh proprietor of Leys in Kincardineshire, had a family of five sons and eight daughters. The third son was Robert, who possessed the estate of Crimond, Aberdeenshire. He was an eminent lawyer, a Member of the Faculty of Advocates, was raised to the Scottish Bench in 1661 as Lord Crimond, and died the same year. He was twice married. By the first marriage he had a daughter who died young. He married for his second wife Rachael Johnston of the Warriston family, whose brother was Sir Archibald Johnston, Lord Warriston.

Of this marriage there were three sons and one daughter. The eldest, Robert, was a Member of the Scottish Bar, and died unmarried in 1662.

Was the second son of Robert Burnet, Lord Crimond.

Thomas the Physician was the second son, and succeeded, on the death of his brother, to the estate of Crimond.

The third son was Gilbert, the divine, the Parish Minister of Saltoun, the Professor of Theology in Glasgow at the age of twenty-six, the Historian, the Politician, associated with the Revolution and King William the Third, and for some time Bishop of Salisbury.

Dr. Thomas Burnet was born in 1638, and died on the 25th March 1704, aged therefore sixty-six years.

Correct dates of his birth and death.

Regarding the dates of his birth and death there appears to be a discrepancy somewhere. My sources of information I consider the most correct,—that for the date of birth was the late

George Burnett, LL.D., Advocate and Lyon King-of-Arms; and for his death the Register of Burials in Greyfriars' Churchyard.

The most recent notice of Sir Thomas Burnet I have seen is that in the *Dictionary of National Biography.* In that notice it is stated that he must have been born between 1630 and 1640, which is rather vague, but correct. The date 1632 is given in Billings' *Surgeon-General's Catalogue, U.S.*, 'but on what authority does not appear.' The notice further states 'he was knighted some time before 1691, and died it is stated in 1715.' In Anderson's *Scottish Nation*, vol. ii. p. 494, the information is equally unsatisfactory: 'The date of his death is unknown.'

The *Dictionary of National Biography* further informs us that, after obtaining the M.A. Degree, he studied Medicine at Montpelier, and obtained the Degree of Doctor of Medicine from that University in August 1659 (a very early age, twenty-one, to obtain a Doctor's Degree in those days), 'and that from the Theses which he thus defended, his medical knowledge was chiefly based upon Galen and Hippocrates.' They were published, the one for his Licence being '*Currus Iatrikus triumphalis, &c. . . . ad Apollinarem laudem consequendam*,' and the other for his Degree of Doctor, '*Quæstiones quatuor cardinales pro supremâ Apollinari daphne consequendâ*,' both in 1659.

Studied and graduated at Montpelier in 1659.

His Theses were published.

He afterwards settled in Edinburgh, and soon attained a distinguished position as a Physician.

In 1662 he married Janet, daughter of Robert Bruce of Blairhall. They had ten children, four sons and six daughters. Many of them died young. Of the sons I can only find trace of one, Gilbert, named after his uncle, and who only of the sons seems to have survived the father. He married Mrs. Oswald, a widow, and the daughter of Sir William Hamilton of Preston. They had a daughter Rachel, and a son Gilbert, of whom I have been unable to learn more. Of Sir Thomas's daughters, the third, Helen, was twice married, and by her second marriage to Sir Ralph Dundas

Married in 1662, Janet Bruce of Blairhall. Family—four sons and six daughters. Survived by only one son, Gilbert.

His daughters.

of Manor, had two sons and one daughter. Sir Thomas's sixth daughter, Euphemia, married James Roberton, the Principal Clerk of Session, and had two daughters and one son. Their elder daughter, Janet, married, in 1726, William eighth Earl of Kincardine—the second instance of a President's female descendant marrying into the aristocracy.

His grand-daughter, Janet Roberton, married in 1726 eighth Earl of Kincardine.

According to the *National Biography*, Sir Thomas is stated to have had a son Thomas who graduated at Leyden in 1691, but according to the family history I have received, none of the four sons bears the name of Thomas—and supposing he graduated about the same age as Sir Thomas, he would have been born about 1670. From my information Helen, his sixth child, was born in 1668, Alexander in 1669, Elizabeth in 1673, Margaret in 1676 and Euphemia later, so I do not see where Thomas comes in. Nor is the name entered in the Leyden Students' *Album*.

Bishop Gilbert had a great-grandson Thomas, who was a Medical Practitioner at Chigwell, and whose daughter Mary was his last descendant in the male line. She died in 1795.

Sir Thomas was a Royal Physician.

Dr. Sir Thomas Burnet, it is said, was not only Physician to Charles the Second and James the Seventh, but in 1693 he was Physician to William the Third, and afterwards to Queen Anne. On the title-pages of some of his books he styled himself 'Medicus Regius et Collegii Regii Medicorum Edinburgensis Socius.' Of course this only applies to those published after 1681. But so early as the first edition of his *Thesaurus Medicinae Practicae*, published at London in 1673, he is 'M.D. et Medicus Regis ordinarius.' As to his title, the Minutes of the College give no information when it was conferred. He was present at the meeting on 22nd December 1684, as 'Dr. Burnet.' When the Minutes are again recorded on 6th December 1694, his name is not entered in the sederunt, nor does it appear till the 14th September 1695, the day on which Dr. Stevenson locked the door of the College and 'deny'd the keys.' On this occasion his name for the first time

His works.

is entered as 'Sir Thomas Burnet.' I conclude therefore the title was conferred by King William probably about 1693, and possibly influenced by the position of his brother the Bishop.

From 'Fountainhall' it is learned that in 1681, when in his forty-third year, he was one of the four chief Physicians in Edinburgh. Being a friend of Sibbald's, he joined him in his attempt to establish the College of Physicians, but he does not appear to have taken a very active part in the preliminary steps towards obtaining the Charter, although enjoying the Royal Patronage as Physician in ordinary to King Charles. When the College was established he soon came to the front.

Was in 1681 one of the four chief Physicians in Edinburgh.

Although younger than some of the other original Fellows, his name stands second in the list, and without title. According to my data he was then in the forty-third year of his age.

He was a Member of the first Council, and was re-elected the next year. According to the Minute of the third sederunt, he and Dr. Robert Craufurd were the first Physicians 'to serve the poore of the city and suburbs,' and they organised the *first* Dispensary in Great Britain. The Royal Physician gave it his personal attendance, when he was also esteemed as one of the leading Physicians in the city, practically illustrating the Christian doctrine towards the needy, and perhaps the poorest, inhabitants of the town. He took interest and participated in all 'The Early Days' Efforts, and obstructed none.

One of the first Councillors, and first 'Physitian to the Poore.'

Took interest in all The Early Days Efforts.

In 1682 he was appointed, on 21st March, one of the additional Pharmacopœia Committee 'to revise the severall partes.' Dr. Burnet was also one of Dr. Kello's Examiners, for along with Sibbald he examined in the second part, upon an Aphorism of Hippocrates, and on 1st December 1684 delivered the first part of his Discourse *De Pleuritide*.

As already stated, he was one of Sibbald's supporters during 1682; and, when Sibbald was raised to the Chair in December 1684, he was in regular attendance at the College meetings, and was a

An early supporter of Sibbald.

Member of Sibbald's Council. But during 1683 and 1684, when Sir Archibald Stevensone was President, he attended very few meetings of the College. That this was due to personal feeling towards Stevensone is indicated by his absence from meetings when Stevensone was again President in 1694. When Dr. Trotter was elected President in 1695, he was not present at the first five meetings, but afterwards was regular in his attendance, when Stevensone and his party had to be opposed. He also supported the Presidential Chair by his presence, when Stevensone and Pitcairn were censured and suspended, the former for his contumacious conduct and the latter for his calumnious Protest. At the Election Meeting in December 1695, he was elected to the Council, and was afterwards regular in his attendance.

His relations with Stevensone.

Regular in his attendance when Stevensone party had to be opposed.

Elected in 1695 to Council.

His Knighthood.

His name first appears, as already stated, in the Minutes on 14th September 1695, as Sir Thomas Burnet; indicating, I surmise, that he received the honour of Knighthood from King William, and not from the Jacobite side.

President in 1696.

He did not attain to the Presidentship until 3rd December 1696, when he had been a Socius for fifteen years. He was then in his fifty-eighth year, and is designated in the Minute as Sir Thomas. He was the fourth of the Knights who graced and dignified that honourable position, and he held it for two years, being preceded in the Chair by Dr. Robert Trotter, and succeeded by Dr. Matthew Sinclare.

The last entry of his name in the Minutes is on 6th February 1699.

His books and writings.

By his writings and books he obtained a European fame. The *Thesaurus Medicinae Practicae* was first published in London 1673, and a second edition soon after, and a third in 1685. Editions were also published at Geneva in 1697 and 1698. A smaller copy was published at Edinburgh in 1703. So that before the College was founded, two editions of this celebrated work had been issued, the first when Dr. Burnet was in his thirty-fifth year. His other chief work, *Hippocrates Contractus,* was published at Edinburgh in 1685, at London 1686, and after his death editions were printed at Venice in 1733, 1737, and 1751, and at Strasburg in 1765.

His fame, therefore, did not perish at his death.

The College seems to have been tardy in conferring its highest honour on this distinguished man, but after occupying the Chair for two years, he was present at only two meetings after his successor was appointed. Sir Thomas lived five years thereafter.

Record of his death, 25th March 1704.

According to the family notes of the late Dr. George Burnett he was born in 1638. I have ascertained from the Greyfriars' Burial Records that he 'dyed upon the 25th and buried 28th March 1704.' His age is not stated, but the entry is, 'Doctor of Medicine.' 'His late Majesty K. W. and present Majesty Q. Anne Pesisian.' 'Lyes interred before Wardlaw's tomb.' At his death he would be therefore in the sixty-sixth year of his age. The statements in the notices of his life in the works previously mentioned regarding the date of his death are vague or inaccurate. The well-preserved Greyfriars' Record is true.

Buried before Wardlaw's Tomb.

Sed omnes manet Nox et via lethi semel calcanda.

SIR ROBERT SIBBALD OF KIPPS, M.D.,

Sir Robert Sibbald of Kipps, M.D. Angers. Born 15th April 1641, died 9th August 1722.

Is the fourth and last of the First Knights of The Early Days of the Royal College. In age he was the youngest, but he was the most important of them all. For not only was the origination of the College due to him, but its success also, as manifested by the results of its four great Efforts to improve the status of Medicine throughout the kingdom.

The origination and advocacy of the movement, as well as the success in obtaining its Charter, were in great degree the achievment of his acuteness and untiring energy; whilst the plan of the College was undoubtedly greatly indebted to him for its completeness, and for its being so thoroughly established and carried out during the early years.

Dr. George Sibbald, his uncle.

He had from his youth had the experience, the example, and the instruction of his uncle, Dr. George Sibbald of Gibliston, a Doctor of Medicine and a former Professor of Philosophy, to guide him. By him he was enlightened as to the causes which prevented the success of the previous attempts, made by his uncle and others, to found a College. As has been shown, the same forces were once more ranged against the last enterprise, and in some respects they had acquired even more power, but Sibbald's ever-present desire was quick to perceive that the chief opponents, the Chirurgeon Apothecaries, were weakened by internal dissension, and that the opportunity had presented itself to revive the idea once more of a College of Physicians in Edinburgh.

No sooner was the suggestion made, than it was with more or less readiness adopted by the assembled Doctors, whilst the enthusiastic proposer of the scheme solicited the help of those who were influential with the King and his Commissioner, and whose counsel was likely to have weight with the Duke of York in Scotland. On the other hand, the town authorities were also anxious to obtain the Duke's interest, and they had endeavoured to gain his favour. This is shown by the large sum of money they spent in his entertainment in the city. And Sibbald, not satisfied with the goodwill of the Commissioner alone, took steps to secure that of King Charles himself through his Physician Sir Charles Scarborough; whilst his intimacy with the Earl of Perth, then rising into power, was made use of to disarm the opposition of the nobility. At the same time, by granting the Scotch Universities certain advantages and prerogatives, which specially benefited that of Edinburgh, he, by his tact, energy, and prudence, with the help of those other Physicians who also were zealous in the object, carried his point. Rapidity of action was essential for success; and, lest the favour of the Duke of York should lessen, he stimulated it at the right time by the production of the mandate which had been given in August 1621, sixty years previously, by King James the Sixth, in favour of a College.

Dr. Robert Sibbald's suggestion to form a College readily adopted.

His procedure.

Sibbald was deeply impressed with the necessity for the erection of a College, as a means for improving Medical knowledge, from his constantly noting the ignorance of those who professed to treat the people. He also saw the injury that was done to them, and that the salutary efforts of the qualified Physicians were thwarted by the unsatisfactory character of the drugs supplied by the Apothecaries, the often exorbitant charge made for them, and the bad consequences which resulted from the want of uniformity in quality in the drugs themselves. There was also this further difficulty in Scotland, that the preparation of galenicals could not be regulated from the want of a recognised Dispensatory, and the purity of the ingredients could not be insisted on, when they were prepared according to a Pharmacopœia issued by the London

Impressed with the necessity for a College.

College of Physicians, but which was not binding on the sellers of drugs in Scotland.

Preparatory step taken by Sibbald and Balfour—the Physick Garden.

He and Balfour had already taken a most important preparatory step, and one for which they had not hesitated to provide at first the necessary pecuniary means, by the establishment of a 'Physick Garden,' in which the various plants then used as medicines might be cultivated, and subsequently were by the intelligent Intendent James Sutherland, so early as September 1676. His *Hortus Medicus Edinburgensis* with Sibbald's help was published in 1683, two years after the foundation of the Royal College. With the aid of Patrick Murray, the Laird of Livingstone, as well as from the resources of Sibbald and Balfour, the garden was stocked with a goodly range of medical plants. Instruction, too, of a certain kind was given, and although very different from that afforded by Professors of Botany of the present day, yet it was the first decided advance in this city. For it gave not only an opportunity to the vendor of drugs to obtain fresh and genuine samples at the garden, but also afforded such students as were apprentices of the Surgeons and Apothecaries in the city, by arrangement, the means of learning somewhat regarding the appearances and characteristics of the growing plants, and some things also, by means of the oral instruction given, regarding their nature and uses, after the manner of the Apothecaries in London, when their improved garden at Chelsea was provided through Sir Hans Sloan's generous benefaction. But it is only right to state that an effort had previously been made to afford instruction in Medicinal Plants in Edinburgh. The 'Medicine Garden,' as originally started by Drs. Sibbald and Balfour, was 'in ane inclosure of some 40 foot of measure every way, obtained of John Brown, Gardener of the North Yardes in the Abby' (Holyrood), and the culture of it was undertaken by a youth named James Sutherland, and with the assistance of the Laird of Livingstone and others a collection of eight or nine hundred plants was made there. Several of the Physicians in

Edinburgh aided the design by yearly subscriptions. Dr. Balfour succeeded in overcoming the opposition of the Chirurgeon Apothecaries, and they too ultimately became friendly and assisted in obtaining from the Town Council a lease to Mr. James Sutherland for nineteen years of the garden belonging and adjacent to Trinity Hospital. Drs. Balfour and Sibbald and others were appointed visitors of the garden. Probably there were members of the Town Council who were friendly to the design; for in the *History of George Heriot's Hospital*, by Dr. William Steven, an extract is given from the *Records* of the Hospital that in the Governors' injunctions to the gardener on the 20th September 1661, 'the Easter Yard, on the South part thereof, be planted with all sort of *Phisical, Medicinal*, and other *herbs*, such as the Country can afford, conform to the fullest Catalogue that can be had, that such who intend to *Study herbs* may have full access there, they not wronging or molesting the samen.' As Sibbald did not settle in Edinburgh till October 1662, and Balfour only came to reside there about 1670, neither of them was connected with this interesting use of one of the fashionable promenades of the city by the Town Council and ministers of Edinburgh, who were the Governors of the Hospital. Nor was Dr. Archibald Stevensone, for he only was appointed Physician in 1666. The idea would appear to have originated amongst the Governors themselves.

Bower on the Physick Garden.

Bower, in the first volume of the *History of the University*, whilst not claiming the Physick Garden as a University institution, observes (p. 375) that a School for Instruction in Botany was the first of the medical classes which may be said to have been founded in Edinburgh. If so, it decidedly was an Extramural Class, when first it was started and for some time after. 'That improvement,' he remarks, 'in Medical Practice, was one chief design of Mr. Sutherland's publication (the *Hortus*), cannot be doubted, because such plants as were used in medicine are differently marked in it, from such as are annual or native in Scotland'; whilst in the

The Botany class was first Extramural.

Considered Sibbald the founder of it. This was his first step in Medical Progress.

Garden the Dispensatory plants were arranged in alphabetical order. Bower concludes that Sibbald must be considered as the founder of that noble collection. This was his first step in Medical progress, and it was a practical one. It was preliminary to his greater project, the foundation of the College.

Was the most important of the Knights.

Naturally, therefore, I hold that Sibbald was the most important of the First Knights. He was masterful, a leader of his Fellows; and, arrayed in his professional armour, he set forth to contend with the ignorance and prejudices around him. And he did it well. For not only were he and his coadjutors, the principal of whom were Andrew Balfour, Thomas Burnet, and Archibald Stevensone, successful in obtaining a Charter and a Constitution for the College, but the plan of, or schemes for, its uses, had all been thought out by him and them and other supporters. Thus in the Preface to the edition of *Statutes and Bye Laws*, issued by the Royal College in 1852, it is stated, 'the two first meetings (7th and 8th December 1681) of the College were occupied with the election of office-bearers.' Immediately (9th December 1681) thereafter, they proceeded under the powers vested in them by the Charter, 'to enact laws for its due government and welfare.' A meeting is also said to have been held on 4th January 1682. All these were held before the sederunts are engrossed in the Minute Book, which begins as I have said on 18th January of that year; and, at one or other of these preliminary meetings, a Committee for the preparation of a Pharmacopœia had been appointed. It must, therefore, have been extremely vexing and even disheartening to Sibbald to find this Effort thwarted, and his friend Balfour in his grave for nearly six years, before the earliest and long completed Effort of the Royal College for the good of the Medical Art in Scotland, and the benefit of sick people, was permitted to be published, through having been 'obstructed by a faction.'

The early meetings of the College before Minutes recorded.

The Pharmacopœia.

The Dispensary.

With the attendance upon the sick poor of the city and suburbs, from which emerged a Sick House, and ultimately the

Royal Infirmary, Sibbald does not appear, either from the College Minutes or from his *Autobiography*, to have been practically so closely identified, as with the other Efforts engaging his attention and time.

As has already been mentioned, Drs. Burnet and Craufurd had taken the most active interest in this Effort; but, as no name is associated with it in the Minutes as the proposer, countenance is given to its having been included in the originally proposed plan of campaign of the Royal College. This opinion is also supported by the fact that the care of the sick poor is mooted at a very early meeting, and at once carried out. From Sibbald's position as Secretary of the College at the time, he must, at all events, have been a helper in arranging and organising the Dispensary; and probably was its first manager.

With Sibbald undoubtedly rests the credit of having originated the first attempt at a Medical Society, by which I mean the association of medical men to read and consider papers or communications upon medical and kindred subjects, and upon which they could interchange their thoughts and express their views, or learn from or correct those of others, and this at regular periods. Or to use his own words, 'to have conferences, to make discourses, the conferences being held monthly, and the discourses inserted in a book called the *Acta Medica Edinburgensia*.' He had instituted such meetings at his own lodging in the Bishop's Land, Carrubber's Close (where he also at a latter date (1706) seems to have taught 'in privatis Collegiis,' that is, in a private course of lectures), before the College scheme was started.

The Medical Society.

The *Acta Medica Edinburgensia*.

This, the fourth Effort of The Early Days, was the arrangement that, at the monthly meetings, each of the Fellows in rotation should give a Discourse. As the originator of this effort, Sibbald contributed more Discourses than any other Fellow. It was also his design that these papers should be handed to the *Secretarius* for preservation, and one can fancy that if there had been an

Edinburgh Medical Journal in those Early Days and Sibbald the editor, they would in due time have appeared in the next month's issue. These interesting contributions to Medical Science are lost. At a later period, when the Royal College obtained its Hall in Fountain Close, the mutual improvement idea was amplified, and the conferences were held weekly, on a fixed day, and at a fixed hour; and these conferences were held at a different time from the business meetings of the College.

Weekly Conferences in Hall at Fountain Close.

Being subsequent to this scheme, Sibbald could have had no personal association with that for the publication of papers, of which the chief projectors were Monro Primus and Dr. Plummer. As I have already mentioned, although Dr. John Drummond, Dr. Plummer, and other Fellows of the College contributed papers, they had not the straightforwardness to refer to the earlier Efforts of Sibbald and others. They must have been well aware of their having been the previous promoters of this system of mutual improvement, and of this means of developing professional knowledge. But I advance a claim for Dr. Robert Sibbald as the first introducer of the 'Medical Society' into the Scottish Metropolis, and indeed into this country, so long ago as the year 1680.

Systematic Medical Examination.

I further claim for Sibbald the credit of introducing a regular and systematic form of Medical Examination for admission to Medical Licence to practise, which included not only theoretical but also practical subjects. No doubt it resulted from his acquaintance with the system followed at Leyden, and from his personal experience of the pre-graduation Examination at Angers, where he obtained his patent of Doctor in 1662. From his having also studied in Paris, he was familiar with Continental forms and methods, and it may be some may detract from his merits for that reason. Yet it must be allowed, that he had the acute intelligence to introduce and to adapt the Examination to the requirements and the capabilities of the College.

I quote from page 16 of his *Autobiography*, as a good idea of his experience at Leyden is there given. It also shows that he was familiar with the expression 'Institutions of Medicine,' the introduction of which title for the first Examination I have already assigned to Dr. Pitcairn, as it was not used until his return from his Professorship at Leyden.

'I (Sibbald) stayed at Leyden one year and a half, and studied Anatomie and Chirurgie, under the learned Professor Van Horne. I studied the plants under Adolphus Vostius, who had been then Botanick Professor thirty-seven years, and I studied *the Institutions and Practice*, under Sylvius, who was famous then.' (The italics are mine.) 'I saw twentye thrie human bodies dissected by him in the Hospitall which I frequented with him. I saw some dissected publickly by Van Horne, I was also fellow student with Steno, who became famous afterwards for his wrytings. He dissected in my chamber some tymes, and showed me there, the ductus salivatis superior, which he had discovered. I frequented one Apothecaryes shop, and saw the Materia Medica and the ordinary compositiones made. I studied Chimie, under a German called Witichius, and after he went away, under Margravius, brother to him who wrote the Naturall Historie of Brasile. Some tyme I heard the lessons of Vander Linden, who was famous for critical learning. . . . I composed ther (the last summer I stayed ther), *Theses de Variis Tabis speciebus.* Sylvius was present when I defended them publickly in the Schools.'

Sibbald's account of his Studies at Leyden.

Here may be observed his acquaintance with the form of reading and defending Theses in public, apart from graduation examinations, and personally recognising the value of such exercises he introduced the Discourses and Conferences into the College.

The form of the Three-part Examination adopted by the College is distinctly an improvement on anything he describes as having met with abroad.

The Three-part Examination a distinct improvement.

Although, as I have stated, the term 'Institutions' was not

The Institutions of Medicine.

used during The Early Days, and indeed not until the College had passed its tenth year, and after the return of Pitcairn from Leyden, the extract from Sibbald's *Autobiography* shows that the word as a designation for the Theory, as distinct from the Practice of Medicine, was in common use at Leyden twenty years previous to the erection of the Royal College, and was not a new word. It was employed by the College to express *more distinctly the theoretical subjects of the first Examination.*

The 'Practicall Caices.'

But the advancement introduced by the College so early as 1682 making the third Examination *systematically and regularly* upon 'two practicall caices,' of which in the Continental Schools visited by Sibbald no mention is made, I claim as an important feature of the College Examination, and as peculiar at this date to itself, they being presumably taken from the patients attending the Dispensary which had been previously organised. One thing is noticeable, and although it is to be afterwards alluded to, I may mention it here, that as years went on, the description, and it is to be presumed diagnosis, of those 'practicall caices,' appear to have been written. In the University of Edinburgh at a later date the form of examination for the M.D. Degree gradually developed into this. When the practical cases ceased to be examined upon, the University, not having a Dispensary, and there being no Infirmary until about 1740 to draw their cases from, a written Thesis, which the candidate was called on to defend, became an essential part of the trial. But in the Royal College of Physicians of Edinburgh, from the very first Examination in The Early Days and afterwards, practical cases were the subjects for the final Examination for the Licence to practise Medicine in the city of Edinburgh and its suburbs. And a very considerable share of the credit is due to Robert Sibbald.

Written Papers on the Cases—as shown in the University.

It was natural that Sibbald, a laureated M.A. at the University of Edinburgh, before he studied Medicine, should have a feeling of disrespect for those graduates in Medicine who obtained a University title of Doctor of Medicine without examination, after payment of charges or dues, and the presentation of testimonials from medical men, often unconnected with the University, before whose authorities it was not always even necessary that the candidate should personally present himself.

Dr. Robert Sibbald's feeling as regards Preliminary Examinations, and Degrees without examination.

In order to conciliate the Scottish Universities, especially those of which a representative of the Church had been Chancellor, the concession that they should be allowed admission to the College without examination was provided for in the Charter. On the other hand, at the English and Continental Universities, the possession of an Arts Degree was necessary before admission to the Doctorate in Medicine, or before any Medical Degree could be obtained. Sibbald showed his feeling very markedly in the advertisement announcing his course of Lectures in the *Edinburgh Courant* of 14th February 1706, for he indicates that they are to be delivered in Latin; and therefore, unless the students had been instructed in Latin and Greek, it was no use for them to attend his 'College.' He had, therefore, a large idea of the necessity for, and the scope of, a preliminary education of a University Graduate or College Licentiate—*for the Medical Examination of both was at first identical in Edinburgh.* A knowledge of Philosophy and the rudiments of learning which was to be certified in their teacher's certificate, were also required from his students. Could he have done more to show his desire that a high standard of preliminary training, equal at least to that of the English and Continental Universities, should be maintained in the Scottish School?

The objectionable concession to the Scottish Universities of admission to College without examination.

Sibbald's view on preliminary education.

One expression in his announcement calls for a word of explanation, for it appears to have puzzled some. Why should he, a University Professor, have given private Colleges? The expression 'in privatis Collegiis' merely signifies a private *Course* of Lectures. It occurs in the Royal College Minutes, in a testimonial

Explanation of 'In privatis Collegiis.'

granted to Dr. Crawford, when he was recommended to the Town Council as fit to be a University Professor. The expression used is, that he desires to give a 'College' of Lectures. In using the words to announce his intention, Sibbald, therefore, is employing a recognised term, and without reference to the place in which the 'College' is to be given.

In '*A New English Dictionary on Historical Principles*, edited by James A. H. Murray, Oxford 1893,' after giving the derivation of the word 'College' and uses, under heading, *b*, he defines it, 'A Course of Lectures at a Foreign or Scottish University,' etc. In illustration he quotes '1700 *Gregory* in Hearne *Collect.* Oxf. Hist. Society, i. 321. He undertakes to teach . . . Mathematicks by way of *Colleges* or *Courses*. The courses or Colleges that he thinks of most . . . use are these.' Further he quotes '1741 *Scots. Mag.* Aug. 372 (Programme of MacLaurin). He gives every year three different Colleges and sometimes a fourth. . . . He begins the third College with perspective,' etc. etc.

Sibbald's course of Lectures—a reason for.

Before passing from Sibbald's course of Lectures, I wish to state that it has been questioned whether he ever lectured in the University or elsewhere previously. From this advertisement in the *Courant* newspaper, to me it is implied that he had not previously given a course of Lectures. He uses the words 'docere in privatis Collegiis incipiet.' Had he been in the habit, would not he rather have employed words to indicate that he would 'resume' his Lectures? Again, the subject of the course was to be Natural History and Medical Art. The words which follow are 'quam Dei gratiâ per annos quadraginta tres feliciter exercuit,' referring distinctly to the years he had been in Practice, which would be rather a singular statement to be made by a regular yearly Lecturer. It occurs to me that, as Sutherland died in the previous year, Sibbald by this course of Lectures on Natural History hoped or intended, in some measure, to supply his place, and until his successor at the Physic Garden was able to do so. Students were beginning to be attracted to Edinburgh, and he desired to retain them. But I reserve my explanation of Sibbald's appointment as a Professor till I come to consider the rise of the University Medical School in the concluding part of this Oration.

Sibbald's views on time occupied in the Study of Medicine.

Again, Sibbald appears to have had views regarding the time which should be occupied in the study of Medicine. I refer once more to his *Autobiography* (page 15), where, after remarking that during the five years he studied for his Degree in Arts, Leighton was Principal, he shortly after states: 'The impressions I retained from Mr. Leighton his Discourses, disposed me to affect charity for all good men of any perswasion' (when this is recalled it will be the more readily understood how his temporary perversion to Roman Catholicism so suddenly occurred when he was emotionally affected), 'and I preferred a quiet life, wherein I might not be ingrossed in factions of Church or State, . . . upon this consideration I fixed upon the Studie of Medicine, wherein I thought I might be of no faction, and might be useful in my generation, if not here, then elsewhere, upon which consideration I resolved to goe abroad to prosecute that Studie, and see the world and know men.' Then as to the duration of study,— I have already mentioned the subjects,—'I obtained the consent of my parents ther to, and went upon the twenty-third day of March 1660.' He stayed at Leyden a year and a half, and, during that time, his father died, which seems to have modified his duration of study; for he continues, 'and I considered I could not stay long abroad, so I applied myself to my Studie with great diligence.' Circumstances, therefore, shortened the period of his study. At the end of the year and a half, in September 1661, he proceeded to Paris and 'stayed some nyne months' there, visiting the Hotel de Dieu and the Hospital of the Charity, and then after a month's study at Angers, he was examined at that University by Sentor junior, Ferrand, Joiselin and Boisenute, and got his patent of Doctor there, so that his period

Impression retained by Mr. Leighton's Discourses.

Reasons for studying Medicine.

Stayed at Leyden. Death of his father.

Proceeded to Paris, then to Angers, where he graduated M.D.

Period of study.

of Medical Study was under two and a half years, but which with his Arts Course gives a University training of upwards of seven years. He graduated in Medicine in his twenty-first year.

Dr. Ralph Winterton's period.

This period falls short by some five years of that proposed by the Professor of Physic, Dr. Ralph Winterton, of the University of Cambridge, who, you may remember, wrote to the Royal College of Physicians of London that they should fix twelve years as the time they required candidates seeking admission to their body to study at a University. But, seeing that so large a portion of the seven years was passed by Sibbald in attendance upon *Medical* classes, and at Hospitals, it is certainly an improvement in Practical training upon that of Winterton. I may also remind you that the great Harvey's period of study at home and abroad was seven years. Sibbald himself implies, that had his family circumstances permitted, his time of study abroad would have been extended; but with close application to his studies, he was successful in passing the necessary Examinations at Angers to obtain the University Degree of Doctor of Medicine.

It would have been of interest to know his more mature views upon the length of time a student should spend in purely Medical study preliminary to examination, for his first motion the Minutes record after he was elected President was upon this subject. On 19th December 1684, the Minute is to the effect it was 'moved by the President Sibbald that the College take to their consideratione the minimum *quid sit* of the tyme that a Licentiat should study before he be Licensed, the same is remitted to the Council and Colledge.' Unfortunately the Report on this subject is not recorded; but it is to the credit of Sibbald and The Early Days, that the period of necessary training and study for a Medical Practitioner had engaged the attention and consideration of the College even at this period.

It is a curious coincidence that when searching for the notice of Sibbald's death in the *Caledonian Mercury*, I noted the following reference to the period of Medical study in the issue of 3rd September 1722, the month after Sibbald's death: 'The Universities of Oxford and Cambridge have desired the College of Physicians in London not to License any Physician who has not been nine years a student; which request the College agreed to.'

The English Universities and College of Physicians, London, in 1722, fix the period as nine years.

This is a reduction of three years from the twelve of Dr. Ralph Winterton's time, but according to its terms, the great Harvey with his seven years, and Scarborough with less attention to Medical studies, and Sibbald with his seven years at home and abroad, would all have been rejected by these sapient authorities. And even at this date, 1722, the English Universities had not increased the means for Medical study.

Harvey and Sibbald never met.

When this investigation into Sibbald's professional views was commenced, I regretted to find that Harvey and Sibbald had never met. On his homeward journey from the Continent, he stayed three months in London; but by this time, Harvey, after a well-spent life, had passed to his rest. That he was impressed with the Harvey spirit of Truth, Progress, and Sociality, his College career shows; and he must also have known Harvey's work, for one of his Discourses made to the College was *De Generatione Univocâ*,—concerning natural generation.

Sibbald and Pitcairne according to Bower.

According to Bower (vol. i. p. 371), Sibbald had excited the animosity of Pitcairne by condemning the Medical system of Bellini, the teacher whom Pitcairne chiefly upheld; and in 1696, he retaliated by a severe criticism of Sibbald's *Prodromus Historiae Naturalis Scotiae*. Although Sibbald would doubtless be familiar with Harvey's discovery and work, possibly through his intimacy in London with Scarborough and other disciples, I find no indication either of his approval or disapproval of Harvey's views on the circulation. Trained at Leyden in his youth, he probably accepted them as correct.

No doubt, in 'A Letter from Sir R— S— to Dr. Archibald Pitcairn,' on title stated to have been published at Edinburgh and printed in the year MDCCIX., the views of Harvey are questioned, and the words occur, referring to Pitcairn's *De Legibus Naturalis Historiae*, 'tho' in this Dissertation you have proposed the solution of *Harvey's* problem, yet I cannot see you have satisfy'd all the difficulties that occur in this matter, for I desire to know how it comes, that an animal breathes when it first comes into the world.' Yet the Reply to this attack on Pitcairn, ostensibly by Dr. James Walkingshaw, though really by Dr. Pitcairn himself, begins with the words, 'I have seen the Libel, rather than Letter falsely written in your Name to Dr. Pitcairn: And I think you may save yourself the Trouble of a Vindication. The sham is too gross to take. None that know Sir Robert Sibbald can ever be induced to believe that such Ungentleman-like Language could have dropt from his Pen.' This is confirmed by a statement written on the board of the book in the Royal College Library which declares, 'This letter which pretends to pass under the name of Sir Robert Sibbald, M.D., was written, at least owned privately, by Will. Cockburn, Physician at London.' Whilst it may be presumed that the writer of it represented Sir Robert Sibbald's opinions, it still remains that I have not met with a distinct statement by Sibbald himself upon Harvey's doctrines; for this letter with its falsities can scarcely be regarded as sufficient evidence of Sir Robert's views.

His later days unnoted, and time of Sibbald's death vague.

Like most of the Knights who have been alluded to, the later days of Sibbald are almost unnoted; and great vagueness has existed as to the place and time of his death, and as to where he was buried. My labours have been rewarded by tracing him to his grave. But it will be well to give a connected record of his career.

Sir Robert Sibbald was the son of David Sibbald, the third

youngest son of Andrew Sibbald of Over Rankeillor in Fife, by Margaret Learmonth, a daughter of the family of Balcomie. David, when the Earl of Kinnoul was Chancellor, held the office of Keeper of the Great Seal. As already narrated he died aged seventy-one years, while Robert was studying at Leyden in the year 1660, and was buried at Edinburgh 'in the Gray Frier church Yard, over against the South West end of the Gray Frier church, where our other relations lye.' He had married Margaret, the eldest daughter of Mr. Robert Boyd of Kipps, Linlithgowshire, an advocate. She is described by her son Robert as 'a vertuous and pious matron of great sagacity, and firmnesse of mynde, and very careful of my education.' She died at Kipps, 10th July 1672, aged sixty-six, and 'was interred in her father's grave, in the isle of Torphichen, and her name inscribed upon the part of the through stone that was voyd.' The 'through stone' as he describes I found in good preservation, but in position, displaced.

Sibbald's history and career.

Two sons and two daughters, who all died under the age of four years, were born before Sir Robert, and were buried in the Greyfriars' Churchyard.

Three children grew up—Robert was born on the 15th April 1641. The place of his birth was 'in a house neer to the head of Blackfriers Wynd, on the left syde.' The house is now removed, the place unmarked. He was a tender child. By the advice of his uncle, Dr. George Sibbald, Physician in Edinburgh, he was nursed for twenty-six months by a foster-nurse, who afterwards died in his service, at the age of seventy. He was a fretful child, and used to be quieted by handling a small copy of George Buchanan's translation of the Psalms of David. To escape the Plague in 1645, the family stayed at Kipps. His classical education began 1650 at Cupar Fife, he being then in his ninth year. The family afterwards removed to Dundee, and were residing there when it was stormed by the English troops. His love of collecting curiosities seems to have been developed at this

Robert Sibbald born 15th April 1641 in Blackfriars Wynd.

1650. Education at Cupar Fife.

Early manifestation of acquisitive disposition.

time; for he tells how his sister Geals, having exposed herself to the fire of the soldiers, he went to bring her into shelter; or, to use his own words, 'I runn after her to bring her back, and they fyred at us in the returning; the ball missed us, and battered upon the street. I took it up and brought it with me,'—an early manifestation of the acquisitive disposition.

Attended High School, Edinburgh.

After his return to Edinburgh his education was conducted at the High School there, under the tuition of Mr. Hugh Wallace. Thereafter he attended the University of Edinburgh for five years. The two last years—the Basler and Magistrant—he was under Mr. William Tweedy who laureated him, in July 1659, at the age of eighteen. The Principal at the time, Robert Leighton,—afterwards Bishop of Dunblane, and after the Restoration of Charles the Second, Archbishop of Glasgow—had a powerful influence upon him, and his Discourses sometimes in Latin and sometimes in English, 'with the blessing of God upon them, then gave me strong inclinations to a serious and good life.' The conduct of the Presbyterians gave him a disgust with them, and he could not therefore gratify his mother's wish to study for the Church. This may have led Bower to the conclusion 'that he had been educated in Episcopalian principles, and associated through life with those whose conduct was in open hostility to the Covenant and its Vindicators.'

Laureated Edinburgh University, 1659.

Went to Leyden to study Medicine, March 1660.

He resolved, therefore, to study Medicine; and, as he could not receive instruction at home, he left for the Continent on 23rd March 1660, in a Dutch frigate. Leyden was the place selected to study at. He stayed there a year and a half, and it was during this time that his father died. He also visited Utrecht and Amsterdam. An abstainer previously by training, whilst suffering from illness, he was advised by a Dutch physician to drink moderately,—'which I did afterwards.'

After nine months' study in Paris where he also attended the Hospitals, he proceeded to Angers; and, after a month's delay, was examined, and obtained the Patent of Doctor of Medicine. He next spent a little time in viewing various towns in France, and thereafter he made his way for the first time to London, where he remained three months, still enlarging his professional knowledge. Sir Charles Scarborough was then lecturing, and at this time that acquaintance was made which Sibbald subsequently turned to so good account.

First visit to London. Met Sir Charles Scarborough.

Considering himself sufficiently equipped to begin professional life, he now turned his face to the North, reached York by coach, and afterwards on horseback arrived at Edinburgh, on the 30th October 1662, in time to find his only brother dying from disease of the spine, the result of an injury, wantonly done, by 'ane Englishe Souldier.'

Returned to Edinburgh 30th October 1662.

Sibbald's early years were somewhat crippled by the losses his father had sustained at Dundee, and by his death, but 'blessed be God all his and my mother's debts were payed by me.'

He then applied himself in a liberal spirit to the practice of Medicine, resolved to be content with a moderate fortune, and prudently and considerately delayed marriage until after his mother's and his sister's deaths. The latter, Giles or Geals, became the second wife of James Chalmers, an advocate, aged about thirty years older than she. Her death occurred soon after the birth of her first child, a son. She is mentioned on Chalmers' Monument, Greyfriars' Churchyard. Sibbald was pleased neither with her marriage nor with the after behaviour of his nephew.

His sister Geals.

Death of.

On 26th April 1677, Dr. Sibbald was married to Miss Anna Lowes who, as he puts it, was the second sister of Master James Lowes of Merchiston. He had then just entered on his thirty-seventh year, whilst she was twenty-two years old. Their married life was happy but too short, for, after a visit to her sister, 'she contracted a malignant fever' and died on the eleventh day, the 27th December 1678.

Married to Miss Anna Lowes, 26th April 1677.

Her death 27th December 1678.

Dr. Andrew Balfour settled in Edinburgh.

'Some four years after' Sibbald had returned to Edinburgh, Dr. Andrew Balfour came home; and, after passing some time in London and a year at St. Andrews, settled in Edinburgh. The intimacy, commenced in France in his student days, was resumed with his kinsman, whom he prononnces to be 'a man of ane excellent wit.'

Have congenial tastes.

Congenial tastes as to Natural History and Botany, as well as the desire to collect specimens belonging to these and other departments of Science, cemented their friendship. Sibbald had previously made the acquaintance of Patrick Murray, 'the Laird of Levingstone,' also a student of Botany, and was a frequent visitor at Livingstone, where Murray had an extensive collection of British and foreign plants, 'near to a thousand.' Balfour was introduced by their mutual friend to Murray; and, on the latter going abroad to travel on the Continent, Balfour wrote him the letters I have referred to, and which were afterwards published by Sir Michael Balfour, his son, under the title of *Letters Written to a Friend*, etc. This intimacy and other correspondence with Balfour gave rise to the design of establishing the Medicine Garden at Edinburgh, as previously described.

Patrick Murray, 'the Laird of Levingstone.'

Introduced to Balfour.

Balfour's letters to a friend.

The Medicine Garden at Edinburgh. The first in the Abbey.

As above mentioned, the years 1677 and 1678 were those in which the chief events were, his marriage to Miss Lowes and her premature death from fever. About this time, 1678, through his cousin, Patrick Drummond, he was introduced to the fourth Earl of Perth, James Drummond. His picture, presented I rather think by Sibbald, hangs in the Hall of the College of Physicians. He presented another picture of him to the University. Dr. Henderson was then the Earl's Physician, but upon his death soon after, Sibbald succeeded to the position. Perth at this time was very observant of the rites of the Church of England, and had Episcopal service in his family. The state of his finances led him to embrace a public career, and to seek appointments. At this time he had just commenced his political life. He subse-

1678. Introduced by cousin, Patrick Drummond, to Earl of Perth.

On Dr. Henderson's death succeeds him.

quently became, first, Justice-General, and afterwards, Chancellor of Scotland.

The year 1680 is memorable as initiating the first dawning of a Medical Society in Edinburgh; for in this year there is another manifestation of Sibbald's possessing the *præfervidum ingenium Scotorum,* since it was that year he induced Drs. Balfour, Burnet, Archibald Stevenson, Pitcairne, and others, to meet at his lodging, once a fortnight, for conferences, as he termed them.

1680. Dawn of the Medical Society.

The next point of importance in his career was, when the division occurred amongst the Chirurgeons and Apothecaries which gave the opportunity wanted by Sibbald to start the formation of a College of Physicians. At the deliberative meeting of the Physicians in Edinburgh, as has been told, his quick wit and perception saw and took advantage of the chance. Although not one of the four Physicians selected by the Court of Session to guide its deliberations on the vexed question, still, as I have shown in this narrative, his position in the profession warranted, and no doubt gave weight, to his action, when he 'down right proposed the establishment of a Colledge to secure the priviledges of the Physitians.' And November 29th, 1681, when he saw the Patent, turned into Latin by himself, given in to the Chancery Chamber by himself, and patiently waited for, till it was written on parchment ready for the Great Seall, and the Seall at last appended, must have been one of the proudest days of his eventful life.

Meeting of Physicians. Sibbald proposes a College of Physicians.

November 29th 1681. The Great Seal appended to Patent of College.

He was appointed, as was meet, the first Secretary of the Royal College, and as such, had the control and organisation of its whole affairs, and being also a Member of the Council had a deliberative vote. How admirably he discharged the duties incumbent upon him, this history of The Early Days has fully disclosed.

Appointed the Secretary.

The honour next conferred upon Sibbald was in March 1682, when through 'the concertion of the Earl of Perth and Sir

March 1682. Knighted at Holyrood.

Charles Scarborough,' one Sunday after forenoon service, he was directed to attend at Holyrood, and to bring Dr. Archibald Stevenson, and Dr. Andrew Balfour with him. They attended, supposing their presence was wanted to confer about the College, but to their surprise, arrangements had been made for the ceremony, and they were each knighted by His Royal Highness the Duke of York, the High Commissioner.

3rd September 1682. Appointed Geographer for the Kingdom of Scotland.

When Sibbald was at first associated with the Earl of Perth, he had just been admitted a Member of the Privie Council. Through his influence, Sir Robert was made by Charles the Second, his Geographer for the Kingdom of Scotland, the Patent being dated 30th September 1682. He seems also about this time to have been appointed the King's Physician in Scotland, and was commanded to publish 'The naturall history and the geographic description' of Scotland. This work was 'a cause of great paines and much expense.' Save the honour, he, however, fared badly, for he tells, when subsequently he became Physician to King James the Seventh—'Yett I obtained nothing except a Patent for ane hundred Pounds Sterling of Salary from King James the Seventh, as his Physician. I gott only one year's payment.'

'The naturall history and geographic description' of Scotland.

Poor remuneration.

November 1682. Married to Miss Anna Orrock.

In November of this year, 1682, Sir Robert was married to his second wife, Anna Orrock, the youngest daughter of the Laird of Orrock of that Ilk, in Fife.

1683. Prospectus of Geographical Work.

Although occupied by so many events, he must also have been diligent in work, for the next year (1683), he published the advertisement of his intended Geographical Work, in Latin and English. It was to be 'ane account of Scotland antient and modern.' In 1684 the work, entitled *Scotia illustrata, sive Prodromus Historiae Naturalis Scotiae*, was published.

1684. *Scotia illustrata* published.

March 1684. Fire in his house at Bishop's Land.

But troubles were mingled with his honours, and his married life was not without its trials. Thus on 20th March 1684, through the carelessness of Lady Rosyth, who occupied the upper flat of his lodging in the Bishop's Land, Carrubber's Close, the house was set on fire, and he incurred the loss of 10,000 merks. In consequence of the alarm from the fire, his wife was prematurely confined in a neighbour's house of a daughter. The child lived only for four years, and it may be observed here that Sir Robert's children all died young. He failed to receive any reparation for the loss he had sustained by the fire.

His loss.

Premature confinement of Lady Sibbald.

Daughter live only four years.

Family all died young.

After holding the offices in the Royal College of Secretary, Councillor, Censor, a Member of nearly all the Committees, and the founder of its Library by the donation of about 100 volumes, and of the rudiments of a Museum, Sir Robert had the highest honour the College could bestow conferred upon him by being, on 4th December 1684, elected the second President, in succession to Sir Archibald Stevenson who had held the position since its foundation. Sibbald's notice of the event in his *Autobiography* is most unostentatious. It is 'I was made President of the Colledge of Physitians at Edinburgh upon the fourth day of December 1684 the day of election that year, and continued till the next election, as appears from the Colledge Minute-book.'

His position in Royal College.

Founder of Library and Museum.

4th December 1684. Elected President.

As indicating the respect and regard which the Fellows of the Royal College had for him, and of their desire to do him honour, in reward for his services rendered to the College before and after its erection, I direct attention to the fact that when the College was first incorporated, Sir Archibald Stevenson, the first President, was in his fifty-second year; Sir Andrew Balfour was in his fifty-first; and Sir Thomas Burnet in his forty-third year. All were senior to Sibbald who was then in his fortieth year. These three, it will be remembered, had been selected as the first Physicians in Edinburgh, to advise the Court of Session. But the College advanced Sibbald rather than Balfour or Burnet. The former succeeded Sibbald in the Chair according to the *Autobiography*. Pitcairne was the youngest of the Fellows, being at the time in his twenty-ninth year.

Age of the Fellows.

When Sir Robert Sibbald in June 1682 was elected Censor,

he 'did take the Oath of Alleadgeance, and did swear and signe the Roll.'

1682. As Censor took the Oath.

There is no record of the election of the first Council and President, but at the Annual Election on 30th November 1682,—after the Minute states the names of those elected to various offices,—it continues, 'and the samen communicate to them, they were admitted to their offices and gave the oath *de fideli*.'

At the election on 6th December 1683, it is stated who were elected office-bearers for the ensuing year, but no statement is made as to the administration of the oath.

When Sir Robert was elected on 4th December 1684, after the election is minuted, at the next meeting on 11th December, it appears 'Sir Robert Sibbald elected Praeses at last meeting, did take his place'; and Dr. Balfour having declined to act as Censor, the Council elected Dr. Learmonth in his place, 'who delayed to accept, but not upon the head of the Test, but for severall other reasons'; but the College adhered to the Council's election, and the Minute further states—'The President and his Censors did take the Oath *de fideli*, and did swear, and signe the Test, and . . . the Thesaurer took the Oath *de fideli*.' It should be observed here that the form differs from the previous elections in this that the President and Censors had to '*signe the Test*.' Further, on the 19th December, Doctor Cranstoune, it is stated, 'gave his Oath *de fideli* as Fiscall, who is appoynted *to take and signe the Test*.'

Dr. Balfour declines office.

President takes Oath and signs the Test. Not previously required.

At election of 6th December 1694 neither Oath nor Test mentioned. Important effect of Test on Sibbald's life.

The next minuted election is that of 6th December 1694, but on this occasion neither Oath nor Test is mentioned. I especially desire to call attention to this; for the signing of the Test, I cannot but think, had a very important effect on Sibbald. In December 1684, he was *free* to sign the Test. At the next election in 1685, he *was unable to sign*, and consequently could not be re-elected President.

The year 1685 is memorable as being the year in which the first Medical Professor of Physick was appointed in the University of King James the Sixth, and Sir Robert Sibbald was that distinguished man. His nomination was an honourable recognition by the Town Council of Edinburgh that one of the city's own children was not only worthy and deserving of being so honoured, but was capable of performing the duties incumbent on the new Professorship. And not only was it a testimony to Sir Robert's eminent professional reputation and talent, it must also be regarded as a great compliment to the Royal College, paid to it by its former antagonists. From the wording of the appointment, I submit it was not only to the first Medical Chair, but the first appointment to the Chair of *Practice of Physick*—held now so ably by one of our present Knights, Sir Thomas Grainger Stewart. It was no mean compliment to the College, that its second President was, whilst in office, selected to found the Medical reputation of this University. It will be observed, too, that *the Chair of Practice of Physick resulted from the erection of the College of Physicians*—one more honour to its originators. The following are the words of the appointment, with an extract of which from the Town Council Records of its sederunts I have been favoured by the courtesy of the former Town Clerk, W. Skinner, Esq., W.S., etc. 'The Counsell, considering that the College of this City, being from the originall erectione and foundatione thereof . . . erected in ane University, and indowed with the privaledges of erecting professiones of all sorts, particularly of Medicen, and that the Physitians have procured, from His lait Majestie . . . King Charles the Second, ane Patent, under his Highness' great Seall, for erecting them in ane Colledge of Physitians, And seeing that there is therefor a necessity ther be ane Professor of Physick, in the said Colledge, and understanding the great abilityes and qualificationes of Sir Robert Sibbald, his Ma'ties Physitian in ordinary, and his fittness to be Professor of Physick in ye s[d] University, Doe therefor as Patrons of the said Colledge and University, unanimously elect,

1685. Appointed Professor of Practice of Physick.

Wording of appointment.

The Chair resulted from the erection of the College of Physicians.

Extract from Minutes of Town Council *re* Chair.

nominate, and choyse the s[d] Sir Robert Sibbald, to be Professor of Physick, in ye s[d] University, and appoynts convenient Roumes in the Colledge to be provydit for him, where in he is to teatch the airt of Medicen, and the said Sir Robert being present and acceptain the said office made faith *de fideli administratione.*' He was elected on the 5th, and 'I was installed and admitted by the Magistrates to the exercise of the charge the 25th of March 1685' (*Autobiography*).

Sir Robert accepts the appointment, 25th March 1685.

As I intend in the concluding part of this Oration to comment upon the early Medical appointments in the Medical Faculty of the University, I refrain from doing so here, except to point out the high position Sibbald must have held in the public estimation, since the discriminating Patrons should have selected him, a man of so pronounced views as regards medical status and education, to be the first Professor of Physick in King James the Sixth's College. He was appointed in the middle of the Winter Session, probably with the intention that he should begin his course of lectures in the winter following. He could have lectured at this time, but he never did. Before the next Session came, *the Test* was in the way and *he could not then sign it.*

The Test prevents him lecturing.

1685. Change in his Church views.

And now I must advert to the great change which occurred during this year (1685) in Sir Robert Sibbald's Church views. I cannot but think this was an emotional alteration in the form, rather than in the principles of his religion. I refer to his perversion to Roman Catholicism, through his wily friend the Earl of Perth. His judgment, during his previous life, led him to see the advantages of the Reformed Church; but it had also convinced him of the injury done to the Presbyterian form, by the great divisions amongst its professors and adherents, and by the conduct of the ministry as being opposed to the spirit of true religion, in that 'they wrote reproachfull discourses against others, and occasional factions in the State, and private families, which gave me a disgust of them.' To the Episcopalians, he also objected

Perversion to Romanism through the Earl of Perth.

for their procedures. It may be remembered that the man of his admiration as a student, was Bishop Leighton. The thing he admired in him most was the tolerance he taught for the views of others. This dissatisfied feeling regarding the Church laid him in some measure open to be influenced by those he loved, and in whom he had confidence. In his youth therefore, and against the desires of his mother, rather than engage in these factions and prepare himself for the ministry of either of the Reformed Churches, it will be recalled that he determined to direct his mind and abilities to the study of Medicine, instead of Theology. It was not to Religion itself—for he was devout—but to the actions of its teachers and professors that he objected. He communicated in the Presbyterian Church, before he went to Leyden, and he afterwards mentions that he had prepared a religious manuscript for his guidance. Then, when he became intimate with the Earl of Perth, he refers approvingly to the strictness with which the home service of the Church of England was observed by him and his household. From the time when he derived comfort, as an infant, from Buchanan's Psalms of David, he was undoubtedly influenced by religious feeling, evidently of depth and sincerity, for it guided his actions.

How brought about.

In course of time, however, he states, 'by my extroversion towards the concerns of the Colledge and great persute after curious bookes, I had lost much of the assiet and firmness of mynde I had previously'; and in his admiration for Perth 'gave full scaith to my affection for him.' This is quite consistent with the rest of Sibbald's nature and disposition, which showed great impulse, warm affection, and devotion where duty seemed to him to require it. He was, as it were, for the time disarmed, and off his guard. He was also fresh from engaging in a controversy with the Bishop of St. Asaph upon the antiquity of our country and our kings; and he states 'this had occasioned in me some contempt of the English clergy upon that account, and some prievaricationes of some of our own folks upon some heads, had lowsed the attachment I had for our owne religion.' For two months, unknown to him, the Earl, although previously many times signifying his aversion to some of the doctrines of the Church of Rome, had become a pervert to the Romish faith. One Sunday when alone, at I presume a professional visit, the Earl confessed with tears that he was of that persuasion, and 'that he was convinced it was the true and ancient Church.' Much surprised at this confession, Sibbald thought there 'could be nothing more contrary to his interest.' Previously he had never spoken 'with any of the Romish clergy upon their doctrine,' he was secure and thought that whatever he (Perth) did, 'I could do better to continue in the Church I was born and bred in.'

September 1685. Death of Lady Perth.

So, in September 1685, he accompanied the Earl to the death-bed of Lady Perth at Drummond. With the neophyte's enthusiasm her husband had 'brought her over to the Romish persuasion.' 'Good lady,' Sir Robert continues, 'she, I believe, did it out of the love she had for him, and took it for granted that ther was no more in it then that she sould be saved only by the merits of her Saviour.' She assented to the worship and service. 'But all she said herself that I heard, was what any Protestant believed, and used in the agonie of death to say.' So she died, and ceremonies were used at her death-bed. And she being gone, the crafty pervert commenced the attack upon the Doctor. The *Lyfes of Gregory Lopez*, and *of Father Davila* were given him to read, and followed by conversation on the Romish religion. Sir Robert expressed his aversion, for their want of charity for those who were out of their Church, but the Earl controverted this by 'they believed that any good man of a different way from them that had a sincere love to God would be saved. I said I was glad to hear that.' The subtle Earl noted the yielding mind, and towards midnight he called Sibbald to his study, and 'there he read to me a paper that the Duchesse of York had writt, upon her embracing that religion, and discoursed very pathetically upon it.' And then 'I knew not how it came about, I felt a great warmness of my affections while he was reading and discoursing and there upon, as I thought, *aestro quodam pietatis motus*, I said I would embrace that religion, upon which he took me in his arms and thanked God for it.'

And thus Sibbald in one of his impulsive moods—his respect for the professors of Presbyterianism and Episcopacy having been lessened by the divisions, factions and prevarications of the clergy—was acted on by the more masterful mind of the watchful and insidious proselyte. He was influenced just at the time when judgment was in abeyance, and emotional sentiment in full force. Thrown off his guard, whilst swayed by his affection and sympathy for his distressed friend deeply and solemnly oppressed by the death of a beloved wife, Sibbald impulsively cast off his allegiance to the Reformed, and declared himself a son of the 'true and ancient' Church.

The hasty and imperfectly thought out change is not difficult to understand. Too trusting, too impulsive, too soft in his ingenuous loving heart, impressed by the place, the silent house, the midnight hour, the death scene of the Countess with its ceremonies so recently witnessed, Sir Robert too weakly resigned his will to that of the Earl, the stronger for the time, who had an object in gaining over so esteemed a man of mark and influence as Sibbald at this period was. Whilst he from sentiment, rather than from conviction, declared his readiness to join that Church, to which the politically aspiring Earl of Perth, to strengthen his scheming selfish ends, had already secretly seceded.

Sir Robert had no selfish ends to gain.

It was a loss to him.

Sir Robert Sibbald had no selfish ends to gain. He was at the height of his ambition. By this step he might have strengthened his personal friendship with the now powerful Chancellor, but otherwise, and in the end, he lost what he had already gained. His Presidency of the Royal College and his Professorship in the

University had to be resigned, at least he could not discharge the duties, seeing that, as a Roman Catholic, he could not now *sign the Test*, and having previously done so, and so resiled from it, he was afterwards charged by his opponents with having perjured himself. Therefore, to this among other reasons, it probably was due that he never lectured in the University, for as a Papist he was unable to take the Test. In November of this year, no doubt, the King had written telling the Council to relieve Papists from taking the Test, but the populace were now against him, and Principal Andrew Cant, a stout enemy to Papists according to Fountainhall, was yet alive when the Session began, and he did not die till December. The University was therefore closed to him.

As regards the Royal College of Physicians, the absence of Minutes may have had some connection with this defection of Sibbald. They do not show how long he was President, but from the *Autobiography* it may be surmised that he only held office till the election day, towards the end of 1685, and within three months after his perversion. This supposition, it seems to me, is supported by the entry in the *Roll of the Royal College of Physicians of London*, by William Munk, M.D., F.S.A., Fellow of the College, etc., vol. i. p. 441: 'Sir Robert Sibbald, as Physician to James II., on the 29th March 1686, during his retirement in London, was admitted a Fellow of the College of Physicians here.' It will be observed he is not designated as President of, nor as having any relation to the Edinburgh College of Physicians.

Admitted Fellow of College of Physicians of London.

Pitcairne, the man of easy religious sentiment, now found his opportunity, and gave free expression to his satire and his sarcasm.

Edinburgh rabble on 1st February 1686, attempt to 'Rathillet' Sir Robert.

The rabble, too, judging that Sibbald had led the Earl of Perth to embrace Roman Catholicism from his secrecy and silence, rather than that the Earl had perverted him, vowed to be avenged on him. Accordingly, on the 1st February 1686, they made the assault while he was sitting in his chamber reading.

They came to his house to assassinate him, or as they termed it, to 'Rathillet' him, as Archbishop Sharp had been by Hackston of Rathillet and others. Calmly he had prepared for death, and, forewarned earlier in the day of their intention, he had made his will, and, instead of trying to escape, sincere in his emotional adoption of the Romish religion, he awaited the attack of an Edinburgh mob of three or four hundred persons. As they approached he 'fell upon his knees and commended his soul to God,' and apprehensive of what they might do to him, he next made his escape from the house. A neighbour, lodging below him, gave him the key of the yard, and leaping the dyke, he got out to the braes between Carrubber's Close (at the top of which, in the Bishop's Land, he resided) and the Calton Hill. He remained there all night, but being found in the morning by his own people, he returned home to find that his wife had made a narrow escape from being murdered by the excited mob. They broke down the outer door, and searched the house, with dirks and axes and hammers. His poor wife was only saved from being murdered by the assailants being assured that she was a Protestant; and the mob left, swearing they would yet 'Rathillet' him. He escaped to Holyrood in General Drummond's coach with Claverhouse (then the Viscount Dundee), and afterwards, in company with Lieutenant Drummond of the Life Guards, he journeyed to Berwick, and thence in six days on horseback to London.

Lady Sibbald's narrow escape.

Sir Robert escapes to London.

I again point out that at this period of his career, at the time of his perversion, it could not be otherwise than an insuperable loss to him. He had gained all the honours he could desire before this. The Royal College, so dear to him, had been completely established. All his pet schemes in connection with it were in full force. He had filled all the subordinate offices he desired. He had been its second President, and might have continued to be so for at least another year. He had been knighted in 1682.

His perversion a loss to him.

Appointed Physician to King Charles the Second and the Duke of York, now James the Second, and was the Geographer-Royal for Scotland, and seven months previously he had been appointed the first Professor of Medicine in the University. He was an author of reputation and renown, the *Scotia Illustrata* having been published in 1684, and he 'had got much practice in the country about upon either side of the river Forth.' He was now also the full proprietor of his cherished Kipps, to which at an earlier period he had 'had ane great inclination to retire there, to enjoy himself in the solitude,' and to apply himself to the country with more conveniency. He had been made a Burgess of Edinburgh in June 1685, a position of more honour and importance then than now, and he was also for the second time happily married.

It is difficult, therefore, to see what further professional honour his accession to the Church of Rome could confer. The only Courtly one he secured, as already mentioned, was 'ane pensione of ane hundred Pounds Sterling for being Physitian to King James the Seventh, given to me by King James, the 12th December 1685,' and he only received one payment.

His perversion must, therefore, be assigned to impulsive religious impressions, brought about in the way I have endeavoured to explain, and not 'to a desire to find favour in the eyes of a bigoted monarch,' as has been alleged. He could gain nothing, but lost largely, for the *Test* stood in his way.

Reached London. Carried to Court to kiss King's hand.

To finish the story, Sir Robert Sibbald reached London in indifferent health. The next night he was carried to Court to kiss the King's hand. 'He spoke very kindly to me, and I prayed God to preserve and bless him, and sayed no more, and never went to him after that,' his reason being 'for I heard, they thought I had gone to Court to sollicite for the Romanists, so I keeped out of it, and gave myself entirely to devotion, while I was at London.'

I do not repeat his meeting with Sir Charles Scarborough, his reception at and admission as Honorary Socius of the Royal College of Physicians of London, nor his interviews with Sir Robert Boyle of the Royal Society.

After two months his health gives way.

After being in the Metropolis for two months or so, his health further gave way, the result of his exposure on the Braes of the Calton Hill and his trials. 'The change too of dyet, keeping Lent, when few good fishes could be had,' also affected him. He was troubled with cough, rheumatic pains, and want of sleep. Ultimately he was seized with rose in the right arm and hand, 'for the aire of the river and city' did not agree with him. The emotional mind was telling on his debilitated physical condition.

Wavers in his allegiance to Romish Church.

He continues: 'I likewise began to think I had been too precipitate in declaring myself of the Faith of the Romish Church, though I joined in the simplicity of my heart, and had no other opinion of the Presence in the Sacrament and of Meat, than what Dr. Holden in his *Analysis Fidei* maintained.'

Noted the error of the Jesuits.

He also saw and noted the error the Jesuits were committing in pressing the King to illegal and unaccountable undertakings, and that they 'were opposeing the takeing of the alledgiance which I was bound to by oathe.' Here the influence of the Royal College upon him is seen, for he had taken the oath of fidelity and signed the Test therein. His judgment was regaining its power. His emotional rashness would not stand the scrutiny of his conscientious and truthful nature.

The Romish faith at variance with allegiance to his country. Resolved to come home and return to Protestantism.

As taught by the Jesuits, the Romish faith was at variance with his allegiance to his country and to his profession. 'Upon which considerations, I repented my rashness, and resolved to come home and return to the Church I was born in.' Reflection had convinced him it was the best for his country and for himself.

Accordingly he returned to Edinburgh by sea, as he was, on account of his recent illness, unable to ride. Immediately upon his arrival, his first duty was to sever the recent tie between him and the Chancellor Perth, by telling him of his resolution to return

First told Chancellor Perth of his return to Protestantism. Retired to Kipps.

to the Protestant Church. He intimated it, also, to others who visited him, and he went no more to the Popish service. He retired to the country, most probably to Kipps, and to worship again in the old Templar Church of Torphichen, in the 'Isle' of which his mother had been interred. Episcopacy was then in power; and upon acknowledgment of his rashness he was received by the Bishop of Edinburgh, took the Sacrament according to the way of the Church of England, and thereafter kept constant to his Parish Church. And so after being Romanist for a year he was able to record: 'I thanked God who opened my eyes, and by my affliction gave me grace to know myself and the world, and to take better heid to my wayes, and amend my lyfe, so that I recovered my health when in the opinion of all men and according to my own, I was past recovery in a decay, occasioned by what is said before, and my regret for my rashness.'

Received by the Bishop of Edinburgh.

His thanks to God for opening his eyes.

After considerable time returns to Royal College.

It was a considerable time before Sir Robert again attended the meetings of the Royal College. He was absent when the split occurred, but seems to have been summoned to attend on the day Stevenson locked the door of the College. He was once more elected to the Council, took his share in the Discourses, and supported the President Trotter by his presence at the business meetings.

1695, superseded as Examiner.

In January 1695, after the Minutes were resumed and preserved, Sibbald does not appear to have been attending; and, though previously one of the yearly Examiners, he was at this date superseded by Sir Archibald Stevenson. From September 14th to 5th December of this year, he was present at every meeting, and on 18th November gave a Discourse.

18th November, gave a Discourse.

During 1696, he was not quite so regular in his attendance, but was present at the Election Meeting and was again voted to the Council. On 5th February 1697 he gave his Discourse on 'Generation,' and although absent from a good many meetings, at the December meeting he was again elected a Councillor.

5th February 1697. Discoursed on 'Generation.'

During 1698 the Royal College met twelve times, and at no meeting was Sibbald present, nor did he hold any office. Sir Thomas Burnet was the President in 1697 and 1698, and was succeeded by Dr. Matthew Sinclare, who held office in 1699 and 1700.

1698. Present at no meeting.

Burnet's last appearance in the College was on 6th February 1699. Sibbald was also present, having been absent, as I have stated, all the previous year. The business does not appear very clearly from the Minutes of that date; but, from preceding and subsequent records, I have come to the conclusion that it must have had reference to the Pharmacopœia, and that Sir Robert, feeling the persistent opposition to its publication, absented himself from the meeting, in indignation and disgust. Burnet was now in the position of King's and Queen's Physician. His sympathies were with the Revolution Government. He had been Regius Medicus to King William, and was also so to Queen Anne. From Sibbald's absence from the meetings one is also warranted to conclude that the previously existing friendship had been interrupted by the position he had taken when he joined the Papists, which was manifestly at variance with the religious views of the Protestant Physician, the brother of the Bishop of Salisbury.

Burnet's last appearance 6th February 1699. Sibbald was present.

Business the delayed Pharmacopœia.

Sir Thomas Burnet never was present again at any meeting of the Royal College, and died in March 1704 as previously stated.

The removal of the Suspension of the Rioters was moved on 31st January 1700, but on conditions, and none of the suspended Fellows took advantage of it. In fact they were still contumacious, and would not give in to the terms offered. On January 7th, 1703, the movement was more successful, but not until the 2nd of December, nearly a year thereafter, did any of the suspended take advantage of the vote. On that day four of them attended, namely, Drs. Eccles, Olyphant, Smelholm, and Robertson.

31st January 1700. Removal of Suspension of Rioters moved.

Also on January 7th, 1703.

30th November 1704. Sir Robert present.

On 30th November 1704, Sir Robert again attended the meetings of the Royal College. There must have been an understanding previously amongst the Fellows; for, with the exception of Dr. Melville, all the other suspended Fellows were present. Dr. Halket was elected President, and Stevensone, Sibbald, and Eccles were elected to the Council. Pitcairn was present, but received no honours. Eccles was further elected a Censor and nominated by Dr. Halket to be pro-Præses; Dr. Smelholm was appointed Treasurer.

Peace restored in the College.

Peace seemed to be once more restored, and the Royal College emerged from the shade under which it had lain for so many years.

Sir Archibald Stevensone present 28th March 1706. Pitcairn last present 12th March 1706. He died in 1713.

Sir Archibald Stevensone continued to attend till 28th March 1706, whilst Pitcairn's last appearance was on 12th March of the same year; and rather than give a Discourse, he kept his name on the College Roll of Fellows, and was fined for absence at every quarterly meeting, till his death in 1713. So that Sibbald's scheme of the Discourses was the means of freeing the College from the sarcastic attacks of this antagonist for many years.

Sir Robert gave Discourse, 29th October 1705.

Sir Robert gave a Discourse on 29th October 1705, and on 13th December seems to have been Convener of the Library Committee, then appointed. But with the collapse of Pitcairn, his regular attendances seem to have been affected. He continued to be tolerably regularly present, till 14th November 1706.

Examined twice in 1706.

He was in the Council, and during 1706 examined twice on Practical Cases, and once upon the Aphorisms.

27th June 1707 present. Mortification of 1250 merks to Dispensary by Mary Erskine or Hair.

He did not again attend till 27th June 1707, when he appears to have been interested in the Mary Erskine or Hair Mortification to the College of 1250 merks 'for buying druggs to the sicke poore who have advice gratis from the Colledge,' which was part of the business before the College at this meeting.

For more than a year, Sibbald is again absent, but resumed attendance in August 1708. The cause of his presence I judge to have been the presentation of the Petition for trial and examination of Dr. Robert Lowes, a graduate of Leyden. I conclude from the same that he must have been a relation of the family of which Sibbald's first wife was a member. On 24th August, in the absence of Dr. Dundas who had been at the previous meeting appointed, he examined Lowes on the Aphorisms, and was nominated one of the Examiners for the final Examination on the Practical Cases—so that he examined candidates when not far short of the threescore and ten years' limit.

August 1708. Present when Dr. R. Lowes presents Petition for Trial.

On November 2nd and 9th, when the admission of Dr. Lowes as 'Socius' was agreed to, he was also present to admit and receive him.

At the following Election Meeting he was put on the Council, when Dr. Sinclare was appointed President; but, from 7th December 1708 till 22nd December 1709, he was present at no meeting. Dr. Montgomery's examination was then in progress. Sir Robert was present when Dr. Montgomery was admitted Licentiat on the 29th December, but henceforth his name never once appears in the sederunts of the Royal College. It may have been on account of this that the confusion regarding the date of his death has arisen, but he lived for thirteen years thereafter.

From 7th December 1708 till 22nd December 1709 not present. Last present 29th December 1709.

Maidment, who edited his *Autobiography*, at the conclusion of it, on page 44, in a footnote states, 'the precise time of Sir Robert Sibbald's death has not been ascertained.' A Catalogue was printed at Edinburgh, 1722, 4to, of 'The Library of the late learned and ingenious Sir Robert Sibbald of Kipps, Doctor of Medicine. To be sold by way of Auction on Tuesday 5th February 1723, at his house in the Bishop's Land in Edinburgh, where placads will be affixed.'

Time of Sir Robert's death. Inaccurate times.

Mr. M. F. Conolly in his *Biographical Dictionary of Eminent*

Men of Fife, Cupar Fife, 1866, observes: 'The period of Sir Robert Sibbald's death is not known, but from the last of his published works being dated 1711 it is supposed to have been in 1712.'

The new edition of *The Globe Encyclopædia* states, 'He died about the year 1712.'

R. Chambers, in 1855, in his *Biographical Dictionary of Eminent Scotsmen*, states that he died about 1712.

Anderson, in his *Scottish Nation*, says, 'period of death' not known, supposed to have been in 1712.

Stark, *Biographia Scotica*, Edinburgh, 1805, neither gives date of Sir Robert's birth nor death.

Dr. William Munk, in *The Roll of the Royal College of Physicians of London*, 2nd edition, London, 1878, has it: 'He died about 1712.' These are all wrong, for there is evidence that he was alive at a later date.

Search for time and place of Sir Robert's death.

To find out the date of Sir Robert Sibbald's death, and where he was buried, has given me a great deal of interesting and earnest labour. For I felt it was not seemly that the last resting-place of 'ane Physitian' so distinguished in himself, in those remote days of scientific darkness, and, moreover, of one to whose untiring energy and determination the Royal College of Physicians of Edinburgh owed its existence, and its early professional distinctions and pre-eminence above the then existing Institutions, should be so slighted and treated with such want of respect and reverence. I therefore devoted a portion of my spare time, as it occurred, to organise and prosecute the search.

Greyfriars' Kirkyard.

Naturally as his father, brother, sister, children, and first wife were interred in the Greyfriars' Kirkyard, I turned first to Mr. Brown's book of Monuments and Records of burials in that historic resting-place of the dead. His sister Geals' name as the wife of Mr. Chalmers was readily found, but of his father, or himself, or other member of his family, there was no trace. I inspected the spot described by himself where his father was buried 'in the Greyfriar Church Yard, over against the south-west end of the Greyfriar Church, where our other relations lye,' but no trace could I find of memorial stone to mark the place. The Superintendent could give me no information; but, in course of time, it occurred to me I was looking at the wrong place. I had inspected the south-west end of the New Greyfriars' Church. When was this built? was it since his death, and if so, were the landmarks then removed? On looking into this subject, I found that in 1681 there was a steeple or tower at the west end of the Old Greyfriars' Church, and that in this year, as there was no bell in the steeple, the Town Council ordered one which had formerly been used in the Tron Church to be hung in Greyfriars'. Unfortunately, at a later date, the economical Town Council considered this tower—being only used once a week for ringing the bell—would be a good place for storing gunpowder, and accordingly made use of it for that purpose. On the 17th May 1718, the gunpowder from some reason exploded and damaged the tower and church. The Sibbald family burying-place, being at the south-west end of the old church, would necessarily suffer; and if a stone had been erected, it would no doubt have been injured or destroyed.

Not in father's burial ground.

Destruction of tower of old church.

Rather than rebuild the tower at a cost of £600, the Council resolved to add a new church to the west end of the old one; and, that both buildings might be of the same length, the original one was shortened.

These changes were finished in the course of 1721. Now, had a monument been erected to Sibbald at the date of his supposed death, Robert Monteith, M.A., in the second part of his *An Theater of Mortality, or a further Collection of Funeral-Inscriptions over Scotland*, would have certainly noted it, for this part of the *Theater* was not published till after his second advertisement regarding the publication of it had appeared in the *Courant*, on 19th August 1713, while the first part was published in 1704.

Not mentioned in Monteith's *Theater of Mortality*.

I therefore concluded that there had been no monument, and that, if dead, he probably was not buried there. On the other hand, had there been a monument within the church it would have been noted, and doubtless some record of it would have been found or recalled when the church itself was restored after the fire of 19th January 1845. If, therefore, as reported, the date of his death was about 1711 or 1712—as even his portrait by Alexander in the Royal College Hall testifies to—had there been any inscription Monteith would have mentioned it; and, if a monument had been erected after 1713, the explosion had possibly destroyed it. But I was not satisfied with this state of uncertainty.

Search at Torphichen Priory.

For some years, so far as record goes, Sibbald was as if lost to sight. Age and illness had probably incapacitated him for the active business of life. He lived in the quiet retirement of Kipps. His mother died there, and was buried in her father's tomb, under the Through or Thruck Stone in the 'Isle' of old Torphichen Church. What place more likely for the Antiquary to choose for his last resting-place? especially when he was one of tender feeling, emotional in sentiment, and loving in nature.

One bright summer afternoon, I made a journey to the Church of Torphichen—hallowed from its associations with the Knights Templars as well as with Sir Robert Sibbald of Kipps—passing as I travelled Carribber Mill and Kipps, both now possessed by others than the Boyd or Sibbald families. Through the polite attention and interest of the Minister of the Parish, the late highly esteemed Rev. John M. Johnstone, admission to the ancient Priory was obtained. It is distinct from the part at present used as the Parish Church, and belongs to Lord Torphichen, whose ancestor having the distinguished honour to be the Superior of the Knight Templar Order, when it was deprived of its prerogatives, had the good fortune to succeed in retaining the Priory and lands.

Entering from the old churchyard, in which are many stones bearing the impress of the lapse of years, I found the Priory to be a desolate-looking place, and bearing little evidence at the time of my visit of being carefully looked after. When almost despairing of finding the stone as described in Sibbald's *Autobiography*, I came upon one seemingly out of place. It lay on the ground, in the shade of the dim—but, from the bare and desolate and untidy surroundings, I cannot say—religious light. It seemed to me, as if this could not be the 'Through Stone' of which I was in search; for the inscription, which was very well preserved, looked too clean cut to have been executed more than two hundred years ago; whilst the letters were peculiar, covered as they were with dust and soil, and when this was rubbed off they were difficult to be understood. We wanted more light. With that thrown by a few matches on the limestone slab, we found we had in darkness been trying to decipher the inscription with the stone in wrong position. The Through Stone had been removed from its original position, placed resting against the wall, with the inscription turned towards it—I presume for its preservation—and had subsequently fallen backwards on the ground, and consequently the inscription was reversed. I found this well-preserved slab was the stone I had come to search for, and that the inscription to Robert Boyd, his grandfather, was there in perfect form, as was also that graven below it by his loving and dutiful instruction to 'Margareta Bodia, denata 10 Julii 1672,' his mother. The inscription was easily read, when looked at in the right way. I found nothing more than the inscriptions as given by Sibbald in his *Autobiography*. There was no mention of the son who had caused them to be graven. I raised the slab, lest there might be some record there. It was smooth and blank. The Rev. Mr. Johnstone kindly interested himself in my inquiry, and afterwards wrote: 'I have looked over the Church Registers and I can find nothing relating to the subject of your inquiry.'

The 'Through Stone' found.

'Margareta Bodia.'

The Rev. Mr. Johnstone communicated with a gentleman (W. H. Henderson, Esq.) in Linlithgow, who some years previously had been interested in the same quest, and he kindly informed me that he 'had reason to think that Sir Robert had died in the vicinity of Dunfermline, and that probably there may be some note of it at the office of the Lord Lyon in the Register House.' Following up this hint, I could learn nothing of 'Sibbald' there; but, on the page where his name was looked for, I observed that of Sir Archibald Stevenson, and so was put on a trace of him to work on—with the result stated in my notice of Stevenson. When the Lyon King, Mr. Balfour Paul's, book, *An Ordinary of Scottish Arms*, was published, I found that Sibbald's arms were registered.

Search at Lyon Office.

Next, I remembered that one of Sir Robert's children by his second marriage with Anna Orrock, a daughter, was still-born in July 1686 'at Baldrick at her sister's house, and was buried in the Church Yard of Dunfermline.' Unfortunately the name of the married sister-in-law was not given, and the ownership of Baldrick has changed since 1686.

At Dunfermline Abbey.

So, as others have done before, I made a pilgrimage to the city of the saintly Queen Margaret, and the shrine of Robert the Bruce. But no trace was found at the Abbey, either of Sibbald or his child, in the Record of Interments in the olden time, in the Abbey Churchyard, and I was referred by the sexton to the Registrar-General's Office in Edinburgh. On inquiring, I learned that the times had been often very disturbed in the days gone by, and that the Records of the presumed years of Sir Robert's death were unfortunately wanting.

In *Courant* Newspaper.

Puzzled but not yet despairing, I read that his books and library had been advertised in the *Courant* to be sold, so I determined to have a look at the original paper. In the file of the *Courant* I had access to, the early volumes were wanting, the first obtainable contained the papers from 31st December 1722, and in that of 1st January 1723, was an advertisement that there was just published '*Bibliotheca Sibbaldiana*, or a Catalogue of curious valuable books . . . being the Library of the late learned and ingenious Sir Robert Sibbald of Kipps.'

Sibbald was dead then on 1st January 1723, but I could not see the volumes of the *Courant* for an earlier year to ascertain when he died. I was again thwarted. There is a copy of the Pharmacopœia in the College, published in 1721. It contains a list of 'Socii, Honorarii Socii, et Permissi,' and is dated 'Prid. Cal. Decemb. 1721.' The original owner of this copy had noted subsequently the dates of death of some of the Socii, but at Sibbald's name he had written 'ob.' but no date. He was, therefore, alive at the end of 1721, and dead at the end of 1722. *He must, therefore, have died in the course of* 1722.

The College Pharmacopœia.

Having ascertained the year, and still desirous to ascertain the exact date, I applied to the Advocates' Library to see the volume of the *Courant* for that year, but was once more disappointed. It did not have that volume, but had a copy of the *Caledonian Mercury*, which was courteously placed before me by Mr. Clark, the Librarian; and, on searching it, my persistent efforts were rewarded by reading in the paper dated Edinburgh, Monday, August 13th, 1722, the following words:—

Notice of Sir Robert's death in *Caledonian Mercury* of 13th August 1722

'Edinburgh, August 13th.—Last week Sir Robert Sibbald of Kipps, M.D., Fellow of the Royal College of Physicians, died here in the 83rd year of his age. He was a person of great piety and learning, and author of many learned and useful books, especially in Natural History.'

I had now got some definite information. He died 'last week,' therefore between the 6th and 13th of August 1722, and in Edinburgh. What was the exact day, and where was his resting-place? It was not at Torphichen nor at Dunfermline—was it in Edinburgh?

In the course of my inquiries I had learned that under the

The Greyfriars' Burial Records.

care of the City Chamberlain (Robert Adam, Esq.) the Records of Burials in Greyfriars' Churchyard were kept, under the charge of a special officer—the Recorder—at the City Chambers, Royal Exchange; and that, if I could read the writing of the time, as they went a long way back, I might find there if the burial had been in Greyfriars'. Mr. Adam at once very kindly gave me permission to examine these well-preserved records of mortality; and with the ready and courteous assistance of Mr. Ferguson, the Recorder, the volume of Index and the Record of Burial for 1722 were placed before me. My labours were at last rewarded when I read: 'Sunday, 12th August 1722, Sir Robert Sibbald of Kipps, Doctor of Medicine, aged 82 years, dyed 9th, buried 12th, lyes the foot of the middle Phesdoes ground, hearse, Turff,' and further, from Records of Interments in Greyfriars' Burying-ground from 1st April 1717 to August 31, 1728—'Sir Robert Sibbald of Kipps, Doctor of Medicine, aged 82 years, died 9 and buried 12 (August) within Phesdoes ground, Middle East End thereof.' So that the conclusion of my inquiry is that he was

Greyfriars' Records. Sir Robert died 9th August 1722, aged 82 years. Buried in Phesdo's Ground.

Born in Blackfriars Wynd, Edinburgh, on
15th April 1641;
Died in the Bishop's Land, Carrubber's Close,
9th August 1722,
in the 82nd year of his age;
And buried on Sunday, 12th August 1722.

The question now presented itself—Who was Phesdo, and where is his 'ground'?

I found in the Register of Lairs Purchased the following entry:—'Allow Mr. John Falconer of Phesdo, Advocate, 12 foot from East to West upon the South dyke of the Greyfriars, to East about 12 foot of Littell of Liberton Tomb, and 14 feet from the Mid dyke upon the South, and the Greyfrier Kirk on

Falconers of Phesdo.

PHESDO'S BURIAL-GROUND, WITHIN WHICH SIR ROBERT SIBBALD WAS BURIED.

the North, for burial Place.' Granted, 15th June 1705. On entering the Greyfriars' Kirkyard, and turning to the left, and following the path by the south wall about ninety paces, Phesdoes ground is reached—a bare and dismal spot. Externally the enclosing wall was intended to be ornamental. It may be judged of by the accompanying photograph, but internally it is bleak and bare, and destitute of 'turff.' On the south wall there is a monumental slab and a smaller one, but they have reference to the Phesdo family and Lord Halkerston's, and not to my Medical Hero. Sir James Falconer of Phesdo died 10th June 1706, and is buried here. He was one of the Senators of the College of Justice, a Member of the Privy Councils of King William and Queen Anne, and one of the first Treaters for an Union.

Reason why buried in Phesdo's Ground.

If it is asked why was Sir Robert Sibbald buried here, the answer is simple. His family ground could not then be got at. It was at the south-west corner of the old Church. Near this had been the tower of the Church, and the erection of the new Church and alterations on the west end of the old were not yet completed. The burial-ground could not in consequence be used. Probably Falconer of Phesdo was on terms of intimate friendship, and his ground being but a little distance to the south and east, and as it were overlooking the old Church, a resting-place for the veteran Physician was found here, after his eventful life. There was probably a sympathy between the Phesdo family and Sibbald in their Church and Political views.

And so the conclusion of the matter is that Sir Robert Sibbald of Kipps—the genial gentleman, the earnest promoter of Medical Progress, the advancer of Natural Science, the projector of a Statistical Account of Scotland, the preserver of Ancient Landmarks, the successful founder of the Royal College of Physicians, the planner of its career and the originator and director of its Early Efforts, and one of its first Knights, the first Professor of Physick in King James the Sixth's University, and the impulsive, sincere, and pious Christian—without a stone or other sign to mark a great man's sepulchre, lies unostentatiously at Phesdo's feet, in alien though in friendly ground in Old Greyfriars' Kirkyard.

Judge leniently his weaknesses, his many excellencies admire. 'He was a man of pure intentions, of amiable dispositions, and of a generous temper.'

PART V

AFTERWARDS

PART V

AFTERWARDS

Y work is done as regards the History of the 'Royall Colledge of Physitians in Edinburgh' before, at the time of its erection, and during The Early Days of its existence. I have still something to add as to the Results which followed afterwards.

I have, as far as the information has been obtainable, reviewed the Lives of its First Knights, and less fully those of its original Socii. The impression conveyed by the retrospect of these men's lives, as deduced from the College Records, has been that each Fellow had his individuality, but that all were at first influenced by the magnitude and importance of the great undertaking they had inaugurated. Disputes, which have so frequently led to the imperfect development or to the annihilation of many a good enterprise, fortunately did not succeed in wrecking the young College. Jealousy and factiousness tried to hinder its course and progress, but its inherent force was too powerful and vigorous to be overcome, and in spite of difficulties it rose superior to them. The effect of the opposition it had to contend against from the time of its inception tended but to nerve its supporters for the fray, and to teach them how best to contend with and overcome its internal dissensions. And when its first projectors, one after another, succumbed to the natural weaknesses of humanity, and Dr. Robert Trotter and Dr. Matthew St. Clair were alone left of the twenty-one originators, they were not called away until the Elected Fellows were imbued with the traditions of The Early

Days, impressed with their responsibilities, and had become capable of discharging the duties of the Trust which, as Fellows, by obligation, they had voluntarily undertaken.

Immediately after its erection the Royal College manifested the desire to conciliate its four former opponents. As soon as the idea of the Dispensary was mooted, it showed that its inclination was to be, and to live, at peace with all men, and that it wished to be on good terms with the Municipality and the Clergy. It approached both with the information that it had inaugurated a new procedure, that it had arranged to attend to the sick poor of the city and suburbs, to aid in relieving their suffering and distress, without charge to them, and without remuneration to itself. To the Clergy it was intimated that cases, certified by the Ministers of the several Kirk Sessions to be poor and sick and 'in severe bounds,' would be served by Fellows of the College gratuitously. But whilst acquainting the Provost and Town Council of the College's intention to undertake and perform this charitable function of looking after the medical care of the poor of their city, it also, as was most natural, required them to nominate 'some person to be Apothecary, and to give some allowance' for his services. A favourable understanding was come to with their *quondam* antagonists, even although the liberality of the Municipality was not conspicuous.

With the Chirurgeons amicable terms were longer of being arranged. It was left for this generation to fully establish a loving and friendly conjunction, and that not only with the Royal College of Surgeons in Edinburgh, but likewise with the Faculty of Physicians and Surgeons of Glasgow. This happy state of concord was brought about through one of the 'Efforts' the Royal College took an early interest in—improved Examinations—and by meeting the wants of the Medical world by the promotion, *Firstly*, of a double examination and qualification in Medicine and Surgery in association with the Royal College of

Surgeons in Edinburgh, and with the Faculty of Physicians and Surgeons in Glasgow. And, *Secondly*, by the Conjoint Scheme, in which the Physicians and the Surgeons of Edinburgh and the Faculty of Glasgow combined to grant a triple qualification in which representative Examiners of all the three Boards take part, and so was completed the desirable and congenial union of those who once were foes, individual interests being sacrificed for the benefit of the country at large, and of the Medical Profession in general.

Still later has the union in the Metropolis of Scotland been further consolidated by the establishment of the Extra-mural School of Medicine of the Royal Colleges of Physicians and Surgeons of Edinburgh.

But not only did the College take the initiative in conciliation. The Town Council took action even during The Early Days. As has been already mentioned, before these were passed, it not only graciously acknowledged the Institution but also paid it the very great compliment of actually rewarding and dignifying its most active agent, Sir Robert Sibbald, when it selected him to fill the Chair of the first Professor of Physick in King James Sixth's (of blessed memory) University, of which they were the Patrons—a most remarkable compliment to the merits and abilities of the man. One can imagine those astute civic representatives saying amongst themselves, He has succeeded in setting our opposition aside, he must be a man of power, therefore. Let us put him into the University to develop a Faculty of Medicine there, as he has developed the College of Physicians! We see what he has already been able to do in spite of us and the University! Better secure him to work in it and for it and us, rather than against its interests and future welfare. I fancy this appointment may thus be explained, though to some it has seemed to present difficulties. The Town Council, on account of Sibbald's relation to the Physick Garden from its inception, must have been aware that it was not a mere pleasure garden for the amenity of the city, but that he and Balfour desired and intended it to be for the study of Botany and for instruction in the nature and uses of the vegetable *Materia Medica*. They must have known that the Intendent selected by them, Mr. James Sutherland, had carried out their views by instructing those who aspired to become Apothecaries—all of whom would no doubt also be apprentices—and such laymen as desired to obtain a knowledge of plants. They must also have been aware that with the exception of the occasional dissection of the body of an executed malefactor (only the importance of the study of Anatomy was not held in as high estimation in those days as it is in these, and was regarded in this city as being in the department of the Chirurgeons rather than in that of the Physicians), and some insight into Chemistry, there were no other public means of acquiring instruction in the Medical Art in Edinburgh. As Patrons they were no doubt also aware that two of the older Universities—St. Andrews, and especially Aberdeen—granted the Degree of Doctor of Medicine with probable benefit to their repute and revenue, and that in the first-named there was no Medical Faculty, and in the other only a Professor of Physick, 'the Mediciner.' If the services of the energetic Sibbald were secured it was reasonable to expect that some of those aspiring to become Medical men would seek the honour of a Degree from Edinburgh. In the hope therefore that Students of Medicine might be attracted hitherward, the Council 'Doe therefor as Patrons of the said Colledge and University unanimously elect, nominate, and choyse the sd. Sir Robert Sibbald to be Professor of Physick in ye sd. University, and appoynts convenient Rowmes in the Colledge to be provydit for him, wherein he is to teatch the airt of Medicen, &c.,' showing clearly he was to teach if he had pupils, and to aid in the University conferring the Degree in Medicine if Candidates came forward. But there were two difficulties. *First*, the absence of Students and Candidates, and *Second*, the views held by Sibbald. It has been seen that it was diplomacy only that induced him and his coadjutors in the creation of 'The Royall Colledge,' to agree to *Scottish graduates* being admitted *without Examination*. His own view evidently was that no one should be admitted to the Profession without examination, and from the perfect form of the Royal College's 'tryall,' more than one examination was required, and that *the Faculty of Medicine, therefore, should consist of more than one Member*. Accordingly we next find that two other Physicians are added, Dr. James Halket and Dr. Archibald Pitcairne. Referring again to the Minutes of the Town Council of 4th September 1685, the following interesting entry is found:—'The which day the Counsell appoynts two professors of Medicine to be joyned,' note the words, 'with Sir Robert Sibbald in the University, and the Professores to be named the next Counsell day, but the professores are to have no Cellarie from the Town or Colledge.' Accordingly, 'on 9th Sept. 1685, the same day, the Counsell considering that by ther act of the dait, the 24th day of March last, had elected, nominate, and chosen Sir Robert Sibbald, Doctor of Medicen, to be professor of Medicen in the University of this Citie, and had thereby appoynted convenient Rowmes for him in the Colledge for teatching the airt of Medicen, and that he had compeired and accepted his office, and made faith, And the Counsell considering that ther is ane necessity ther be more Professors of Medicen in the sd. University, and understanding the abilityes and great qualifications of Doctor James Halkit and Doctor Archibald Pitcairne, Doctors of Medicen, and ther fitness to teatch the airt of Medicen in the said University, Doe therefor elect, nominate, and choyse ye sd. two Doctors to be joyned with the said Sir Robert Sibbald, his Majestie's Physitian in Ordinary, to be professores of Medicen in ye University with ye sd. Dr. Sibbald, and appoynts convenient rowmes in the Colledge to be provydit to them for teatching the said airt of Medicen, But the Counsell declaires the sd. Professors are to have no Cellaries from ye good town, nor from ye sd. University, and the sd. Doctor Halkit and Doctor Pitcairne being pret. (present) and acceptain ye offices, made faith de fidei administratione, Lyk as the Counsell appoynts Baillie Brand to install them in ye offices.' There is no evidence in the Royal College Minutes, as there is in some of the subsequent appointments, that the Royal College suggested these men. They seem to have been proposed by the Town Council itself.

It does not appear that any one of those three taught in the University. Were not the two 'joyned' with Sibbald to form a Faculty of Medicine? As yet there were no Students, but the Faculty was now there to examine for a Degree in Medicine when applicants applied for it.

Sibbald was appointed on 25th March 1685, in the middle of the Winter Session; and before the next returned, he was disqualified. He had joined the Romish Church in September, and could not now take the Test. Pitcairne, it may be presumed, was preparing himself to Lecture; but he, too, never seems to have had any one to instruct; and before he had, his reputation had gone abroad, and he was called to fill the position of Professor in the University of Leyden. From the Lectures on record he delivered there, it may be concluded that the department he was to fill was that of the Institutes or Institutions of Medicine. But all three were to teach 'The Airt of Medicen.' In Sibbald's first appointment the term used is 'Physick.' It seems, however, to have been left to each to choose the department of 'The Airt of Medicen' he preferred, and was fit to teach.

Whether Halket intended to Lecture does not appear, for there is no evidence, although he was not disqualified, that he ever did.

Having the power to erect a Faculty of Medicine, though the term is not mentioned, the Patrons exercised it. But the time had not yet come for the kind of Students to present themselves, and indeed no Candidate for a Medical Degree presented himself for several years thereafter. The easy acquisition of that obtainable without trouble, at the two older Universities, possibly helped to save the University of King James the Sixth from conferring its Medical honours too easily. All honour to it that it was so! and that it never condescended to soil its reputation by trafficking in the sale of Medical Degrees without Examination, and the personal appearance of the Candidate before its Faculty or its representatives. That the University of Edinburgh did not do so, it has especially to thank the Royal College of Physicians and its first Medical Professors.

The Examination of Dr. Kello having been so recent, and the style of it so new, it would doubtless be the subject of talk in the small would-be scientific community of the city; and from the terms of their appointment, and the readiness with which Drs. Halket and Pitcairne were appointed, one would conclude that the Patrons from the first were prepared for Medical Candidates being examined.

Before passing on, I wish to remark, that Sibbald's selection shows the repute in which he was held by the Patrons; for although, at this time, Drs. Balfour and Burnet, both his seniors, were in practice in the city, and as 'Physitians' seem to have held a higher reputation than he, yet in the eyes of the Patrons, neither of them possessed the kind of abilities required to establish a Faculty of Medicine. Is not this another testimony to the acknowledged pre-eminence of Sibbald? Nor was Archibald Stevenson, a son of the former Regent, mentioned. It was only in the learned, energetic, and versatile Sir Robert Sibbald, that the Patrons—shrewd business men—saw the qualities they considered to be requisite for the first Professor of Physick.

A few months upset the Scheme, as has been shown in Sibbald's Life; and, after several years had passed, Medical

Degrees were conferred, before there were Students to teach or teaching Professors to give instruction.

This was the second tribute of approval the Royall Colledge received from the University of Edinburgh, its former strenuous and powerful opponent. *It solicited the aid of the Royal College to examine the Candidates for its Degree in Medicine!* The compliment was paid too, before there was any other Medical Faculty than that constituted by the Town Council appointing Sir Robert Sibbald and Drs. Halket and Pitcairne, Professors of 'The Airt of Medicen.' It had fallen into abeyance, if it was ever constituted; for when at last a Candidate presented himself for the Degree of Doctor of Medicine, it was not called on by the University to act, nor had it any say in the matter, except as individual Fellows of the College of Physicians. But before entering on the subject from the College of Physicians' side, it will be proper to consider the views of Sir Alexander Grant on the growth and development of the early Medical School in the University of this city.

Sir Alexander Grant's account of the beginning of a Medical School.

Sir Alexander Grant in *The Story of the University of Edinburgh*, etc., in the first volume treats of the 'Beginnings of a Medical School.' He states that after 'the establishment of the Physic Gardens and of the College of Physicians . . . the Town Council took in the Keeper of the Physic Garden to be Professor of Botany in their College, and three chief Members of the College of Physicians to be Professors of Medicine. These last appointments were almost entirely honorary; class-rooms were provided for the so-called Professors, but teaching was left optional, and certainly none of them taught systematically. This, however, was the tentative outset—a sort of false dawn—of the University Medical School' (p. 294). At page 220, after describing the steps 'so judiciously taken' by Sibbald and Balfour, he continues: 'A few years later what had been done was associated with and incorporated into the College, for in 1676 the Town Council passed an order that, 'considering the usefulness and necessity of encouragement of the art of Botany and planting of Medicinal herbs, and that it were for the better flourishing of the College that the said Profession be joined to the other Professions, they appoint a yearly salary of £20 sterling to be paid to Mr. James Sutherland, present Botanist, who professes the said art; and upon consideration aforesaid, they unite, annex, and adjoin the said Profession to the rest of the liberal Sciences taught in the College, and recommend the Treasurer of the College to provide a convenient room in the College for keeping books and seeds relative to the said Profession.'

It may be observed that no room is mentioned for teaching in—only for storage. The teaching was presumed to be done elsewhere, probably in the Garden. Sir Alexander further states: 'Nineteen years later, in 1695 (fourteen years after the erection of the Royal College), the Town Council, after stating that the "Physic Garden is in great reputation both in England and foreign nations, by the great care and knowledge of Mr. James Sutherland," appointed him still more formally Professor of Botany in the College, with all the emoluments, profits, and casualties, and with the "pension" of £20 sterling annually, which had been formerly granted him.' It is somewhat remarkable that Sibbald, whilst adverting to the remuneration of Sutherland, in no way indicates that he had been assumed as one of the University Professors, and one concludes it was rather as Intendent of the Garden that he received his stipend, than as a University Professor.

The Physic Garden preceded the erection of the Royal College, and with it the College had nothing in the way of business connection or relations further than the Socii taking interest individually in the remuneration of the Intendent. In the Minutes there is no reference to Mr. James Sutherland, nor to his appointment in 1695 as a University Professor.

Mr. Alexander Bower, in his *History of the University of*

Mr. Alexander Bower on Mr. J. Sutherland. On his retirement.

Edinburgh, published in 1817, when referring to Mr. Sutherland's retirement, mentions that he had been Professor of Botany for thirty years; and that he probably retired from want of proper encouragement, and had resolved to live in greater retirement, to quit the Profession of Botany, and to apply himself to the study of Medals; but it does not follow from his statement that he had been a Professor in the University for that length of time. He was succeeded on 1st May 1706 by Dr. Charles Preston, a Fellow of the College of Physicians. He held a Scottish Medical Degree, and was admitted Licenciat on 21st November 1704, and Socius on 1st December, without examination. According to Grant, he succeeded Sutherland in 1706, and in 1707 advertised in the *Edinburgh Courant* on 16th May: 'Dr. Preston teaches his lessons of botany in the Physick Garden at Edinburgh the Months of May, June, July, and August 1707,' etc., vol. ii. p. 380. It will be observed that he styles himself 'Doctor,' not Professor. The date of his death is given as 1711, which seems to be borne out by what follows. In the Royal College on 4th October 1705 he was appointed one of a Committee, with Sir Robert Sibbald and others, to 'revise the books and rarieties of the Colledge, put them in order, and make inventories of them, and by whom they have been gifted, with such other regulations yr anent as they shall find expedient,' and on 6th December, in the same year, he is appointed Secretary and Library Keeper, and on 13th December a Library Committee was appointed, with him as Chairman.

Succeeded in 1706 by Dr. Charles Preston, F.R.C.P.E.

His advertisement in *Courant* 1707, as Doctor not as Professor.

His death in 1711.

Under 6th May 1712 the following is noted: 'The said daye the Colledge appoynted Wm. Riddell, the Clerk, to make inquiry as to what was resting by the Town of Edinburgh to the deceased Doctor Prestoun of his Salary, and how it be affected, and to report to the next quarterly meeting.' It will be observed that no reference is made to his connection with the University, either in that or the succeeding Minutes. On

5th August 1712, I find the following 'Report as to Dr. Prestoun's Salary. The Clerk was informed that there was resting to the Doctor about 20 lb. star., and that the same with some other debts due to the Doctor were confirmed by his brother George Prestoun the Botanist for payment of the funeral charges and others.' From this Dr. Charles Preston does not appear to have found the profession of Botany to be remunerative, and did not die possessed of large means, and the probability of the College receiving cash for his Bond was very doubtful.

Report by Committee of Royal College as to his salary.

He was succeeded by his 'brother-german' Mr. George Preston, Apothecary and Druggist, on 2nd January 1712. In the Minute of his election as quoted by Bower, vol. ii. p. 119, the commencement is—'The Council considering that the office of Professor of Botany of this City and Master of the Physick Garden thereof is now vacant. . . . Therefore the Council have nominated and elected the said George Preston to be Professor of Botany and Master of the Physick Garden of this City . . . and the Council allowed to him the sum of ten Pounds Sterling of yearly salary for his encouragement, to carry on the said Profession of Botany and cultivate the said Gardens,' etc. This does not read as if the Council regarded him as a Professor in the University, but 'of this City.' If he was so regarded it does not appear that he was appointed as a Professor of a Medical Faculty. George Preston had evidently an eye for business, for the opportunity of securing the Royal College's sympathy and assistance was not to be lost; accordingly 'The same day the College having heard the Representation given in by George Preston, Intendent of the Physic Garden, by Aut[ie] (Authority) of the Magistrates of Edinburgh, giving ane account of the improvements he had made of New Plants and herbs, with a list of the samen plants and herbs in the said Garden—and craving ane act of the Colledge recommending him to all noblemen, gentlemen, and others, the Colledge recommend the consideration of the said representation to a Committee with

Succeeded by Mr. George Preston, his brother-german, 2nd January 1712,

as Professor of this City and Master of the Physick Garden.

His representation to the Royal College.

power to them to grant the recommendation as they shall see cause and to drawing the samen in his favour without the necessity of its coming back to the Colledge.' This is a rather undignified appeal by a University Professor, though proper enough from the Intendent of the Garden, and a dealer in plants and herbs. On 4th November 1712, Dr. C. Preston's Bond is directed to be given up to 'George Prestoune, bottanist, Intendent of the Physick Garden, his brother-german, gratis, with a discharge yr of.' From this it may be held that Dr. Preston died poor. If a Professor at this time, the position does not seem to have been on a like level with that of the Professor of Medicine; and I judge it was not so regarded till a later day when Alston was appointed, also as Professor of Medicine in 1738.

Dr. C. Preston's Royal College of Physicians Bond given up to Mr. George Preston.

As regards the Chair of Anatomy, with the exception of the extract referred to in Monro's application, the subject did not come under the province of the Royall Colledge; and as Grant (vol. i. p. 294) observes, 'the first impulse having come from the newly created College of Physicians, the second came from the College of Surgeons, who, having got a fresh Royal Charter in 1694, and also a grant from the Town Council of unowned dead bodies, opened an anatomical theatre in 1697.' I have already, in the notes on Dr. Archibald Pitcairne, shown the part he played in stimulating the College of Surgeons to teach Anatomy more systematically and thoroughly.

The Chair of Anatomy, according to Sir Alexander Grant, came from College of Surgeons.

Their Anatomical Theatre opened, 1697.

After this digression I return again to the consideration of the Minutes of the Royal College, its connection with the University of Edinburgh, and the conferring of its Degree of Doctor in Medicine. This may be best stated in narrative form.

Consideration of the Minutes of the Royal College connected with the University.

Dr. Dundas on the Election day, 3rd December 1702, had been 'choysed for President,' and re-elected 2nd December 1703. The Minute of 13th July 1704 records: 'The same day upon a representation made by the President that he had spoke both to the Principal of the Colledge of Edinb^r and Glasgow anent ane

Dr. Dundas, President, 1702.

agriement betwixt the Colledge of Physitians and the four Universities. The Colledge appoynts Doctors Eccles, Dicksone, and Monro (John, M.D. Aberdeen), or any two of them togither with the President, to meet with the fore named Principal or any deputed by the said Universities to confer upon the said agriement and report.' From the Minutes, it does not appear what was the nature of the proposed conference. It may be supposed that it had reference to the Degrees conferred by some of the Universities without examination, and the compulsory admission of the possessors of them to the Fellowship of the College. For, shortly before this conference, it is learned from the Minutes that Dr. John Drummond, after being remonstrated with (7th July and 21st August 1701) by the College for practising in Edinburgh illegally without its Licence, set the College at defiance, was prosecuted, 13th December 1702, and then having really obtained a Degree from Aberdeen claimed his rights as a Scotch graduate from the Royal College, and was admitted *without examination*, 11th January 1704.

Agreement betwixt Royal College and the four Universities.

Dr. John Drummond's prosecution and subsequent admission.

There is no entry concerning the Report of the conference; but, on the 19th July 1705, there is a Minute which evidently has reference to that of 13th July 1704. It is to the following effect: 'The whilk day, the Colledge appoynt Sir Robert Sibbald, Dr. Sinclair, elder, Dr. Eccles, Dr. Mitchell, Dr. Dundas, Dr. Dicksone, a Committee to sie what agriement they can make with the Universities of the Kingdome upon the terms of the proposalls formerly made to the said Universities, and lyke wayes to take into their consideration, some other things relating to the order of the Society,' etc. This would indicate that the previous conference had been held, and terms proposed, regarding which no agreement had been come to; and at the next meeting of the Royal College, a practical and material matter was also remitted to this Committee, 'to consider what those who apply to licentiat without examination shall pay to the Colledge for their Licence,'

Further consideration of the Agreement.

Fees to be paid for Licence without Examination.

a remit which suggests that the holders of Scotch University Degrees had been demanding in virtue of their qualification, to defraud the Royal College of its fees, for the Licence to practise.

To finish this preliminary subject, I may observe that after it had been before the Royal College by motion, at three meetings (without there being any further reference to the Universities), it was brought to a conclusion, very much I should suppose to the annoyance of the Universities, 'The sd. day (October 29th, 1705), the act anent Licentiats entering without examination being read a third tyme, and approven of, *nem. con.*: that such Physitians as shall apply to the Colledge, to be made Licentiats without submitting themselves to the examination, shall pay ane thousand merks Scots to the Colledge for the Licence.'

Shall pay 1000 merks Scots for Licence.

Meantime the Edinburgh University of King James the Sixth of Blessed Memorie, and who also favoured the erection of a College of Physitians, acted towards the Royall Colledge in what, to it, must have been a very pleasing and satisfactory way, especially when it is remembered that more than twenty years had passed since the Town Council showed its good feeling by appointing from their number the first Medical Professors.

Dr. James Halkett, President.

Dr. James Halkett (one of those Professors) was now President, and occupied the Chair; whilst Sir Archibald Stevenson, Sir Robert Sibbald, and Drs. Trotter, Lauder, and Pitcairn of the original Fellows were, with others, present.

5th April 1705. Letter from Mr. William Carstairs, Principal of the College of Edinburgh, applying to Royal College to examine Mr. David Cockburn.

The Minute of 5th April 1705 reads: 'The whilk day a letter from Mr. William Carstairs, Principle of the Colledge of Edinburgh, directed to the President was read—bearing that Mr. David Cockburn, Student of Physick, haveing addressed for the Degree of Doctor of Medicine, the Professors of that University desyre the Colledge of Physitians to give themselves the trouble to examine him, and that the President wold lett him know their opinion. The Colledge ordered the said letter be kept amongst the Records of the Colledge, and Mr. David Cockburn to give in his bill to be admitted to examination, and that he doe it next Meeting of the Colledge, which is appoynted to be the tenth instant (April) at thrie o'clock in the afternoon.'

A Candidate, the first for the Medical honours of King James the Sixth's University, had at last come forward. The Medical Faculty, for the constitution of which the Town Council had elected the elements in 1685, had either never been constituted, or, if so, had from disuse fallen into abeyance; and in its extremity the University Authorities sought the aid of that Institution it had done its best in former years to oppose being formed. Little wonder that Principal Carstairs' letter was ordered to be 'kept amongst the Records of the Colledge,' whilst the form and method of the Royal College three-part Examination received the stamp of University approbation and approval.

The first Edinburgh University Candidate.

Five days thereafter, on 10th April, 'The Colledge, having heard the Petition, given in by Mr. David Cockburn, craveing that some of their number may be appoynted to take tryall of his qualifications and progress in the Study of Medicine which way and manner as they shall think fitt, and to report their opinion to the Principall and Masters of the University of Edinburgh, that he may have the Degrie of Doctor of Mediceen conferred upon him, which petitione being redd and considered by the Colledge, they grant the desyre thereof, and ordered Doctor Smelholme and Doctor Mackenzie to examine him upon the Institutions this day eight dayes, at thrie o'clock in the afternoon.' Accordingly on the 17th April, David Cockburn was examined on the Institutions, and the College was satisfied. He was examined in presence of seventeen Fellows, including Dr. Halkett the President, Sir Archibald Stevenson, Dr. Lauder, and Dr. Pitcairn; but Sir Robert Sibbald was absent, as also were Drs. Trotter and Sinclair elder.

The Royal College grant the desire of Mr. David Cockburn's Petition.

Is examined on the Institutions.

The second Examination, upon two Aphorisms of Hippocrates, was conducted by Dr. Dundas and the President Halkett, one of the Professors appointed in 1685 as was fitting, whilst Dr. Pitcairn, also one of the then appointed Professors, with Dr. Lauder, examined him upon two Practical Cases, for his third and final Examination on the 1st of May. Being satisfied with 'his explanation' conducted before the sederunt of eighteen Fellows—the same three Fellows being absent from all his Examinations—the College 'find him duly qualified to practise Medicine, and recommend to the President to make Report of their opinion to the Principall and Masters of the University of Edinburgh, in order to have the Degrie of Doctor of Medicine conferred upon him; and the said Mr. David, being always obliged to give in his Petitione to be admitted a Licentiat of the Colledge, after he has got his Degrie, before he practises.'

He graduated on the 'thretten of May,' on 29th June was admitted Licentiat of the Royal College, and on 30th August, all in 1705, was admitted Candidat and Socius in the ordinary form.

This is the history of the admission of the first Candidate for the Degree of Doctor of Medicine in the University of Edinburgh, and of the first Fellow of the Royal College holding that Degree, cementing that union which, then begun, should always continue between these two national Institutions. The Royal College taught the University how to examine, and gave the initiative to a long line of honourable and distinguished graduates *after examination.*

Minute 26th December 1710. Letter from Principal Carstairs regarding examination of Mr. Jonathan Harley.

After an interval of five years, a communication was again received from the University. The Minute of 26th December 1710 records—'The which day the President haveing received a letter from Mr. William Carstairs, Principall of the University of Edinburgh, to the effect underwritten, whereof follows:—"Edinb. Decr. 25, 1710.—Sir, Mr. Jonathan Harley, a persone of great probity and worth, and of singular accomplishments in learning, having applyed to the Professors of this University for the Degrie of Doctor of Medicine, and we not haveing at present a Facultie of that useful Science, Doe desyre the favour of your honorable

Societie, to take such a Method as they shall think fitt, for knowing how he is qualified for haveing the Degree that is desyred, which upon your recommendation we are all heartilie willing to bestow upon him. The inclination that we have to keep a friendlie correspondence with your College, and to doe nothing that is irregular, or may give any just ground of offence to you, is the cause of yore haveing the trouble of those lines, in the name of the Professors in the Universitie, from him who is with great respect, Sir, yore most humble Servant, sic subscribitur, W. Carstares." Which letter being read and considered, by the Colledge, they doe appoynt Doctor Mitchell, Doctor Dicksone, and Doctor Forrest, with the President (Matthew St. Clair) or any two of them, to take tryal of the said Mr. Jonathan Harley his qualificationes in all the parts of Medicine, and if he be found to be qualified to recommend him to the Principall and Professors of the said Universitie of Edinb[h], that the Degrie of Doctor of Medicine may be conferred upon him in such manner as they think fitt.'

6th January 1713. Letter from Principal Carstairs regarding the examination of Rev. Mr. Caleb Threlkeld.

After an interval of a little more than two years, on 6th January 1713, another communication was received from the University. 'The whilk day the President having received a letter from Mr. William Carstairs, Principall of the University of Edinburgh, to the effect underwritten, whereof the sense follows:—"Edinb., Jany. 5, 1713.—Honoured Sir, The constant desyre that the Professors of this University have, to keep a friendly correspondence with your honourable Societie, is the cause of my giveing you the trouble of these lines, that you may know that the Rev[nd] Mr. Caleb Threlkeld applyed to us for the Degrie of Doctor of Medicine. We delayed to give him an answer, till you should, after tryall, approve of his sufficiencies, and to recommend him to us as one worthie of that degrie. We relye so much on your kyndness as not to doubt of your granting our desyre, which will oblidge us, and par[lie], honored Sir, your most faithfull and most humble Servant, sic subscribitur, Wm. Carstares," directed on the back thus:—"To the honored Dr. Sinclair, President of the Colledge of Physitians at Edinburgh." Which letter being read and considered by the Colledge, they doe appoynt the President, Dr. Stewart, Dr. Riddell and Dr. Craufurd,—two with the President to be a quorum,—to take tryall of the said Mr. Caleb Threlkeld his qualifications in all the parts of Medicine, and if he be found qualified, to recommend him to the Principal and the Professors of the said University of Edinburgh that the Degrie of Doctor of Medicine may be conferred upon him in manner as is usual in the lyke caice. Signed Matthew St. Clair, P.C.R.M.E.'

The Records of the University show the Examination was successful, and that the Degree was conferred upon him on 26th January 1713. It may be noted that these Examinations were conducted in the Hall of the Royal College.

But a change in the relations between the Royal College and the University was not far distant, and it happened in this way.

23rd November 1710. Dr. James Crawford, M.D. Leyden, petitions for trial.

On 23rd November 1710, Dr. James Crawford petitioned for 'tryall'; he was a graduate of Leyden. On 28th November the Royal College were satisfied with his answers in his Examination on the Institutions and also with his explanations, on 5th December, of two Aphorisms, and on 12th December being 'well satisfyed with his explication of two Practical Cases,' he was admitted Licentiat. He was received as Socius on 13th February 1711. At the Elections on 6th December, of the same year, he was elected Secretary and Librarian. He filled these offices till 14th April 1713. In the Minute of that date, 'the President represented to the Colledge that Dr. Crawford, Secretarius yr to, had informed him that he was going abroad furth of the country, within a fourtnight, about his lawful affaires, and that he might be a considerable tyme before he returned, and therefore desyred that

6th December 1711. Elected Secretary and Librarian.

14th April 1713. Resigns office as he was going abroad.

the Colledge might name one of their number to be Secretarius in his place,' etc.

The College approved, and Dr. Montgomery was appointed in his place. Dr. Crawford was present at meetings on 5th May and 24th July; but, on 23rd November, a communication is once more received from Principal Carstares. The Minute regarding it is as follows:—'The which day (23rd November 1713), a letter being presented to the Colledge from Mr. William Carstares, Principal of the Colledge of Edinburgh, to Dr. Sinclair, President, dated 20th November 1713, where in he represents, that it might be of Publick advantage, to have a Professor of Medicine established in their University, and that Dr. James Crawford being mentioned to them, as being peculiarlie fitted for that post, the University thought it proper to acquaint the Colledge of Physitians with the affairs, that they might be favoured with the character of that gentleman, before they made application to their Patrons about it": which letter being read in presence of the Colledge, they were very well pleased with the qualifications of the said gentleman, as very fitt for that post, and gave him a very ample character, and recommended the President to give a return to the said Principal of the Colledge of Edinb. his said letter, in favour of the said Dr. Crawford, who is a Fellow of the said Society of Physitians, and they also recommend that the President give thanks in name of the Colledge to the Principal and Masters of the said University, for their civility to the Colledge.' And of course by this time Dr. Crawford was at home again, and at the following Election, on 3rd December 1713, resumed his position of Secretarius and Bibliothecarius; and for the third time the office of Secretary was filled by one who was advanced to Professorial dignity.

23rd November 1713. Letter from Principal Carstares regarding the appointment of a Professor of Medicine.

Requesting Royal College's opinion of the character of Dr. James Crawford.

3rd December 1713. Dr. Crawford resumes office in the Royal College.

At the following meeting, for some reason not stated, but possibly from the check the raising the fee for Licence without Examination had made upon Scottish University Entrants, it was

Fee for Licence reduced to 500 merks.

On 4th May 1714 Dr. John Clerk, M.D. St. Andrews, petitions for Examination.

determined that they in future shall pay 500 in place of 1000 merks. The difference in the value of fee on a good, well-qualified man, is shown on 4th May 1714, by Dr. John Clerk, who *although a graduate of St. Andrews University,* petitions for a 'tryal,' although he could have been Licensed by payment of the still high fee without Examination.

Four University graduates admitted M.D. *ad eundem.*

Between January 26th, 1713, and November 1718, the University Roll of Graduates shows that four gentlemen had the Degree of Doctor of Medicine conferred upon them. Of these there is no mention in the Minutes of the Royal College, and none of them appears to have petitioned for the Licence to Practise. The *ad eundem* Degree was probably conferred upon them, and they did not settle to practise in Edinburgh.

4th November 1718. Letter from Principal Wishart requesting the Royal College to appoint Examiners to join Dr. Crawford in examining Mr. James Eccles in the Library of the University.

On 4th November 1718, there is a Minute to the effect—'The same day the President having produced a letter from Mr. William Wishart, Principal of the University of Edinburgh, to the effect under written and yr of the tenor following, "the Facultie here having appointed our Professor Doctor Crawford, to examine a young gentleman, in order to his receiving the Degrie of Doctor of Medicine and there being no other Physitian in the University at present, it is humbly desyred by the Faculty, that your Royal Society may be pleased to appoynt one or more of their number to joyn with Dr. Crawford in the said Examination in the Library of the University. The tyme for it may be either to-morrow, or Friday, or any other tyme that may be judged most convenient, only you will be pleased to acquaint me, that I may advertise Doctor Crawford. I am, Sir, your most humble Servant, sic subscribitur Will. Wishart. Edinb., October 29th, 1718." Directed on the back, thus, To Doctor William Stewart, President of the Royal Colledge of Physitians in Edinb. Which letter being read and considered by the Colledge, and the person's name, upon whom the Degrie of Doctor of Medicine was desyred to be conferred, being, Mr. James Eccles, son to Doctor Eccles, the Colledge therefor approve of the said letter and appoynt Doctor Drummond and Doctor Pringle to meet with the said Doctor Crawford at the place named by the letter forsd—upon such dayes and dyets as they shall find convenient, and there to take tryal of the said Mr. James Eccles his qualifications, in all the parts of Medicine, and being found qualified to recommend him to the Princ[l] and Professors of the said University of Edinb., to have the Degrie of Doctor of Medicine conferred upon him, in such manner as is usual in the lyke caice. Signed, Will. Stewart, C.R.M.E.P.'

Upon this letter it may be remarked that 'the Faculty' is quoted—but obviously that does not refer to a 'Medical Faculty,' but only to the governing authority in the University. Also Dr. Crawford is mentioned as 'our Professor,' but of what is not stated; but at the time of his appointment, on 23rd November 1713, his position is noted as 'a Professor of Medicine.' The only one of the four appointed, namely the first, Sibbald, is titled 'Professor of Physick.' The effect of the one Professor being in the University is evidently to weaken the character of the Examination. When the first University Candidate for the Degree of Doctor of Medicine presented himself, thirteen years before, he was examined by six Physician Examiners in the usual manner *in* the College, and in presence of the Fellows; but the effect of an acting Professor being in the University is that the Candidate is examined *within the University, in the Library,* by *only three Examiners,* and *the Practical cases are not mentioned.* The Examination being conducted away from the College Hall and the Dispensary, the characteristic of the old Examination, 'the Practical cases,' were probably dropped, and they seem, for many years thereafter, to have been omitted from the University Examination. In Dr. Gibney's Reminiscences of his Edinburgh University days in his *Eighty Years Ago,* edited by Major Gibney, London, 1896, he describes how his Examination was

The Faculty is not a Medical Faculty.

Dr. Crawford is Professor of Medicine.

Effect of his appointment to weaken the Examination.

It was in private.

The Practical cases were dropped and absent from the Examinations for many years.

Dr. Gibney's Reminiscences of 80 years ago.

conducted about the commencement of this century. It was at the house of one of the Professors, the others sitting in a semicircle around the Candidate. The Examination was carried on in Latin, each Professor asking questions, apparently upon any subject, but he states that usually the Examination began by the Candidate being questioned *on the circulation of the blood.*

Edinburgh University Examinations.

How inferior this was to the original Royal College 'tryall,' extending over three distinct subjects and conducted at three separate 'Dyets,' with special attention given to both Theory and Practice.

In 1719 three University Examinations.

The records of the year 1719 show that the aspirants for the University Degree were increasing in number. Three were examined; and, as each Examination shows variation in some details, I have extracted the notes of them. The Minute of 24th March 1719 is to the following effect: 'Dr. Stewart, the President, reported to the College, that Dr. Crawford, Professor of Medicine in the University of Edinburgh, and some of the Professors yr of, had acquainted and signified to him that there was a young gentleman named Robert Stoddart . . . had applyed to the Princip[l] and other Members of the said University, to have the Degree of Doctor of Medicine conferred upon him, and that the said Dr. Crawford being present, acknowledged the samen, and there being no other Physitian in the said University at present . . . he, in name of Princip[l] and Professors, desyred that the President and Members of the Colledge of Physitians might appoynt one or more of their number, to joyne with . . . Dr. Crawford in the examination of Mr. Robert Stoddart . . . within the Bibliotheck of the said University . . . and that the Princip[l] of the University would wryte a letter to the President yr anent . . . appoynted Dr. Rule and Dr. Young to meet with Dr. Crawford . . . to take tryall of Mr. Stoddart his qualifications, in all the parts of Medicine, . . .' etc.

Robert Stoddart's Examination.

Attendance of Examiners requested by Professor Crawford in name of Principal and Professors.

'The same day, the Colledge allow the President in caice of the like occasione of any recommendation from the Princip[l] and

University of the Colledge of Edinburgh to the Colledge of Physitians for any of their number to joyne with the said Dr. Crawford in the Examinatione of Medicine . . . that the President, by himself, appoynt one or two Physitians for that effect, without the necessity of calling a meeting of the Colledge, he always giveing ane account of the name and designationes of such persones, as desyre to be examined . . . with the Physitians names . . . appoynted to be Examinators . . . the samen may be recorded in the Colledge Sederunt Book, and this to continue till next Election day.'

President in like occasion to appoint one or two Examiners without calling meeting of College.

From this it is learned that more Candidates for the University Degree were in future expected; that the Royal College considered a modified Examination sufficient for them, with which the University was satisfied; and that no Practical cases were examined. Their own Licentiat's Examination went on as of old, however.

Although University Examination a modified one, that for the Licence was unchanged.

On the same day, the 24th March 1719, the admission to the Royal College of Mr. James Eccles, Doctor of Medicine, took place. It is of interest, as he had been examined for the University Degree by Fellows of the College, and also that he was the first son of a Fellow who received the Licence. His petition states that he had for several years studied Medicine in foreign Universities, and that he had been examined and approved by some of their own number, and had received the Degree of Doctor of Medicine in the University of Edinburgh, 'therefore craving to be made a Licentiat of the Colledge of Physitians.' The desire of the Petition was granted, and he was admitted 'to practise Medicine within the Citty of Edinburgh and Liberties yr of, with all the Privileges,' etc. 'He having satisfied the Thesaurer for his dues as a Licentiat, and the Clerk and Officer.'

Dr. James Eccles admitted to College, 24th March 1719, with only the one Examination for University.

There were two other Candidates for the University Degree this year—the one in August, and the other in October. Application for assistance in their Examinations was made to the Royal

4th August 1719. Dr. John Burnet's Examination for University Degree.

College. The first is entered thus—'4 August 1719. Committee appoynted to Examine Dr. John Burnet with Dr. Crawford, Professor of Medicine, with view of getting the Degree of Doctor of Medicine conferred upon him.' Thereafter the following Minute is entered:—'10 August 1719. The Colledge having heard the petitione of Mr. John Burnet, Doctor of Medicine, mentioning that after severall years studie of Medicine in forraigne countris and Universities, he had received the Degree of Doctor of Medicine (after his return to his native country) by the University of Edinburgh, at which he was examined and approved of, by some of the Members of the Colledge of Physitians, appoynted to joyne in his examinatione, as his Diploma of Graduation dated the seventh of August instant, bears, and seeing that his efforts abroad, did not allow him to stay here at present, and practise Medicine within the City of Edinburgh and suburbs yr of. But that he was resolved, when he should happen to returne, to practise Medicine within the samen and therefor craveing to be made a Licentiat of the Colledge, . . . which petitione being read and considered by the Colledge, they agried to grant the desyre yr of, and therefor admitted the said Mr. John Burnet a Licentiat of the Colledge . . . and that in regard he is to reside in forraigne parts for some tyme, the Colledge, out of favour to the said Doctor, and in consideration that he may be servicable to the Colledge, by keeping up a correspondence with them, and sending what curiosities the places may afford he shall reside in, to the Colledge, have agried to immediately admitt the said Dr. Burnet a Fellow of their Society, and accordingly the said Doctor Burnet having retired to another room, and y^r after called in again, The Colledge unanimously admitted and hereby admit the said Doctor Burnet, a Fellow of their Society,' etc., 'he having instantly payd Dr. Cochrane, Thesaurer of the Colledge, 200 Merks Scotch Money as the half of his dues, and given bond . . . to pay the other half . . . howsoever, and

Craves to be made a Licentiate of College.

Reasons for immediately admitting him a Fellow.

whensoever, he shall return, and reside within any part of Scotland. This the Colledge has done out of mere favour, and on the consideration above said—the laws of the Colledge anent Licentiation and Fellowship remaining full in force, without allowing what has been done in this partic. caice, to be drawn in precedent in tyme coming. The said Doctor Burnet having also payed the Colledge officers their dues.'

The spirit of this transaction is quite that of the Early Fellows. The desire to use Dr. John Burnet as serviceable for the advancement of knowledge and the benefit of the College by having communications from him and curiosities sent to them, recalls the reasons Sibbald gave for, and the subjects considered at, the meetings at his lodging of the Medical Men of Edinburgh before the College was erected. The liberality of the College should also be noticed. Without Examination the dues were 500 merks, but apparently this Examination for the University having been joined in by Fellows of the College, is rated as if Dr. Burnet had been admitted directly by Examination. Quite in the spirit of The Early Days' Fellows.

On the 27th October 1719, there is a Minute to the effect that—'The President represented to the Colledge, that Dr. Crawford, Professor of Medicine in the University of Edinburgh, had applyed to him for two of ther number of the Colledge of Physitians, to assist him in the Examination of Mr. John Hamilton, sone to William Hamilton, Professor of Divinity in the said University, in order to obtain the Degrie of Doctor of Medicine conferred upon him by the said University. Therefor the President with the consent of the Colledge appoynts Dr. Mitchell and Dr. Forrest, to join in the Examination, and to examine him upon all the parts of Medicine to the effect foresaid,' etc. 27th October 1719. Mr. John Hamilton's Examination for Degree of Doctor of Medicine.

The Minute of 2nd August 1720 testifies to further indications of activity in the University, for 'The same day the President represented that Alex^r Monro, Professor of Anatomy, had by his

2nd August 1720. Alexander Monro, Professor of Anatomy, craves a recommendation from the Royal College to the Magistrates of Edinburgh.

petitione, applyed to the Colledge, craving a recommendatione from them to the Magistrates of Edinburgh in his favour, as a fitt persone, deserving further encouragement in that matter. The Colledge after the hearing of the said petitione read, granted the desyre there of, and appoynted the President to signe a recommendatione in name of the Colledge in his favour.—JAMES FORREST, P.C.R.M.E.'[1]

1720 and 1721. Two *ad eundem* Candidates for University Degree.

During 1720 the University Degree was granted to one Candidate on 21st July, and in 1721 on 18th May to another;

[1] John Monro, the father of Alexander, was admitted Fellow of the College of Surgeons on 11th March 1703, and died about 1737. Was he the same John Monro as joined the Physicians? The time of death does not agree. The name of Monro appears for the first time in the Physicians' Minutes of 11th January 1704, when the petition of Dr. John Monro was read to be Licensed and admitted a Fellow as he had been admitted a Doctor of Medicine at the University of Aberdeen, and desired he might be Licentiat without any previous examination in respect of his Patent, which he produced. The usual forms in such cases were gone through. (On the same day Dr. John Drummond, also of the University of Aberdeen, was admitted.) For some time he was a regular attender at the Meetings, and on 13th July 1704 was a Member of the Committee appointed with the President to meet the Principals of Edinburgh and Glasgow Universities to confer 'anent ane agriement' betwixt the Royal College and the four Scottish Universities. After this his name does not appear regularly. In the second Committee for the same purpose his name is not mentioned. He does not appear to have ever held office in the College. On 6th May 1718, the Minute states, 'the same day the President represented that John Monro, Chirurgeon in Edinb[h], had made a present of some *anatomical preparations* to the Colledge, for which the Colledge appoynt the President and Thesaurer to give him thanks in their name for the samen.'

After this the name of 'John Monro' does not appear till 3rd November 1724, when there is an entry—'Dr. Monro, deceased, debt to the Colledge for Bond, composition approved of.' In the *List of Fellows of the Royal College of Surgeons of Edinburgh from the year* 1581, there is no indication that John Monro also joined the Physicians' College. After 1704 Dr. Monro's attendance was irregular. From his being on the University Committee he was probably interested in that question. The Surgeon, John Monro, was their President in 1712 and 1713.

Alexander Monro and the College of Surgeons.

Sir John Struthers, M.D., late Professor of Anatomy in the University of Aberdeen, in the *Historical Sketch of the Edinburgh Anatomical School*, at p. 21, referring to Alexander Monro, observes: 'Returning to Edinburgh in the autumn of 1719, he was examined and admitted by the Surgeons (20th November 1719), and two months afterwards (29th January 1720), on their recommendation to the Town Council, elected Professor of Anatomy in the University.' 'He had eight months to prepare for his first course,' but if already appointed by the Magistrates and Town Council a Professor in the University, it is not very clear why he applied to the Royal College in August of the same year for a recommendation to the Magistrates in his favour.

but neither of them is referred to in the Minutes. Probably they had received the *ad eundem* Degree.

13th April 1721. Royal College fees for Licence without 'tryall' restricted to 400 merks.

Evidently the high fee for non-examined Licenciats had been objected to, for on 21st March 1721 the Minute has it, 'the fees to be payed by every Licenciat admitted without tryall restricted to 400 merks and ye act read a first time.' This act applied to 'every such Physitian as are or shall be graduat in any of the Universities within Scotland who shall at any time there after apply to be Licentiat by the Colledge without subjecting their selves to be previously Examined.' This act became law on 13th April 1721.

Dr. Charles Alston, M.D. Glasgow, petitions for Licence, 13th April 1721.

On this date Mr. Charles Alston, Doctor of Medicine, petitioned, mentioning that he being graduat Doctor of Medicine in the University of Glasgow, as the Patent of graduation dated 'the 2nd day of Decr. 1719 years, which he then produced, desyring that in respect of the said Patent he might be Licentiat to practise Medicine within the City of Edinb[h], etc., without any previous examination. Which desyre the College thought reasonable and therefor admitted, etc., He having satisfied the Treasurer for his dues,' etc.

1738. Became Professor of Medicine and Botany in Edinburgh University.

This is the first time a graduate of Glasgow University presented himself. On 1st August 1721, after taking the obligations, he was on this day admitted Socius. Dr. Charles Alston afterwards, in 1738, became Professor of Medicine and Botany in Edinburgh University, and lectured on Botany in Summer, and in Winter on *Materia Medica.*

1722. Another graduate admitted to University Degree.

In 1722, on 20th September, another graduate was admitted to the University Degree. No mention is made of him in the Royal College Minutes, but they were not kept very accurately that year. Thus the President, Forrest, died in the early part of it, and Dr. W. Eccles acted as Præses till next Election day, but no remark is made regarding the President's death in office; whilst Sir Robert Sibbald, who passed away in August of this year, is allowed to be carried to his unnoted grave without even one

No remark on deaths of President Forrest and Sir Robert Sibbald.

New Pavilion at Fountain Close and New Edition of Pharmacopœia.

memorial word. The building of the New Pavilion at Fountain Close, and the preparation and issue of the New Edition of the Pharmacopœia, seem to have been enough to engage the attention of the College about this period.

1723. University Examination of Mr. William Wood.

In 1723 the University received an increase of Candidates for its Degree, and accordingly, on 29th March, Dr. John Drummond being now President, we read: 'The President had letter from Principal Mr. William Wishart, dated 15th March, regarding conferring the Degree of Doctor of Medicine on Mr. William Wood, who is to be examined there to by the Professor Dr. Crawford, and there being no other Physitian in the University of Edinburgh at present, that the President be pleased to bring the same before the Colledge, that they may, if they think it expedient, to appoynt one or more of their number to joyn with their Professor in the Examination in the Library . . . to take tryall of the said W. Wood in all the Parts of Medicine. . . . President to have power to nominate Examiners in future untill recalled by College.' A Medical Faculty had not therefore been as yet constituted, even although Alexander Monro had been Professor of Anatomy since 1720. There is no evidence that the Professor of Anatomy examined Candidates for the Degree till a much later date, nor did the so-called Professors of Botany. The Degree at this time may have been regarded as purely Medical only.

President to have power to nominate Examiners.

No Medical Faculty yet though Professor Monro acting since 1720.

On 7th May, 'the President reported that Drs. Riddell and James Eccles had met with Dr. James Crawford' (Monro is not mentioned), 'in the Library of the Colledge of Edinb^{h} and assisted him in the examination of Master William Wood as to his qualifications, in order to obtain the Degree of Doctor of Medicine in the University of Edinb^{h}, and that the said Mr. William Wood was examined accordingly, and they had recommended him to the effect forsaid.'

21st November 1723. Dr. George Oswald

On 21st November 1723, it is recorded that Dr. George Oswald was admitted Licentiat, he being a Doctor of Medicine of 1696, 'as also that he was admitted *eundem gradum* by the University of Edinburgh on the 16th day of November inst. 1723 years—craves admission as Licentiat—granted and admitted.'

admitted Licentiat after being admitted to *ad eundem* Degree.

'The same day all the Members of the Colledge present signed a recommendation in favour of Dr. William Porterfield, to teach the Institutes and Practice of Medicine, which is as follows in these words, "Wee the President, Censors, and other Members of the Royall Colledge of Physitians in Edinb[h], taking into our serious consideratione the great losse our youth sustain, from their not having Medicine in all its parts taught in this place, and the great advantage that would redound to such of the inhabitants of the Good Toun of Edinburgh, as have sons who are to follow Medicine, by having them compleatly instructed in that Science at home, at no greater charge than a small gratification to the Undertakers, as also, that in the event good numbers of Students not only from all parts of our own Country, But lykewyse from England and Ireland might be induced to come here, for their improvement in Medicine, and spend that money amongst us which otherways they are oblidged to carie abroad to forraign Universities. And we, being informed, by Doctor Wm. Porterfield one of our Members, that he designed to give Colledges upon the Institutes and Practice of Medicine, provyded that he got suitable encouragement, doe applaud his designe, and think ourselves oblidged, in justice to his merits, to recommend him to all concerned as a person well qualified for such an undertaking, and worthie of all encouragement, in witness whereof Wee have subscribed the presents att our Hall in Edinburgh, the twenty-one day of November, 17 hundred and twenty thrie years, *sic subscribitur* Jo. Drummond Præses, Robert Trotter, And. Melville, Wm. Stewart, David Dicksone, Thomas Young, Wm. Learmonth, Jo. Riddell, Fran. Pringle Censor, Robt. Lowis Censor, Jo. Clerk, Jo. Learmonth, James Eccles, Charles Alston. Members not present at the sederunt subscribing afterwards—*sic subscribitur*,

Recommendation in favour of Dr. William Porterfield to teach the Institutes and Practice of Medicine.

Great loss from Medicine in all its parts not being taught in Edinburgh.

Students might be induced to come to Edinburgh.

Ed. Eizat, Gilb. Rule, Jas. Robertsone, Wm. Cochrane.—J. DRUMMOND, P.C.R.M.E."'

5th December 1723. Dr. Porterfield elected Secretary and Librarian.

At the next Election day, 5th December 1723, Dr. William Porterfield was elected Secretary and Librarian.

No better means for learning Medicine than when Royal College was established.

The foregoing is a most interesting testimony not merely as to the character of Dr. William Porterfield, his desire to give Colledges upon the Institutes and Practice of Medicine, of his qualification to do so, and of his being worthy of encouragement, but also as showing that in the year 1723 there was no better opportunity for the aspirant to Medical knowledge to be had in Scotland, England, or Ireland, than there was in the days of Harvey, and before the Royall Colledge in Edinburgh was established forty-two years previously. There were individual teachers, but no complete instruction in all the parts of Medicine; and, handicapped as it was by the terms of its Charter, the College, unable to teach itself, did its best to encourage the University to do it. The Fellows of The Early College, as I have shown, effected great changes by their four Efforts, and in the course of its progress other improvements which I have not mentioned, for they were subsequent to The Early Days; but the Fellows were wise, intelligent, and prospective, and had not the jealousy of its opponents prevented the College obtaining power to teach, to me it seems highly probable that a Medical School would have been founded in Edinburgh at a much earlier date than this. Here the Union of Scotland and England, it cannot be doubted, was reviewed with satisfaction by the Fellows, for seeing that the students of Medicine of Scottish origin might be limited, they boldly, in the early Sibbald spirit, speculate upon attracting them from England and Ireland. Those would support and encourage the School of Medicine, its teachers, and the citizens generally; whilst the sons of Scottish Medical men, and those aspiring to become 'Physitians,' would get their education at a much less outlay and waste of money, time, and labour, than if they had to spend their time and money and physical energy in travelling to and residing at 'forraign Universities.'

The Testimonial is genuinely Scotch, and, at the same time, it testifies to the *præfervidum ingenium* and the longsightedness and 'canniness' *Scotorum et Medicorum*, to which reference has previously been made.

How gratified the founders of the 'Royall Colledge' would have been could they have witnessed the progress of the Edinburgh School of Medicine, and that not only Scottish, English, and Irish students, but men of varied hue and nationality, and even students of the fairer and gentler sex (whose admission the Royal College was amongst the first of Licensing Boards in Great Britain to regard with favour), have been induced to resort to Edinburgh for their general as well as their Medical education, and to spend their money amongst the citizens. What a glorious realisation of their ideal vision of the future Medical School of Edinburgh, a realisation towards which others contributed in the Sister College, and amongst these John Monro, the careful educator and developer of the talents of his greater son, the anatomist.

The progress of the Edinburgh Medical School. Realisation of the dream of the Fellows in 1723.

Dr. William Porterfield's recommendation was given by the Royal College on 21st November 1723, and evidently it had been submitted to the Town Council, the Patrons of the University, for in Grant's *Story* we read at page 307, vol. i., that the Town Council 'passed an act *in August* 1724' (nine months afterwards), 'where in considering the great benefit and advantage that would accrue to this city and kingdom, by having all the parts of Medicine taught in this place; and likewise considering that hitherto the Institutes and Practice of Medicine, though principal parts thereof, have not been professed or taught in the said College: therefore they hereby institute and establish the foresaid profession of the Institutes and Practice of Medicine in their said College and do elect, nominate, and choose, Mr. William Porterfield, Doctor of Medicine in Edinburgh, to be Professor.' They granted him all

Town Council nine months afterwards passed an Act and elected Dr. William Porterfield Professor.

'powers, privileges, and immunities enjoyed by any other professor,' but at the same time no salary; and mindful how the Professorships of Medicine which they had created in 1685 had borne no result in the shape of teaching, they inserted the clause that 'Dr. Porterfield, by his acceptation, binds and obliges himself to give Colleges (*i.e.* courses of lectures) regularly, in order to the instructing of Students in the said Science of Medicine.' Dr. Porterfield, according to the same authority, did not do this, however, and Sir Alexander Grant speculates as to the reasons, which he attributes to peculiarities in Porterfield, but it does not appear to have suggested itself to him that Porterfield only designed to give Colleges 'provyded that he got suitable encouragement.' Now if he got the position of Professor, but without rooms to lecture in, and no salary, and if Students in sufficient number did not present themselves, was he likely to lecture? He was appointed Professor in August 1724 to lecture, I presume, when the next Session began, and in that year Alexander Monro, backed up by all the efforts of the College of Surgeons and his previous experience and reputation of four Sessions, had, according to Dr. Struthers' *Historical Sketch*, page 23, only fifty-eight Students, which was a decrease of ten from the previous Session; and in the next, the number was still further reduced to fifty-one. It does not follow that all these Students would attend Colleges on the Institutes, and Dr. Porterfield may not have considered the number of Students proposing to attend his course as 'suitable encouragement.' Seeing he was so well recommended by all the Fellows of his College, it is rather hard on him to place all the blame on his 'personal peculiarities.'

And bind and oblige Dr. Porterfield to give Colleges regularly.

Sir Alexander Grant's view of Porterfield.

1724. Number of Students attending Professor Alexander Monro.

Since the date of Dr. Porterfield's application to the Royal College (November 1723), the following Physicians who subsequently took part in the formation of the Edinburgh Medical School, and contributed to the advancement of the University, were by 5th May 1724 admitted to the Royal College:—Dr.

Andrew St. Clair, M.D. Angers; Dr. Andrew Plummer, M.D. Leyden; Dr. John Rutherford, M.D. Rheims; and Dr. John Innes, M.D. Padua.

5th May 1724. Andrew St. Clair, M.D., Andrew Plummer, M.D., John Rutherford, M.D., John Innes, M.D., admitted to Royal College.

They were all examined in the three subjects, and at the three diets; and, in addition to the statutory fees, each paid before taking his seat at the table as Socius, as had been previously enacted, 'twenty shillings sterling to the Treasurer for the use of the Dispensary belonging to the College.'

Each paid 20 shillings for use of the Dispensary.

On this day, too, President Dr. John Drummond reported 'he had received a letter from Mr. William Wishart, Principal of the University of Edinburgh, dated the 18th day of March last (1724) desyring the favour of one or two of the Members of the College of Physitians to meet and joyn with Dr. James Crawford, Professor of Medicine in the said University, to examine one Mr. Aaron Wood in order to his receiving the Degree of Doctor of Medicine from the said University, and that the President according to the powers given him by sederunt of the Colledge dated 19th day of March 1723 years, did appoynt Dr. Oswald and Dr. Porterfield to meet with the said Dr. Crawford and joyne with him in the examination of the said Mr. Aaron Wood, which accordingly they did and had recommended him as sufficient to receive the degree of Doctor of Medicine from the University.' It should be noted that Dr. Porterfield was not yet Professor. He became so in the following August.

18th March 1724. Letter from Principal Wishart for examiners of Aaron Wood.

The Minute further states that—'The said day, the Colledge ordered that here after when the President shall appoynt any of the Members of the Colledge to meet with Dr. Crawford, Professor of Medicine in the University of Edinburgh for examining any persones that shall desyre the Degrie of Doctor of Medicine conferred upon him by the said University that before any such Physitians be appoynted that the Clerk to the Colledge shall have a Crown for his paynes yr anent.' From this it would seem as if the University had not been very liberal in those

In future a fee of a Crown to the Clerk to be paid for each University Examination for his 'paynes.

days, and as if the Examiners received no payment for their trouble, but only thanks for the honour of assisting the University! Or does it bear this suggestion—that by verbal understanding the Royal College insisted on the graduates being examined previously to the conferring of the Degree?

Mr. John Nicoll examined for M.D.

Under date, 6th August 1724, it is reported, 'that a Committee attended the University at an examination of Mr. John Nicoll, A.M., and recommended him for the Degree of Doctor of Medicine.'

3rd November 1724. Dr. John Monro's Composition for Bond debt.

On the 3rd November of the same year, there is an entry concerning the deceased Dr. John Monro's Composition for Bond debt to the College. It is mentioned as being approved of. This was referred to in the Note on Dr. J. Monro, and differs from the date of death of John Monro as entered in College of Surgeon's list of Fellows. There must therefore have been two John Monros in Edinburgh alive at the same time, and both of them interested in the subject of Anatomy.

Two John Monros in Edinburgh.

4th May 1725. Examination of Dr. Gibson for University.

On 4th May 1725, a 'Committee to joyne the Professor in the University in Examination of Dr. Gibson, by letter from Mr. William Hamilton in absence of Principal Wm. Wishart, the President had appoynted Drs. Dicksone and Oswald to assist Dr. James Crawford in his Examination of him for the Degree of Doctor of Medicine. He having given a Crown to the Clerk and ane shilling gratuity to the Officer as their dues.' It is notable that the form of words still used is 'to joyne *the* Professor,' even although Porterfield had been Professor of the Institutes and Practice of Medicine since the preceding August; and in all these Examination transactions, whilst even the officer is rewarded with the gratuity of one shilling, there has never been any reference to the Examiners receiving a fee. The Candidate paid the Clerk's dues, but what pecuniary gain the University obtained does not appear.

Words used, 'to joyne the Professor.'

Never any mention of fee to Examiners.

But this friendly aid was at last becoming no longer required.

Medical interests in the University were now being developed—the Anatomy Class had risen to sixty-five pupils, but the Professor does not yet appear to have assisted Crawford at the Examination of Graduates. In the Minute of 1st November 1726, when the Royal College had almost completed its forty-fifth year, we find recorded, 'Thanks from the University of Edinburgh, which has now sufficient number of Professors to examine, Mr. Stewart and Mr. Drummond, Regents, convey the thanks to the Colledge.'

Medical interests in the University developing.

1st November 1726. Thanks from the University, which has now sufficient number of Professors.

This was brought about in the following manner (see Grant's *Story*, etc., vol. i. p. 310): 'In February 1726, Rutherford, Sinclair, Plummer, and Innes presented another petition to the Town Council "craving the Council to Institute the Profession (of Medicine) in the College of Edinburgh, and appoint the petitioners to teach and profess the same."' 'In their preamble they stated that they had already, "under the Council's protection, undertaken the professing and teaching of Medicine in this city; and, by the encouragement which the Council had been pleased to grant them, had carried it on with some success."' Sir Alexander further observes: 'Apparently the petitioners had been supplying Porterfield's place as a lecturer, by giving lectures on Medicine in the town; or if Porterfield lectured, then they had been playing the part of extramural rivals with the sanction of the Town Council.'

February 1726. Application to Town Council to institute Profession of Medicine.

Relations of Rutherford, Sinclair, Plummer, and Innes to Porterfield.

The Town Council (page 311) enunciated afresh that 'it would be of great advantage to this College, City, and Country' (the idea suggested in the previous recommendation of the College of Physicians, but amplified), 'that Medicine in all its branches be professed here, by such a number of Professors of that Science as may by themselves promote students to their degrees, with as great solemnity as is done in any other College or University at home or abroad.' 'These were important words, and the acts in which they were contained, passed under the Provostship of George

Town Council repeat the idea in previous recommendation of Royal College. Sir Alexander Grant's account.

Drummond, constituted the Charter of the Medical Faculty of the University of Edinburgh. . . . Now for the first time the Town Council showed that they understood what is necessary to make a University Medical School—namely, a sufficient staff of Professors to instruct students in all the main branches of Medical Science, and then conduct them to graduation with all the guarantees that the degree of any other University could give. And such a staff the Town Council were now resolved to create.'

Dr. John Gairdner's statement.

From the statement of Dr. John Gairdner, in his *Historical Sketch of the Royal College of Surgeons of Edinburgh*, published in 1860, it appears (page 21) that—'After 1720 various other departments of Medicine were added to the School at our Theatre. Theory of Physic was taught by St. Clair, Practice of Physic by Drs. Rutherford and Innes, Chemistry by Dr. Plummer.'

Dr. Struthers' statement.

According to Dr. Struthers' *Historical Sketch of the Edinburgh Anatomical School*, page 17: 'Four Members of the College of Physicians, Drs. Sinclair, Rutherford, Plummer, and Innes, who had been preparing for the duty by study at Leyden under Boerhaave, now joined Monro at the Surgeons' Theatre, and taught the Theory and Practice of Medicine and Chemistry. Left behind by the removal of Monro, five years afterwards' (that is, after 1720), 'to the University buildings, they petitioned the Town Council to be made Professors in the University, and this the Council did on 9th Feby. 1726.' The Minutes of the College of Physicians suggest a little more definiteness in the date of their connection with the College of Surgeons' Theatre. The nature of the subjects they proposed to teach indicated that they were Physicians, and could not, therefore, practise in the city till they were Licentiat by the Royal College. As I have just shown, they only obtained Licence in February and March 1724, and became Socii on 3rd November of the same year. They could not, therefore, have lectured more than

Minutes of Royal College suggest more definiteness as to date of connection with Surgeons' Theatre.

one, or at most two, Sessions as extramural lecturers, but may have lectured in the Surgeons' Hall, as Monro did at first, after being appointed University Professors.

Sir Alexander Grant, I think, appears to undervalue the attempt the Town Council made to form a Medical Faculty so far back as 1685, when they elected three Professors. In 1726 (*Story*, page 313), 'They proceeded accordingly to "unanimously constitute, nominate and appoint Drs. Andrew Sinclair and John Rutherford to be Professors of the Theory and Practice of Medicine, and Drs. Andrew Plummer and John Innes to be Professors of Medicine and Chemistry in the College of Edinburgh; with full power to all of them to profess, and teach Medicine, in all its branches—to examine Candidates, and to do every other thing requisite and necessary to the graduation of Doctors of Medicine.' They conferred these appointments *ad vitam aut culpam*; but they were to be unaccompanied by any salary out of the city's revenues.

Sir Alexander Grant undervalues the attempt to form a Faculty in 1685.

Thus in 1726 a Medical Faculty was constituted in the University by the Senatus Academicus recognising the five Professors of Anatomy, Institutes of Medicine, Practice of Physic, and Medicine, and Chemistry.

In 1726 a Medical Faculty at last constituted in the University.

Twelve years afterwards, the Chair of Botany was placed in a more distinctly University status, by the appointment of Dr. Charles Alston, a Fellow of the Royal College, to be Professor. Grant (*Story*, vol. i. p. 318) states he had devoted his life to the study of that subject, and had 'especially embued himself at Leyden with the views of Boerhaave on this science.' On the death of George Preston in 1738, the Town Council 'considering that were a Professor of Medicine and Botany elected and installed in the City's College it would in a great measure contribute to the advancement of learning, etc., they therefore appoint Dr. Charles Alston,' etc.; and so the teaching of Botany and Materia Medica was established in the University, and, for the second

Dr. Charles Alston appointed Professor of Botany in 1738.

time, the Botanist was selected from amongst the Fellows of the Royal College. This, however, was a good many years after the College had ceased to examine the University Candidates.

1st November 1726. Royal College Minute. President's statement. Regents Stewart and Drummond commissioned to give thanks to the College through the President, Dr. J. Drummond.

After this digression—returning again to the Royal College Minute of 1st November 1726—I find that after other business, it continues: 'There after the President represented that Mr. Stewart and Mr. Drummond, Regents, in the University of Edinburgh, were commissioned by a General Meeting of the said University, to give thanks to the Colledge of Physitians for lending some of their Members to joyne with ye Professor for trying and examining those who were to receive the Degree of Doctor of Medicine from their University; but now that there was a sufficient number of Professors of Medicine to make a Facultie of Medicine, that they should not trouble the Colledge any more upon that head. But were thankful for what favours they had received, and desired to live in good correspondence with the College. This commission was delivered by the named gentleman to the President to be reported to the College at the first meeting, which accordingly was done as above.—J. DRUMMOND, P.C.R.M.E.'

Conclusion after twenty-one years' co-operation.

And so, after twenty-one years' co-operation, the University of Edinburgh having obtained all it required from the Royal College by borrowing, thankful for past favours it had ungrudgingly received, and with the laudable desire to live in good correspondence with the College in the future, having now got a Faculty of Medicine from amongst the Royal College Fellows, needed to trouble it no more. And, without the faintest allusion to the dignity the Royal College had enabled it to attain to, nor to the trade in Medical Degrees the Royal College had been instrumental in saving it from falling into, with scant ceremony and politeness, dropped further association! The aid given by the Royal College, in enabling the University of Edinburgh Degree of Doctor of Medicine to attain its distinguished Medical value, was apparently of small consequence in its estimation; but nevertheless it was the spirit of the original founders of the 'Colledge of Phisitians,' then all, save Dr. Robert Trotter and Dr. Matthew St. Clair, gone to their rest, which placed King James the Sixth's College in its high and proud position of being for many years the most important Medical School in the United Kingdom, and the great conferrer of honourable Degrees in Medicine, with reputation unstained and lustre untarnished, and from the first bearing the impress of the 'Royall Colledge.'

The Institutes of Medicine holds its distinguished place, even with increasing reputation, to the present day. The Aphorisms of Hippocrates gave place, through Leyden in whose University Archibald Pitcairne taught, to the views of his great pupil, Boerhaave; and then, as years rolled on, to those of our own yet greater Cullen. But, after the lapse of a century, the acute perceptions and intuition of the founders of the 'Royall Colledge' were once more recognised; and the early use in the third 'tryall' of the Dispensary of the College in improved form, because of improved means, was reintroduced, by the 'judging' of 'two practical cases' being replaced by the Clinical Examinations conducted in the Wards of the Royal Infirmary, itself one of the later important developments of The Early Days and First Knights of the 'Royall Colledge of Phisitians' in Edinburgh.

Towards the close of the seventeenth century the College arose as a guiding beacon. Well has it performed the duty incumbent on it during the intervening years; and now, in the closing decade of the nineteenth century, it can proudly point to its last great Effort—the establishment, endowment, and maintenance of the Laboratory for the Prosecution of Original Scientific Research.

free and without fee not only to the Fellows, Members, and Licentiates of the College, but to all Medical Men desirous of prosecuting scientific investigation.

The Harveian spirit of progress and goodwill and of disinterested and enlightened liberality is as characteristic of the Royal and philanthropic College in the present age, as it was in the first of The Early Days—upwards of two hundred years ago.

INDEX

Printed by T. and A. CONSTABLE, Printers to Her Majesty
at the Edinburgh University Press

www.ingramcontent.com/pod-product-compliance
Lightning Source LLC
Chambersburg PA
CBHW021110270326
41929CB00009B/816

* 9 7 8 3 3 3 7 1 6 1 4 0 8 *